MW01382046

MOURNING, MEMORY AND LIFE ITSELF

WORKS BY THE SAME AUTHOR

A History of Art Therapy in the United States
(With Paige Asawa)

Creative Realities, the Search for Meanings

Architects of Art Therapy, Memoirs and Life Stories
(Edited with Harriet Wadeson)

Mourning, Memory and Life Itself: Essays By an Art Therapist

MOURNING, MEMORY AND LIFE ITSELF

Essays by an Art Therapist

By

MAXINE BOROWSKY JUNGE

With a Foreword by

Helen B. Landgarten

CHARLES C THOMAS • PUBLISHER, LTD.
Springfield • Illinois • U.S.A.

Published and Distributed Throughout the World by

CHARLES C THOMAS • PUBLISHER, LTD.
2600 South First Street
Springfield, Illinois 62704

© 2008 by CHARLES C THOMAS • PUBLISHER, LTD.

ISBN 978-0-398-07827-0 (hard)
ISBN 978-0-398-07828-7 (paper)

Library of Congress Catalog Card Number: 2008024368

With THOMAS BOOKS *careful attention is given to all details of manufacturing
and design. It is the Publisher's desire to present books that are satisfactory as to their
physical qualities and artistic possibilities and appropriate for their particular use.*
THOMAS BOOKS *will be true to those laws of quality that assure a good name
and good will.*

*Printed in the United States of America
LAH-R-3*

Library of Congress Cataloging-in-Publication Data

Junge, Maxine Borowsky.
    Mourning, memory, and life itself : essays by an art therapist / by Maxine
Borowsky Junge ; with a foreword by Helen B. Landgarten.
      p. cm.
    Includes bibliographical references.
    ISBN 978-0-398-07827-0 (hard) -- ISBN 978-0-398-07828-7 (pbk.)
    1. Art therapy. I. Title.
    [DNLM: 1. Art Therapy--Personal Narratives. 2. Art--Personal Narratives.
3. Grief--Personal Narratives. 4. Women--Personal Narratives. WM 450.5.A8
J95m 2009]
    RC489.A7J86 2008
    616.89'1656--dc22
                                                                    2008024368

In memory of Robert Ault.
And for my grandson Henry Petrie who is the future.

FOREWORD

Helen B. Landgarten, DAT, MFT, ATR, HLM

Maxine Borowsky Junge's curiosity about art and issues related to it, led her to explore numerous thought-provoking subjects. The amalgamation of new material and previously published works make this book impressive.

The author establishes ART as a basic prism. Its reflective facets encompass: "Psychology of Art," "Creativity," "Social Action," "The Profession of Art Therapy," and "Clinical Applications of Art Therapy."

Many chapters are written from a feminist point of view. Junge's interest in female artists and art therapists is revealed time and again. Factual contents are flavored with her own opinions.

The author's willingness to expose herself through personal material is a bold step in art therapy literature. In the past, art therapists tended to record their clinical work and sometimes included how they were affected by their clients and the outcome of cases. This was an appropriate model for education. Nevertheless, there is room in art therapy and mental health for a more personal type of writing. It helps to provide a place for empathy and the validation of feelings for students and colleagues.

As I read this book I found myself having an inner dialogue with Junge. At times I was in agreement; at other times I argued with some of her statements. This type of involvement with an author's thinking process is a major asset for readers. It encourages silent readers to become engaged. The value of this book is the author's extraordinary talent to make us think!

Art therapists, artists, mental health practitioners and the general public will find *Mourning, Memory and Life Itself, Essays by an Art Therapist*, fascinating and a worthwhile book to read.

Helen B. Landgarten is Professor Emerita, Loyola Marymount University and formerly Senior Staff Member, Thalians Community Mental Health Center, Cedars Sinai Hospital. She is the author of many art therapy books.

INTRODUCTION

The room where I write is up seven stairs in my house on Whidbey Island north of Seattle. It is the only second story room in my house and feels a bit like a tree house. Sitting at my computer and looking out the windows, I see very little built architecture, but there is a stand of evergreen trees taller than the house, and these autumn days I see trees with leaves turning orange and yellow. This morning on my way out through the courtyard to my red Suburu to take my Golden Retriever Moka to the dog park, I noticed that the deep maroon leaves of the flowering plum are starting to fall and cover the ground. In a few months the tree will be winter bare, brown-black branches instead of the plump round of leaves I can see from my window now. When it rains as it is today, I hear soft and hard fingertips of sound pounding and playing on my roof and through the windows I can see sheets of rain coming down.

Inside, my work room is cozy. Occasionally, my beloved dog climbs the stairs to sleep near me curled on the oriental rug while I work. She is here now. There is the blue Victorian love seat with a Georgia O'Keeffe pillow, in black and white, I bought in a museum shop in Milwaukee and another throw pillow, black with strong colorful abstract patterning of flowers and leaves, given me by an art therapist friend whom I treasure. There are overflowing bookshelves and my mother's teak desk, with the desktop barely seen through the mass of papers (I have found that putting away something where I can't see it, means it no longer exists for me and therefore, doesn't get attended to–so I leave stuff out and the stack grows ever higher). On the wall in front of me, is a quilt made by my students at Loyola Marymount University and presented to me at my retirement. Above the blue couch is a John Marin-like watercolor of New York City by my father and a story framed by my daughter from an old *Life* magazine about "Pride of the Marines" a movie written by my Dad. Folk art, a long-lasting love affair of mine, stands on ledges of my writing room–some figures–acrobats, largely– are from Cirque de Soleil, and there are figures from a crocheted nativity scene, including donkey, lambs and Baby Jesus in a crocheted manger made by an elderly woman on Whidbey Island. I see photographs of my son Ben on the wall, one on a bluff in Ireland and one of him sitting in a replica of the Oval Office on the set of "The West Wing" which he visited when my daughter was writing for the series. There is a framed poster from a musical "Galileo" written by my daughter Alexa when she was in her early 20s and a bulletin board with drawings and sayings: "I'll be a post-feminist in post-patriarchy," "To create one's own world in any of the arts takes courage," (Georgia O'Keeffe), "The strongest drive is not love or hate. It is one person's need to modify, revise, alter, change, rewrite, amend, chop to pieces another's copy," and "Life is not a journey to the grave with the intention of arriving with a pretty and well-preserved body, but rather to skid in broadside, thoroughly used up, totally worn out and loudly proclaiming, WOW! What a ride!" I have no memory of who said this, or who sent it to me, but think it might have been my mentor for my doctoral work, who died recently.

My filing system is evidenced by the stacks of papers and books strewn about the floor of my workroom. From my constant and comfortable seat at the computer, I can see books about Arbus, O'Keeffe, Kahlo, Henry Darger, a pile of books of essays including those by Kinsolver, Rodriquez and Page Smith, with Arnheim's *New Essays on the Psychology of Art* on top. Gaston Bachelard's *Poetics of Space* and Joyce Cary's *The Horse's Mouth* are on the couch. With the familiar pleasures and safety of family and friends around me, I have written this book.

Many of the essays here were originally published in art therapy journals. I consider them old friends of many years returning for a family reunion. Their sometimes scattered and often inconspicuous appearances, "briefly flowering and recycled tomorrow," in Barbara Kingsolver's words, did not cause me to love them any less and their return has been cause for a tender celebration. Since their first debuts, all have been substantially altered for this book and brought up to date. Reading them in their original forms, I was often saddened to discover that 30 years after a first publication, times have not changed as much as I could wish. There are six new essays for this collection. Writing these has enabled me to think about ideas that have been assaulting my brain and consciousness—some for a long time. I have reproduced patient artwork.

A few years back, a student of mine said that she thought I was opinionated. I said that at my "advanced" age, surely she didn't expect me not to have opinions. She didn't mean her comment as a complement. What she meant was if I held strong opinions, she feared I might be judgmental of her if she differed. I DO hold strong opinions, but I would like to believe I frame them as hypotheses and that I am open enough to change my mind. I love to discuss disparate ideas with people I respect as thinkers and often find a wealth of wisdom that might bump up enough against my own to change my opinions. I discovered long ago that most psychotherapy theories and ideas, persistent though they may be, are anecdotal at best and cannot be "proved" to work. This is one reason the nature/nurture pendulum of etiology and child development has swung to the *nature* end, with most serious mental health disorders now being defined as "diseases" amenable to medication. It is one reason why these days the field and managed care are commonly afflicted with behaviorism, cognitivism and their offspring. I support attempts to improve psychotherapy and counseling and to make them more accountable, but this switch to nature is presumably based on our increasing knowledge of brain chemistry. Although I believe in historical progress, I was married to a brain researcher who was possibly more of a skeptic even than I am, and he taught me to watch for the huge changes in brain research which are not necessarily improvements, and that what we think we know in that area changes about every ten years. So I will reserve judgment.

It isn't hard to understand that the complexities of the human condition do not make any of this easy. I have spoken out to the art therapy profession to gather it's "self esteem" together, to ask it to *define itself* instead of following and attempting to adapt to the trends, and they *are* trends, in mental health–not "truth," (e.g., I was trained before there *was* a *Diagnostic and Statistical Manual*, and consider it mostly a political document, sometimes useful, but certainly not to be employed, as many therapists today do, as information given by God (or Godly psychiatrists) and not to be ignored or used in concert with therapeutic experience and common sense).

Many writers salute the libraries and librarians that first provided a home for them and their imagination. Like them, I remember the pleasure when I was an adolescent and bored to tears in school, of picking books off the library shelf to take home and read, to return them and choose more. I didn't follow any list of great books, nor gather anyone's opinion of what to read. I simply read what interested me. I would read the first few pages and if they held me, I took the book home. I remember the tenth grade English teacher, Mrs. Bruce who told us we were going to read *Arrowsmith*. The only reason she gave us was that she liked it. I loved it! And it set me off to reading everything Sinclair Lewis ever wrote and all the biographies of him I could find.

From my library treasures, I got a broad if eccentric and eclectic education and have been a reader all my life. Over my years as a mental health practitioner and as a teacher, I have read much of the psychology and psychotherapy literature which I have found generally wanting. I believe that art, music, theater and literature tell us more about human life and how it is lived and should be lived.

Since I discovered him in adolescence and found someone who believed what I did, I have always been interested in John Dewey's innovation of progressive education, learning from experience. I have discovered that I learn that way myself. While I have had a few great teachers whom I revere, mostly, with their tender guidance, I have taught myself. I call myself "a skeptic who will try anything" and that is primarily true. The various ideas and theories I hold are framed as *hypotheses* to be tested in the real world with real human beings, and perhaps altered or changed entirely. Nevertheless, I have been in the psychotherapy and art therapy fields for almost 40 years now and there are certain assumptions that have been tested and seem to work so far and which provide the often tacit bedrock on which my work exists and expands—some might call them "biases." These assumptions will be found in my essays, but I want to frankly acknowledge them here for the reader:

- *My major theory is systems.* It seems to me a shame that after all these years and with the global network increasing in complexity and influence and national boundaries becoming more permeable, most art therapy and psychotherapy training programs in the United States are still individually conceived and taught. Individualistic America in which a John Wayne type conquers the western territory by molding it to his will is still a prevailing paradigm in most psychotherapy and art therapy thought and practice. Once integrally trained in individual ideas, it is very tough for a therapist to change directions to become a systems thinker, though not impossible. It is one of the main reasons that mental health is all too often about social control.

I believe:

- In the *unconscious.* I have never seen it and do not know exactly how it works, but I believe it exists and must be considered in any concept of change, large or small. Not too many years ago, I was around a number of bright people attempting to be change agents in their businesses and organizations. That the organization probably had an "unconscious" seemed obvious to me, but was a new idea to many of these people.

I believe that:

- A person's *history* is important and is played out in their adult life. I think that the first five years of life are extraordinarily important and that a human being develops and grows through a lifetime. Although I certainly wouldn't call myself any kind of Freudian, I am primarily a psychodynamist. I believe Freud's ideas still prevail in American culture for better or worse: Every time we hear a parent asking a young child "why did you do that?" we are hearing the cause and effect *ideas* of Freud.

I believe:

• *The relationship* is the essential element of change.

I believe:

• *We cannot predict, nor control the future, nor even much the present.* This means to me that while a person's history may have been horribly damaging, there are too many mysteries about human life and culture to predict outcome with any certainty.

I was born in Los Angeles and lived there most of my life–long enough to see it covered over with buildings and cement. My early years were influenced by The Great Depression's web on my parents and World War II. I have lived through many things: the Civil Rights Movement, The Women's Movement, Lyndon Johnson's War on Poverty, the beginnings of the Peace Corps, Vista, Head Start, Legal Services for the Poor, the massacre at Kent State and the Vietnam War. It was a time of rioting in ghettos and barrios in over 100 United States cities (some call the riots "revolutions"). Stonewall and AIDS are of my time and I watched on TV as an astronaut landed on the moon; I witnessed *Roe v. Wade*, the turbulent revolution of the '60s, the resignation of a president and the impeachment of another. It was the time of the assassinations of John and Bobby Kennedy and Martin Luther King within a few years of each other. I have been around to see 9/11 and its ramifications. All have influenced and formed me and I have noticed that life keeps bobbing up and getting in the way of plans. I consider the term "planned change" an oxymoron. There are always surprises.

I believe:

• *Education can be transforming of individuals and cultures*, but usually isn't.

I believe:

• *Humor* is essential–in life, teaching and in therapy. Almost anything can be said, if it is done with humor. And it helps if the person feels *understood*. Humor is a virtually unstudied but tremendously important asset of human life.

• I am passionate about *art therapy*. Because it is innovative, magical, mysterious and because the created image is always surprising and sometimes life changing. Art and the creative process are as important to life as breathing.

And I believe:

• *Hope* is the cauldron in which most change occurs.

In many ways, this book of essays *Mourning, Memory and Life Itself*, includes my life's work. While it may not contain all, it certainly represents ideas that have been most fascinating and important to me and reflects the variety of interests that have startled and provoked me over time. When I look at the essays as a whole, that certain themes unaccountably persist over my almost 40 years as an art therapist surprised me. Many go way back and are the very same themes that intrigued me as a child and as an adolescent. Although sometimes disguised or couched in different terms, they are the very same themes that plague and interest me now. Themes here appear as topic headings for the essays. They are: Psychology of Art, Creativity, Social Action, Clinical Applications of Art Therapy, and Art Therapy as a Profession.

As I wrote this book of essays, I hoped I would be able to discover something different than that written by the sometimes wonderful multidisciplinary writers and theoreticians about art and creativity, art historians, educators, mental health practitioners or even philosophers. I am satisfied and pleased that this book is clearly the work of an art psychotherapist who while including ideas from disparate sources, hopes to conceptualize and "see" within her own idiosyncratic focus. *Mourning, Memory and Life Itself* is first for my art therapy colleagues and students. In addition, it is for other mental health professionals who I hope will find some of their questions echoed here. It is also a book for people interested in the psychology of art and for those who love wondering about the combination of art and people, as I always have and as I do now.

Now it is almost spring on Whidbey Island. The winter tree's bare branches are covered with buds which will be bursting into fabulous pink in another week or so. The leaves from bulbs in my garden—tulips and daffodils—have come up, fanned by the little sun we have had, with their abundant flowers not far behind. This morning it rained, but in the afternoon sun appeared for awhile.

Maxine Borowsky Junge
Whidbey Island, Washington
April 2008

ACKNOWLEDGMENTS

First, my profound thanks go to Helen B. Landgarten, my art therapy mentor, colleague and friend, who wrote the Foreword for this book at a time I know, was very difficult for her.

My sincere thanks go to my publisher Michael Thomas of Charles C Thomas, Publishers, Ltd. Michael has worked with me on two books and has been unendingly kind, supportive and helpful. I believe he has greatly contributed to the profession of art therapy in his consistent publication over the years of art therapy literature. Claire Slagle, my editor at Thomas, gave my manuscript an important read and improved it considerably. She was a major help.

My son, Benjamin Junge, was my "computer consultant." When I couldn't make the computer behave, he knew how to straighten out my messes. With his cheerful demeanor, Ben was always there when I needed him. Even when he was up to his ears in work as an Assistant Professor of Anthropology at SUNY, he never turned me down. In addition, he designed the graphics for this book. I am very grateful.

Jason Calk efficiently and effectively transposed onto CD the images for this book, easily rescued me from a huge computer glitch and has been invaluable as a backup person. He deserves my thanks as does David Wilder who took photos of my art for the cover. A number of friends gave me valued feedback and support on parts of the manuscripts–in particular Wendy Lambeth. They know who they are, but I want them to know how enriching their help has been to me.

I owe thanks to Bob Ault who died before this book was completed and to whom this book is dedicated along with my grandson Henry Petrie. Bob was a great art therapy friend for over 30 years. He called art therapy a "movement," and meant it and he worked tirelessly for it over its history. He was a prime mover in the formation of the American Art Therapy Association (AATA) and was its second President. With Bob's encouragement and support, I was spurred on to spend nine years writing *A History of Art Therapy in the United States.* His pioneering work as an art therapist at the Menninger

Foundation in Topeka, Kansas and his founding of the art therapy Masters program at Emporia State University inspired us all. I loved that he collected jokes and would tell me his latest so we could both chortle over them. (They were usually bad, powerful and extremely funny.) But it was his enduring and remarkable friendship over the years and that of his wife Marilynn which meant and mean a great deal to me. I owe them a lot.

And to Jim, thanks for the pen.

I am deeply indebted to those who have granted permission to print some of the material in this book. Their names are listed below:

Art Therapy, Journal of the American Art Therapy Association in a different form published "An inquiry into women and creativity including two cases studies of the artists Frida Kahlo and Diane Arbus," "The book about daddy dying: A preventive art therapy technique to help families deal with the death of a family member," "Door at Abiquiu," "Guest editorial for stories of art therapists of color," "The art therapist as social activist," and "Themes and reflections on the stories of art therapists of color"

Andrew Lownie, for the Joyce Cary Estate.

Anna Belle Kaufman, art therapist, for her moving account of her son's panel for the AIDS Quilt.

Art Resource in New York, for the Frida Kahlo image and Estate of Diego Rivera and Frida Kahlo, Banco de Mexico, Mexico D.F. for permission to print it.

Basic Books for quotes from Arieti's *Creativity, the Magic Synthesis.*

Don Lambert and the Lawrence, Kansas Arts Center for permission to print Elizabeth Layton's "Husband on scales."

Elsevier Press *The Arts in Psychotherapy* in a different form published "The perception of doors: A sociodynamic investigation of doors in 20th century painting," "Mourning, memory and life itself: The Vietnam Wall and the AIDS Quilt," and "Feminine imagery and a young woman's search for identity." In addition, they gave permission to print a quote from Golub's "Symbolic expression in post-traumatic stress disorder: Vietnam combat veterans in art therapy"

Estate of Alice Neel for permission to print the image of "Mother and child, 1957."

Farrar, Straus and Giroux, for the quotation from Fritz Stern's *Five Germanies I have known.*

Harper Collins for quote from Herrera's *Frida, a Biography of Frida Kahlo.*

Istock international, Inc. for the photos accompanying Chapter 1.

Jessica Kingsley Publishers for the chapter in a different form "The art therapist as social activist: Reflections on a life," first published in Kaplan's *Art Therapy and Social Action.*

Minneapolis Institute of Arts for permission to print Pierre Bonnard's "Dining room in the country, 1913."

NAMES Project Foundation for permission to print the image of the AIDS Quilt.

Oxford University Press, for quotes from Ashton's *About Rothko*.

Orion Press, Inc. for quotes from Bachelard's *The Poetics of Space*.

Sophie Bowness for the Barbara Hepworth Estate.

University of California Press for quote from Sturken's "Tangled memories: The Vietnam War."

University of Chicago for quote from Hawkins' "Naming names: The art of memory," *Critical Inquiry.*

Whitney Museum for permission to print images of Edward Hopper's artwork.

Yale University Art Gallery for permission to print Edward Hopper's "Sunlight in a cafeteria, 1958."

W.W. Norton & Co. for permission to use the quote by Rainer Maria Rilke.

And my colleagues Janise Finn Alvarez, Anne Kellogg, Chris Volker and Janise Hoshino with whom I wrote Chapters 8 and 9 of this book.

CONTENTS

PART IV. THE PROFESSION OF ART THERAPY

PART V. CLINICAL APPLICATIONS OF ART THERAPY

MOURNING, MEMORY AND LIFE ITSELF

Art is personal; it makes people think about their secret lives.
–Joan Acocella

The reward of writing is learning.
–Fritz Stern

Part I
PSYCHOLOGY OF ART

Chapter 1

MOURNING, MEMORY AND LIFE ITSELF: THE AIDS QUILT AND THE VIETNAM VETERANS MEMORIAL[1]

The Vietnam Veterans Memorial and the AIDS Quilt represented our most profound cultural yearnings of memory and forgetting at the end of the twentieth century. In this essay, I attempt to make connections between these memorials' artistic meaning-making at the individual level as it springs from and expands into remarkable and powerful societal concerns about healing. Along with the Women's Movement, the Vietnam War and the AIDS epidemic are the distinguishing events of the latter half of the twentieth century. They represent two markers of what America meant at this unique historical moment.

Artwork and other articles of remembrance have been left by visitors to the Wall since its inauguration. These "offerings" are collected by the National Park Service, taken to a secret[2] warehouse, catalogued and stored. Some years ago, a student of mine as her thesis project, studied the artifacts left at the Wall. As I accompanied my student through her thesis exploration, I grew fascinated that people at the Wall created and brought their own offerings to the dead. (We have observed this phenomenon again with the spontaneous offerings left after Princess Diana's death and, increasingly, at the sites of accidents and deaths across the United States.) The AIDS Quilt is another

---

1. This essay is printed with changes from "The AIDS Quilt and the Vietnam Veterans' Memorial Wall" (1999). *The Arts in Psychotherapy*, 26, 195–203. Used with permission.
2. "Secret" because the was is still controversial.

important memorial first created in the United States during the last decades of the twentieth century as a response to the pandemic of AIDS.

As I thought and read about these phenomena, I came to believe that the mourning process as it is expressed and enacted, and the mourning objects of individual and collective memory, can be thought of as metaphors for art therapy processes because, as with art therapy, these memorials embody our deepest sufferings juxtaposed with an intrinsic impulse toward creativity, existing paradoxically and simultaneously within the bounded container of the therapeutic relationship.

The art therapist provides art materials, a listening heart and mind—and a surround in which suffering exists but simultaneously can be contained. Created artwork, its particular intent or direction notwithstanding, represents the dark and the light, the known and the unknown, consciousness and unconsciousness. And it represents the creator's reinterpretation of *memory*. Within the boundaries of art materials, the concrete and imagined art product expresses safety and continuity. It represents and stands for a life lived and one still living. It echoes a voice of continuity in the face of loss and death.

ART THERAPY LITERATURE

Much art therapy literature has dealt with loss, grief and trauma, but these studies seem to fall into two major categories: First, are the individual or group case histories of clients undergoing grief from loss, trauma or post-traumatic stress syndrome who through their involvement in art therapy with a sensitive art therapist (often in a workshop setting) are able to alleviate suffering and lift depression (e.g., Case, 1987; Kornreich, 1993; McIntyre, 1990; Speert, 1992; Stronach-Buschel, 1990; Zambelli, Clark & Heegaard, 1989).

The second category is art therapy literature on trauma at the societal level (e.g., Berkowitz, 1990; Felber, 1993; Golub, 1985; Jones, 1997; McDougall, 1992; Roje, 1994). In her paper, Berkowitz (1990) wrote about art therapy treatment with returning veterans of the Vietnam War. Golub (1985,) also working with this population, stated that art therapy was a natural form of expression for "the devastating anguish surrounding visual memories . . . because there are no works to describe such extreme situations." In 1991 in "Art Therapy in a War Zone," Sherebrin described her work with Israeli children whose homes were destroyed in SCUD missile attacks during the Gulf War. Felber (1993) wrote about art therapy as a way to ease psychological trauma in Tijuana, Mexico after giant floods. Her study concerned an art therapy group with mental health workers on the front lines after the tragedy. McDougall (1992) worked with children who survived the Andover, Kansas tornado, and Roje (1994) described art therapy with children after the 1994 Los Angeles earthquake. Jones (1997) discussed art therapy with Oklahoma City bombing survivors; Franklin (1993) described the AIDS crisis and its art imagery and persuasively argued the connection between AIDS art and its social context. For an interesting story of the making of a Quilt panel within the context of art therapy, see Kerewsky's (1997) "The AIDS Memorial Quilt: Personal and Therapeutic Uses."

A third category of literature is the art therapy response to urban violence. A precursor of this ilk was published by Landgarten, Tasem, Junge and Watson (1978) in "Art Therapy as a Modality for Crisis Intervention" in which a team from a community mental health clinic conducted art therapy sessions in a public school after the Symbionese Liberation Army's kidnapping of Patti Hearst and the burning of people and houses in the student's neighborhood in Los Angeles. I was a member of this team.

My own writing in these areas has taken me from clinical work into the social arena. In 1985, I published "The Book About Daddy Dying: A Preventive Art Therapy Technique to Help a Family Deal with the Death of a Family Member" (Junge, 1985, Chapter 13 in this book). I described the making of a book in which all the family participates and which gives expression and concreteness to the dead person as still, part of the family. I spoke of the book as a ritual memory object. In 1989, in "Social Applications of the Arts" (Ault, Barlow, Junge & Moon), I wrote of the "sweeping power of the arts for change." "The Art Therapist as Social Activist" (Junge, Alvarez, Kellogg & Volker, 1993, Chapter 7 in this book) describes a clinical project in which art therapists worked with Nicaraguan refugees and one art therapist's experience of being a union organizer and striking against her clinic management.

Relevant to my essay here is Kaufman's 1996 paper "Art in Boxes: An Exploration of Meanings." Through artmaking, Kaufman, a talented art therapist, explores the relationship of art and suffering through research based on the loss of her child to AIDS. By making a sculpture the author confronts her own sense of loss and separateness and transforms it through art and meaning-making. Kaufman's work is very close to the exploration of meaning in this paper of the Vietnam Veterans Memorial and the AIDS Quilt: She sees art as a response to suffering and a container for feelings. She establishes art as having the potential both to memorialize and to transform.

HISTORY AND ORIGIN OF THE VIETNAM VETERANS MEMORIAL AND THE AIDS QUILT

After World War I, allied forces determined that every fallen soldier should be commemorated individually. Major architects of the time put names on gravestones, or incised them on a monument. In 1924, Sir Edward Luyten constructed arches at Thiepval in France containing 73,367 names to memorialize those who had died at the battle of the Somme. On the Mennen gate which leads out of Ypres in northwest Belgium, there are 54,896 names.[3]

A Vietnam veteran, Jan Scruggs, initiated the Vietnam design competition through grassroots efforts to build a memorial to honor and remember those who served in that conflictual war. Criteria for designs were that the future monument be nonpolitical and that it include *all* who were killed or missing in action from 1959 to 1975. An eminent jury of eight art experts judged the submissions.

Maya Lin, a Chinese-American, who grew up in Athens, Ohio was an undergraduate architecture student at Yale University at the time. She became fascinated with monuments commemorating the ordinary lives of fallen soldiers. As a senior design student, together with each member of her design seminar, in 1980 she submitted a design to the Vietnam Veterans competition—a design shaped by her study of World War I cemeteries. Lin designed a simple V-shaped panel with roughly 58,000 names inscribed in 140 panels. The names, themselves, she decided, would be the memorial.

Lin's design contrasted with and functions in opposition to the established methods of remembrance on the Mall in Washington, D.C.

---

3. This history of memorials has been culled from a variety of sources including Hawkins, (1993), Ruskin, Heron & Zemke, (1988), Sturken, (1997), and The NAMES Project, (1996).

where the Vietnam memorial would be placed. Previous memorials were of white marble, often contained realistic figures and included towering shapes, such as the neighboring Lincoln Memorial and Washington Monument. Lin's wall of names was a minimalist sculpture, an earthwork cut into the sloping earth. Made of highly polished black granite, the Wall in effect acts as a mirror: Here the living see themselves superimposed upon the names of the dead. The names on the Wall are represented chronologically instead of alphabetically as was typical; they are like a Greek epic, representing the continuing chronicle of the war.

Although the jury was unanimous in its selection of Lin's design, a firestorm of controversy was ignited. At first, the focus of the controversy was on the modernist character of the monument itself. But when Lin's identity became known—she was not only young (21 years old) and uncredentialed, she was Chinese-American and female—she was defined not as American, but as "other." The jury's selection of someone with "marginal" cultural status as the primary interpreter of a controversial war inevitably complicated matters. Lin's design was characterized as passive and female. The aesthetic was seen as Asian and therefore not appropriate for an American memorial. In addition, Lin's refusal to glorify war led her to an aesthetic statement of pacifism, not a very popular stance then or now in America.

Maya Lin's design reflects war's violence as the Wall cuts into the earth. Despite its initial deep flaying for the construction of the Wall, the land itself remains constant and endures. Although the still-visible cut is part of Lin's design, grass has grown back around it. Later, a more traditional monument depicting soldiers was added to the Mall area and recently a monument to women of the Vietnam War has been established. Both face the Wall.

What was unexpected was the stream of reverent visitors filing past the black granite wall, often in tears. Soon after the inauguration of the Memorial, the controversy fell away attesting to the Wall's aesthetic power. Since its dedication, people have been unable to keep from touching it. They look for names familiar to them, and touch them as if tenderly caressing skin. Often they leave behind teddy bears, flowers, model cars, letters, photographs, and dog tags. Even women's underpants and a Harley Davidson motorcycle have been left at the Wall or pushed into a seam near a name.

Lin believed that the names themselves would be the memorial.

What she did not foresee was that the simplicity and power of the Wall was so strong that an interactive process would often play out in which mourners would leave intimate identity keepsakes as if to restore to the dead the worlds they had lost. In so doing, mourners could express grief, their connection to the lost, and their refusal to forget. In this way, they were potentially able to move on–walking slowly down the wall itself connecting with other names, sometimes backing away from contact. The silence at the Wall is indicative of the presence and deeply-felt experience connecting the living and the dead.

Cleve Jones' motivation to name names, in his innovation of the AIDS Quilt was the threat to oblivion of another lost generation, like the Vietnam veterans returning to an America intent on forgetting them. In November 1985, it was announced that the AIDS death toll in San Francisco was 1,000. But that tragic loss of life had been large-ly unnoticed nationally except among gays. It occurred to Jones that if that many corpses were laid out in a field, people might then notice the loss. In the widespread denial about the disease, he worried about the massive numbers of largely hidden dying and the lack of acknowl-edgement of those who had died. Most people then who died of AIDS-related causes did not have funerals and their remains were typ-ically refused by funeral homes and cemeteries.

At the annual candlelight march in San Francisco, held in honor of the slain gay politician Harvey Milk, Jones asked participants to make signs with the names of someone they knew who had died of AIDS. The signs were hung on the façade of the federal building where they provided a stunning "wall of memory that, simply by naming names, exposed both private loss and public indifference" (Hawkins, 1993.) The wall of names looked like a patchwork quilt.

Jones recalled a patchwork quilt handed down in his family. As American folk art, quilts may represent not only family but America itself. In our national consciousness, they are connected to nineteenth century sewing bees and a longing for past community symbolizing collective, national unity. The family quilt implies warmth and com-fort. Above all it implies continuity with the past and the future. It is linked to nostalgia for a feeling of community which may never have really existed–certainly not for gays. In the nineteenth century, when women had little public voice and could not vote, quilting bees were community meetings. Susan B. Anthony made her first speech on women's suffrage at such a gathering. Communal family quilting pro-mises a *future* in which the quilt and all that it means can be handed down the generations.

In 1987, Cleve Jones made the first panel for what was to be called the NAMES Project Quilt. Using a sheet the size of a grave, 3' x 6', he spray-painted the name of his friend Marvin Feldman as a memorial. Since then, like a solemn and hilarious quilting bee, families and friends of those who have died and sometimes the dying person meet to create a panel to contribute to the Quilt. Since 1987 40,000 3' x 6' panels bearing 70,000 names have been sewn into the Quilt and the AIDS Quilt has become the largest ongoing community arts project in America. In October of 1996, the Quilt, equal in size to 54 football fields was shown in its entirety on the National Mall in Washington. Among the visitors were President and Ms Clinton and Vice President and Ms Gore. This marked the first time in 11 years and the Quilt's display in Washington five times that a United States President or Vice President had visited a Quilt display. Previous Presidents had turned away, even left town, as they refused to acknowledge the national tragedy represented by the Quilt. The Quilt was nominated for a Nobel Peace Prize in 1989 and as it lies on the Washington Mall has been called a national cemetery for those who have died of AIDS.

Figure 1-1. "The AIDS Quilt on the Mall in Washington, D.C. and the Washington Monument. The AIDS Memorial Quilt, © 2008 The NAMES Project Foundation.

NAMING

Human beings are unique in that they can imagine their own deaths. In addition, they remember the dead and keep on remembering them. This immediate act of memory and imagination is often tied to the name of the deceased as a symbol of identity. Naming keeps memory alive. The names written on the Wall and Quilt signify voices of the dead and our refusal to forget them. To name is to give voice to memory. To name and remember the name is to live on after death. To name is to draw a boundary around something or someone–to accent individuality, separateness, identity, even within the crowd. The names of the AIDS Quilt and the Vietnam Veterans Memorial pose a counterpoint to the anonymity of lives tragically lost. On the two memorials, names express both private, personal loss and the public's indifference to that monstrous loss. When the Quilt is displayed, the reading of names is now a tradition. Reading–saying aloud–the names from the Wall has also become an intense tradition.

The power of the Wall is due to the 58,196 names inscribed on it as a roll call of the dead. The names were read aloud at the dedication ceremony of the Wall and on its tenth anniversary. The Wall's design creates spaces in which visitors are invited to touch the names and to thereby see themselves mirrored among the names and among the dead.

Within the context of AIDS, naming is connected to a potential immense risk. In the early days of the illness (and unfortunately, often still today) there was stigma and anonymity. The acknowledgment that one had the disease might mean the loss of medical coverage, job, and/or family and friends. Naming meant coming out of the closet. It was a brave act of defiance, a courageous affirmation of identity and a life lived and a vivid action against discrimination. A gay psychiatrist friend, also an AIDS doctor and painter and I have talked about the impact of the hiding of self-image on the development of personality. Telling the lie and hiding behind the mask, the person feels increased loneliness, isolation and self-hatred. An article by Pert, Dreber and Ruff (1998) describes research with gay men, equating the stress of secrecy and being in the closet with a negative progress of their HIV infection. The AIDS Quilt is called "The NAMES Project." The name represents everything and it represents nothing. It illustrates memory and remembering as a *political act.* While the AIDS Quilt includes many panels for those dead who were not gay, it remains largely thought of as a gay representation. Naming often provides relief through telling a history that has previously been taboo. It embodies the act of bearing witness.

The Wall and the Quilt illuminate a collective body count. When the Quilt is shown on the Mall in the nation's capital, it symbolically includes those typically cast out of America–homosexuals, drug users and the poor. In both memorials naming is the act of inclusion of the plurality–many different individual threads come irreparably together. In their ethnic diversity, some have seen the names on the Wall as representative of the diversity of America itself.

MAKING QUILT PANELS AND ARTIFACTS LEFT AT THE WALL

The Vietnam Veterans Memorial of names memorializes the dead from a war that many consider lost or at least, not won, but a war that is over. The panels of the AIDS Quilt reflect a war still ongoing, a disease that thus far we cannot cure. The Wall's names mourn the dead. The AIDS Quilt panels personalize, memorialize and celebrate individual lives *lived.* This difference may explain why so many artifacts of personal and individual memory loss are left at the Wall: The need to offer intimate memory objects representing a particular life fill the names with individual meaning.

The Vietnam Veterans Memorial is the only site in Washington where artifacts are left. Brought to it are such things as photos, letters, poems, teddy bears, dog tags, combat boots and helmets, MIA/POW bracelets, clothes, medals of honor, headbands, beer cans, plaques, crosses and playing cards. These objects were originally classified as "Lost and Found." Later, the Park Service realized that they had been left at the Wall intentionally and began to save them.

The Wall is a place to speak to the dead and where, by implication, the dead are present. Many letters left are addressed to the dead and often reflect the lives the dead were unable to live. Sturken (1997) describes some of the keepsakes–such as a watch and a Vietcong wedding ring–carried for years and finally placed at the Wall. Artifacts are left as symbols of loss, anger, guilt and redemption. They often thank those who "died for us" or offer apologies to the dead. The ritual itself of leaving something behind may provide a transformative process wherein the long process of healing can begin.

The majority of objects are left at the Wall anonymously. The Park Service, by collecting cataloging and treating them as precious, transforms these objects from individual artifacts to aesthetic objects of memory; with a subtext of emotion they are no longer common objects. They have become art icons representing the mystery of the past; they are objects which bear witness to pain and suffering.

Figure 1-2. "Boot at the Vietnam Veterans Memorial." Photograph by Jim Pruitt.

The NAMES Project of the AIDS Quilt does not restrict the number of panels that can be made for one person. Some panels are made by strangers. Some people with AIDS make their own panels before they die. Often, in the making of a panel, a compassionate community is formed that did not exist before, when friends, lovers, family, strangers come together for the making of the Quilt panel. Each panel reflects and answers the question "How can this person be remembered?" The only criteria for the panel are that it be 3' x 6', the size of a grave and that it bear the name of the person to be remembered. Otherwise, there is no control of form or content, no necessity for skill in design or execution. Kitsch, humor and high camp coexist with expressions of rage and sentiment. The importance of laughter in the face of the epidemic's horror is a key element of the Quilt. That humor and playfulness which are essential to life can exist simultaneously with the tragedy of loss indicates that living can go on. The Quilt makers' refusal to subsume AIDS tragedies under the common rubric of loss, but instead to contain in their panels the ironies and tackiness of a life fully lived illuminates and celebrates the complexities of living and not merely the death. Hawkins (1995) writes of the Quilt as a place which tells the story of individual lives. No spiritual intermediary is necessary to face death here. The growth of the Quilt and that it cannot be seen all at once reminds us of the multitudes lost. Many panels bear witness to the details of a life. Many function as testimony, quite simply, that this person was here "But the individual panels show what the AIDS epidemic has been powerless to destroy: quirkiness, sensuality, humor, the bonds of relationship, the value of private life, love" (Hawkins, 1995).

It is natural to believe that children should outlive their parents. But many parents have buried their children with AIDS. Art therapist, Anna Belle Kaufman, whose son was given a tainted blood transfusion at birth, died of AIDS at age five. She tells this story of Zack's panel for the Quilt:

> My sister had sent Zack a red kite with a green train and a pink heart for Christmas, but he died before he received it. I thought of a kite being up in the sky as an appropriate symbol for the soul of a child taking flight. I painted sky and white clouds and included his actual handprints in the clouds. . . . Zack's passion was trains, so I knew I had to have trains. . . . The train track represents infinity, in that it has no beginning and no end, but simply keeps going. . . . The name "Zack" in red is his signature, in his handwriting. In my handwriting, I added dates. I wanted people to know it was a child—that children die of AIDS. [For the UCLA ceremony in 1988] Zack's father and I brought the panel into a workshop where we put them together to make a square. There was a panel in the group for another child, a baby. For the ceremony, families with new panels unfolded the squares. Then the lights went out. They thought it was sabotage because of the rampant homophobia and fear of AIDS at that time. We were sent home and came back the next night for the ceremony.
>
> During the ceremony, everybody was weeping. But it felt like a community embrace, expressing pain but knowing you are not alone. Because we scattered Zack's ashes, the Quilt displays are the only place

I have to go and mourn, the only place where I know I can find my son. (Anna Belle Kaufman, personal communication, April 2007.)

IN THE FACE OF DEATH, THE IMPULSE TOWARD CREATIVITY

The Vietnam Veterans Memorial and the AIDS Quilt depend upon the presence of the image. In Quilt panels created for the dead and in the individual objects left at the Wall, creativity in the face of numbing grief and death are expressed in compelling imagery. The Quilt had no permanent home for many years,[4] but travels and can be said to embody within it a location, a *site of memory*. The Vietnam Veterans Memorial in the nation's capital is the location of American memory of this war. The creativity evoked in the presence of the dead is the remarkable attempt not only to remember the dead as a process of remembering and marking the meaning of their lives but to create something from that loss.

The desire to express and share personal experiences plays a central role in the creation of the image as a representation of memory and of meaning. Through creating as a social act, mourners make ritual memory objects to bring to the dead. Personal moments of a life are sewn into panels and are brought to the Wall. Through their impulse to create, mourners give meaning to their own lives. The act of creation in the face of death is a compelling *act of connection* between a community of mourners and the community of the dead.

Panel making for the Quilt and the selection of artifacts for the Wall are paradoxically cathartic and painful. For mourners, they provide an intense confrontation with grief and a deeply profound creativity that can help the artist/mourner begin to heal. As a panel is finished and sewn into the Quilt, as the intimate object is left at the Wall, a psychic mourning process continues of hypercathecting, detaching, connecting and letting go. And some form of preliminary closure can be expressed.

---

4. The Quilt is too big to travel whole, so pieces of it go around the country. It has found a home and is stored in Atlanta where there is now a NAMES Foundation and a museum.

MOURNING AND MEMORY: CONVERSATIONS WITH THE DEAD

Our thinking about memory has dramatically changed in a very short time. In mental health and in life, research has challenged many long-held assumptions about memory. Still we must acknowledge both the fragility and the endurance of memory. As with art therapy, memory is articulated through the processes of representation–in the image. The Vietnam Veterans Memorial and the AIDS Quilt are unusual memory objects in that they depict two shared national tragedies of the late twentieth century, representing two markers of what America was at that particular point in history. The Wall and the Quilt are forms that memory takes. In the waning years of the twentieth century both created communities of shared loss.

The AIDS Quilt and the Vietnam Veterans Memorial manifest *sites of memory*. Both memorials offer opportunity for an outpouring of loss and grief about traumas that had not been previously sanctioned. Their joint message is that memory has *purpose*–to remember is to give consolation to the living. In these instances, to remember has meant transforming public opinion in an America intent on forgetting returning veterans and focused on making invisible what was perceived to be a gay disease. The memorials express the value of making intimate reality *public.* Oblivion and forgetting are death in life. The Wall and the Quilt keep us from the death of forgetting.

When we visit and revisit these memorials which represent vast cemeteries of the lost, we reopen our grief once again–we open the wound so that it may bleed freely to blend with our tears, to perhaps eventually heal, although we may bear scars forever. This process of mourning is at once transformative and rehabilitative. A wife of a Vietnam veteran tells of her husband who goes to the wall when he has something he wants to think about (Sturken, 1997). Through ritualized remembrance, the Quilt and the Wall have become places to visit memories, to have a conversation with the dead. But the Wall and Quilt are as much about survival and about life itself, as they are about mourning.

The transformative and rehabilitative process of mourning enabling a return to life is enacted through the creativity of the Quilt panels and through the intimate and ritualized memory objects left at the Wall. These memory objects can have many conflicting interpretations and are ultimately mysterious in meaning. Created memories represent a form of interpretation. But within the essential process of mourning, people reenact the trauma and their reactions to it and participate in giving meaning to the past and the present and, therefore, to the future.

The Quilt and the Wall act as forms of collective remembering and contribute to a cultural memory which is outside the mainstream; they express a sense of American culture not typically accepted because it symbolically represents those who have been marginalized and excluded. The memorials are about personal cultural memory, not about generalization. The AIDS epidemic and the Vietnam War produced new stories and radical resistance. These stories confronted and interrupted the dominant historic narratives of the United States, those of science and technology, masculinity and American imperialism. The contested histories of the Vietnam War and the AIDS epidemic are still fluid and formative and still contested. They demand unique forms of commemoration to give presence and voice for mourning and for memory. The Vietnam Veterans Memorial and the AIDS Quilt are these unique forms. Sturken (1997) argues for cultural memory as an "inventive social practice" and not a representation of the truth of an experience. According to Sturken, memory as an individual and social act is invention and meaning-making; it includes fantasy and remembrance. To remember is an imaginative reworking of the traumas of the past, creating new meaning and value in the present.

CONCLUSIONS

The lessons from the Vietnam Veterans Memorial and its artifacts and the AIDS Quilt are many. They focus on the inclusion of disenfranchised and marginalized people, and they remind us of the tremendous importance of the ritual of creativity. Creativity in the face of death offers a spectrum of life-enhancing possibilities. These possibilities can ward off a meaningless conclusion to a life, give meaning and hope to a life lived and to a future in which the dead, through memory, still exist. In the Wall artifacts and the Quilt panels, creativity is not merely about remembering the dead. Unconsciously or consciously, it is an effort to create something new from that loss. The power of the created memory image remains a talisman and a touchstone. It is both a symbolized ritualized process and an art product inherently full of meaning. Its singular power lies in its ability to portray a life. The art image reminds us of the personal complexities beneath a surface—of a human life lost and remembered,

Implications for clinical practice are cultural and systemic. The clinician must recognize that they and their clients are bound to a unique cultural moment. They are part of it and structured by it. It lives in them and is inescapable. Paradoxically, the culture also changes minute-to-minute. The old mental health treatment notions of "adaptation to culture" no longer hold. They have not been effective for a long time now. Art therapists must reconfigure themselves to become change agents whose materials and media are not only the human life in front of them, but the *culture itself.* They must strive to enhance and "grow" a positive environment that will not only sustain but will nurture. This comes about because of who the therapist is, what they do in the world and what their clients do.

To be of real help, I believe the therapist must pay close attention to these larger community and systemic concerns. The creation of community art projects as exemplified in the Vietnam Veterans Memorial artifacts and the AIDS Quilt engage people together in the remarkable power of the arts for change through the creation of meaning. It is my hope that the art therapy and creative arts therapies communities can begin to more clearly define themselves to act as arts communities and activists with special skills and a special purpose: to use the arts as agents of change for a world sorely in need. Arguably, the most important lesson the memorials teach, is about human beings yearning to be part of something bigger than themselves. Coming together with many others and leaving one's mark on the whole is both transformative and transcendental. In the process of collaboration one leaves one's imprint through the image connecting the person to the community of others who have undergone the tragic consequences of suffering. Through the creation of *meaning and hope,* our common bond can continue on—like life. In this way, the therapist and client become co-creators, an interconnected community so to speak. Suffering cannot be eliminated, but in art it can be expressed, given voice and thereby transformed. The client and therapist come together to create an image which weaves a path through trauma and suffering, which engenders hope and which finally may enable life to go on.

REFERENCES

Ault, R., Barlow, G., Junge, M. & Moon, B. (1989). Social applications of the arts. *Art Therapy, Journal of the American Art Therapy Association, 5,* 10–22.

Berkowitz, S. (1990). Art therapy with a Vietnam veteran who has posttraumatic stress disorder. *Pratt Institute Creative Arts Therapy Review, 11,* 47–63.

Case, C. (1987). A search for meaning: Loss and transition in art therapy with children. In T. Dalley (Ed.), *Images of art therapy: New developments in theory and practice.* New York: Tavistock/Routledge.

Felber, M. (1993). *Using art therapy in treatment of psychological trauma: An introduction manual for latin american mental health professionals.* Unpublished Masters Thesis. Los Angeles, CA: Loyola Marymount University,

Franklin, M. (1993). AIDS iconography and cultural transformation: Visual and artistic responses to the AIDS crisis. *The Arts in Psychotherapy, 20,* 299–316.

Golub, D. (1985). Symbolic expression in post-traumatic stress disorder: Vietnam combat veterans in art therapy. *The Arts in Psychotherapy, 12,* 285–296.

Hawkins, P. (1993). Naming names: The art of memory and the NAMES Project AIDS quilt. *Critical Inquiry, 19,* 753–779.

Hawkins, P. (1995). Stitches in time. *The Yale Review, 83,* 1–15.

Jones, J. (1997). Art therapy with a community of survivors. *Art Therapy, Journal of the American Art Therapy Association, 14,* 89–94.

Junge, M. (1985). The book about daddy dying: A preventive art therapy technique to help a family deal with the death of one of its members. *Art Therapy, Journal of the American Art Therapy Association, 2,* 4–10.

Junge, M., Alvarez, J., Kellogg, A. & Volker, C. (1993). The art therapist as social activist. *Art Therapy, Journal of the American Art Therapy Association, 10,* 148–155.

Kaufman, A. (1996). Art in boxes: An exploration of meanings. *The Arts in Psychotherapy, 23,* 1–11.

Kerewsky, S. (1997). The AIDS memorial quilt: Personal and therapeutic uses. *The Arts in Psychotherapy, 24,* 431–438.

Kornreich, S. (1993). Group art therapy intervention with bereaved children in the elementary school. In E. Virshup (Ed.) *California Art Therapy Trends,* Chicago, IL: Magnolia Street Publishers.

Landgarten, H., Tasem, M., Junge, & M., Watson, M. (1978). Art therapy as a modality for crisis intervention. *Journal of Clinical Social Work, 6,* 221–229.

McDougall, H. (1992). Finding the light at the end of the funnel: Working with child survivors of the Andover tornado. *Art Therapy, Journal of the American Art Therapy Association, 9,* 42–47.

McIntyre, B. (1990). Art therapy with bereaved youth. *Journal of Palliative Care, 6,* 16–25.

Pert, C., Dreher, H. & Ruff, M. (1998). The psychosomatic network: foundations of mind-body medicine. *Alternative Therapies, 4,* 30–41.

Roje, J. (1994). L.A.'94 earthquake in the eyes of children: Art therapy with elementary school children who were victims of disaster. *Art Therapy, Journal of the American Art Therapy Association, 12,* 237–243.

Ruskin, C., Herron, M. & Zemke, D. (1988). *The Quilt: Stories from the NAMES Project.* New York: Simon & Schuster, Inc.

Sherebrin, H. (1991) Art therapy in a war zone. *Art Therapy, Journal of the American Art Therapy Association, 8,* 30–32.

Speert, E. (1992). The use of art therapy following perinatal death. *Art Therapy, Journal of the American Art Therapy Association, 9,* 121–128.

Stronach-Buschel, B. (1990). Trauma, children and art. *The American Journal of Art Therapy, 29,* 48–52.

Sturken, M. (1997). *Tangled Memories: The Vietnam War, the AIDS Epidemic, and the Politics of Remembering.* Berkeley, CA: University of California Press.

The NAMES Project (1996). Too many names to forget. *On Display, 9,* 5–12.

Zambelli, G., Clark, E. & Heegaard, M. (1989). Art therapy for bereaved children. In Wadeson, H. & Durkin, J. (Eds.), *Advances in Art Therapy.* New York: John Wiley & Sons.

Chapter 2

THE PERCEPTION OF DOORS, A SOCIODYNAMIC INVESTIGATION OF DOORS IN 20TH CENTURY PAINTING[1]

If the doors of perception were cleansed everything would appear to man as it is: infinite. For man has closed himself up, till he sees all things thro' narrow chinks of his cavern.
William Blake (1757–1827)

If one were to give an account of all the doors one has closed and opened, of all the doors one would like to re-open, one would have to tell the story of one's entire life.
Gaston Bachelard[2]

In this essay I present a sociodynamic investigation of doors as boundary in twentieth century painting. Within a phenomenological perspective, using paintings as visual semiotic reflections of psychological states, I explore meaning to penetrate and illuminate interpretations of space. Images of doors by painters Georgia O'Keeffe, Pierre Bonnard, Edward Hopper, Alice Neel, Elizabeth Layton, Ben Shahn and Mark Rothko are used to plumb dimensions of the human being's relationship to the environment and to speculate about balance, intimacy, separation, limits and boundaries. The artist's visual

---

1. This essay is printed with changes from Junge, M. (1988). The perception of doors: A sociodynamic investigation of doors in 20th century painting. *The Arts in Psychotherapy, 21,* 343–357. Used with permission.
2. Quotations from Gaston Bachelard are from *The Poetics of Space*, translated by Maria Jolas, copyright © 1964 by The Orion Press, Inc. Original copyright © 1958 by Presses Universitaires de France. Used with permission of Viking Penguin, a division of Penguin Group (USA) Inc.

topology is seen as metaphor—a doorway if you will—through which to encounter deeper levels of meaning hidden beneath the surface. This inquiry is based on the assumption that experiences of personal space and boundary are intrinsically linked to human development, psycho-pathology and psychotherapy and therefore have direct relevance for arts psychotherapists and the mental health community. The investigation is driven by an essential tenet of expressive therapies: that created artwork is a visual map of the person's inner world, of their world view and their reality. Entering deeply in and dwelling in the world of the visual product, we may gain understanding useful to us as psychotherapy clinicians and to our clients and enriching to us and to them as human beings. When asked why he chose certain subjects, painter Edward Hopper spoke of his art as the outward expression of *his inner world* and painting as a *synthesis* of this inner experience. Artists have much to teach clinicians about the psychological vicissitudes of space and human personality.

PERSONAL

When my son was 17 years old in the spring semester of his senior year in high school, he began to leave open the front door of the house as he went out to school in the morning. Then, upon returning in the late afternoons, dropping his things as he went, he would strew his school books and jacket from the door on down the hallway to his room. Neither of these behaviors was typical of Benjamin who since a small child had known well to close and (with two working parents and the increasing dangers of city life) lock the front door. Although he was not famous in the family for any exceptional neatness, Ben had previously managed to contain his messes within the confines of his room behind his closed door. But that spring was different. Along with anxious high school students across the country, he was waiting for answers to his applications to college; he was hoping for admittance to his first choice—a college on another coast—3000 miles from Los Angeles and home. And he was approaching that essential rite of passage of June—high school graduation—with its co-existing excitement for a future with new experiences of independence and growth and its sadness of leaving old friends and familiar comforts. Ben was fast-reaching the boundary that separates childhood and the beginning of adult life.

Ben's struggle to maneuver through the shoals of that ambivalent transition was expressed in many ways, but no more dramatically than through the metaphor of the door. As he left it open in the morning to adventure out, he symbolically kept open the possibility of returning to a known and comfortable environment. As he re-entered the door in the afternoon and scattered his belongings inside, he created for himself a trail, like a reverse Hansel and Gretel's bread crumbs, to mark the way back to the door and its beckoning future of independence and potential. Bachelard (1964), a French philosopher, wrote: "Memories are motionless, and the more securely they are fixed in space the sounder they are."

Western thought has historically dichotomized person and environment whereas Eastern tradition conceptualizes a wholistic reality with few such separating boundaries. Some have written of *birth* as the first experience of boundary—of inside and outside, of self and world, of person and environment. Artists use this concept in their understanding of aesthetic space as not dichotomized—not empty nor filled—but instead positive and negative space as two equally important sides of the same coin. The artist may paint an object, but the object defines the space around it as the space around it defines the object and it is *together* that they create meaning. Artistic space is never merely vacant; it is full of potential in a contextualized relationship.

Based in an environmental psychology perspective, in this inquiry I explore the sociodynamic implications of doors as boundary in some visual artist's work. Resting on the assumption of the human being as actor on the environment and the environment as actor on the human being, this essay is frankly explorative and speculative. My exploration is based on the belief that the artist's *work* reflects a social-psychological milieu and provides important *artifacts* of social phenomena, which reciprocally, may influence and define our environment. My speculations represent the eye and heart of an art psychotherapist at work. My thinking about art in this essay is not unlike my conversations with therapy clients regarding their creative work as our verbal dialogue back and forth compares the client's comments and validating thoughts with the viewer/therapist's reactions. This essay does not pretend to offer answers; it suggests that a framework for thinking and experiencing from different fields and disciplines can be useful and that evidence from art may take us closer to unconscious meanings about self and environment.

THE DOOR AS DIALECTICAL INTEGRATION OF INSIDE AND OUTSIDE

Spatial experience is acquired by infants much earlier than human speech. First, they perceive mother and self as same. But soon they reach out to touch, to grasp, to explore–a breast, a finger, a rattle–and to acquire firsthand knowledge of their environment. Before infants are many months old, they crawl. As children mature, they venture out. We begin with these early experiences and our referent for environmental scale is always the human body.

Our first home, our total environment is within our mother's womb. After birth, each of us inhabits an essential personal universe radiating out from our own body and with our most important boundary of the skin. It is from this *self as home* that we encounter, experience and interact with the larger environment. Writers from many disciplines have developed the model of the house as self. Jung (1969) emphasized the house as a self symbol and defined the self as both individual and social, existing within a social context. Bachelard (1964) elaborated on the theme in his suggestion that as the self and the non-self represent the basic divisions of psychic space, they are represented by house and non-house (environment) as basic divisions of geographical space. The house both encloses and excludes space. Its dialectical opposites are reflected in interior and façade, inside and outside. A house defines an intimate interior revelation of self which may be protected, controlled and revealed only to those invited inside. Its exterior (in Jungian terms, the Persona or mask) expresses a metaphor for the public self we choose to show to others. Writing on the history of religion, Eliade (1959) expanded this assumption. He wrote of *the threshold* as the division between known and unknown. According to Eliade, outside is chaotic space, sometimes peopled by demons and ghosts; chaotic space is distinctly foreign. Inside the house is the world the person constructs. He states that it is not easy to change houses because it means an abandonment of one's world.[3] Describing the entrance to a temple as the division between the profane of the outside universe and the consecrated inner world, Eliade says the threshold is suitably embellished to ward off evil spirits that might seek to invade.

---

3. Much of contemporary interior design, in my opinion, is intentionally impersonal and thus in opposition to this idea. A celebrity writing in a magazine recently expresses that he wanted his home to be as much like a fine hotel as possible. If we are to read meanings expressed in personal space, what are we to make of this lack of personalness?

As with the human body, essential elements of any building or house are the *openings* between interior space and the outside world which permit interchange to support and renew life. The location of the threshold and its unique configuration varies in different cultures and offers a symbolic metaphor for the individual's relationship with the world outside the door. Greenbie (1981) writes that the nature of openings define whether they are boundary or barrier, home or a prison, allowing the world to come in or walling it out.

The following speak of the writer's awareness of the psychological and symbolic implications underlying one's sense of boundary and of door: As a child, French author Collette was told not to eat with her mouth open. Anais Nin writes about seeing a closed garden gate from her window which felt to her like a prison and was, she thought, a reflection of her projected inner obstacles keeping her from a full life outside. At times she saw this gate as invitingly half open. And, of course there is Robert Frost in his poem "Mending Wall" who famously spoke of knowing whether a wall was keeping something in or out.

At the dialectical poles of self and other—of house and universe— stands the pull of inside and outside as felt through the artist's imagery of the door. Bachelard (1964) described some dialectics of inside and outside as "this side and beyond," "here and there," running toward the center or escaping," void and non-void," "within and without," "open and closed," "surface separated from region of other," "the 'yes' and 'no' which divides everything" and he questioned:

> But how many daydreams we should have to analyze under the simple heading of Doors! For the door is an entire cosmos of the Half-open . . . [it] accumulates desires and temptations: the temptation to open up the ultimate depths of being and the desire to conquer all reticent beings. The door schematizes two strong possibilities which sharply classify two types of daydream. At times, it is closed, bolted, padlocked. At others, it is open.

Georgia O'Keeffe bought her house at Abiquiu near Santa Fe, New Mexico because of her obsession with a door she saw in a wall there. She painted it over and over. In Chapter 3, "Georgia O'Keeffe: Themes and Resonances" I write about O'Keeffe's art as visual metaphors symbolic of psychological personality struggles concerning independence and intimacy, separation and attachment. I speculate that the viewer of her art catches a painted image of these struggles through O'Keeffe's extreme sensitivity to distinctive boundary and edge in her art and to the relationships between filled space and void. O'Keeffe, in a 1944 exhibition catalog, described her ongoing awareness of the pulls of this spatial quality of *interaction*: "I was the sort of child that ate around the raisin on the cookies and around the hole in the doughnut" (O'Keeffe, 1976.)

O'Keeffe's many paintings of the door in her house at Abiquiu in New Mexico are *open spaces,* not closed opaque separators.[4] In one painting, we see the Abiquiu door from an undefined interior patio which speaks of the intimacy and secrecy of enclosure. Yet in the mysterious dark of the painting, we find ourselves simultaneously held and intrigued with a world outside. True to the built architecture typical of a particular culture, time and place—adobe houses of the southwest— as was typical of her work, the painter has reduced detail to essence, creating a sense of timelessness and the appearance of an archetypal symbol. One can hardly imagine the hand of a human being using tools in the construction of O'Keeffe's house. And if ever a wooden door for the opening we see, existed here to close and to open, it has long since faded away with only the essential shell remaining. We are reminded of O'Keeffe's famous paintings of skulls bleached white by the desert.

The composition's center of interest is the beautiful shape described by and seen through the door. Thus, the viewer remains bound in space between inner comfort and outer adventure. O'Keeffe's door at Abiquiu invites contemplation, daydreaming, but not action, and it exerts a feeling of tension and a bit of danger; it is not a door one wants eagerly to walk through. Human behavior within O'Keeffe's spaces would need to be careful, quiet, meditative and adult. The loud, messy habitation of children cannot be imagined within them.

An example of exterior doorways from O'Keeffe's paintings of Canadian barns also illustrates the point of the continuity of the painter's psychological vision. We sense a cool, neat life within the buildings. It is difficult to imagine that "real" farmers or livestock live or work inside. The artist holds us at bay; we are caught in the boundary of the threshold of picture frame. No imagistic paths are offered that provide entry. O'Keeffe's doors are apparently open but, paradoxically, they serve to keep us at an edge that we are not permitted to cross. Simultaneously, they invite us in and they keep us out. The struggle to cross the threshold keeps the viewer bound in a dialectical tension.

---

4. Unfortunately, the Georgia O'Keeffe Estate refused permission to reprint images of her artwork and therefore I refer the reader to the prints in O'Keeffe, 1976. It was said that she didn't want her work having to do with anything psychological.

O'Keeffe wrote: "The black door held a horrible fascination for me . . . You find a door and you are bound to it. It's a curse the way I feel that I must continually go on with that door" (1976).

INTERIORS AND THE EXPERIENCE OF INTIMACY

Crossing the threshold into the personal space of interiors, filling our vision and our psyche with a sense of more private intricacies inside, we nevertheless remain aware of the dialectical pull of the universe *outside* the door. Asymmetrical though the tension is when inward (or outward), there remains a dynamic sense of counter-energy to the prevailing focus. Our houses provide privacy, the regulation of human interaction, shelter and an environment for the deepest of human relationships—family life.

The sense of the separate family dwelling as a revelation of self may be particularly American. For example, many Americans still hold the image of the individualistic frontiersman of the last centuries in the wild, clearing the land to build a house for his family. Studies in England, Australia and the United States have shown that when asked to describe their ideal house, people of all incomes and backgrounds tend to describe free-standing, detached family homes (Cooper, 1976). In 1968, in a survey of 748 people in 32 urban areas in the United States, 85 percent stated that they preferred to live in a separate family house rather than in an apartment (Michelson, 1968). This survey is almost 40 years old, and the uses of urban space and of lifestyle have changed dramatically in that time, but it may be that the myth of the self-made man, carving out his home in the wilderness and protecting his family against ever-encroaching intruders, remains a psychologically pervasive paradigm.

Studies of personal space, territoriality and crowding perpetuate the notion that we carry with us an innate sense of space. Although these studies are based on differing assumptions about the etiology of a person's spatial needs, there is agreement that to deprive one of the essential sense of space usually leads to psychopathology and even, ultimately to breakdown in the sense of self. Bachelard wrote:

> . . . [the] house shelters daydreaming, the house protects the dreamer, the house allows one to dream in peace. Thought and experience are not the only things that sanction human values. The values that belong to daydreaming mark humanity in its depths. (1964)

French painter Pierre Bonnard is known for his benign and intimate scenes of family life and for his luxurious, decorative compositions that often combine landscape with interiors of everyday French life. Figure 2-1 is a painting of the dining room in Bonnard's country home.

Figure 2-1. Pierre Bonnard's "Dining Room in the Country, 1913," Minneapolis Institute of Arts. Reprinted with permission.

Through his use of color and structure, Bonnard renders the interior centrally important in this composition. The middle-value blue of the table extends into the middle-value green of the door. The two structures together create a central shape that divides the picture plane to effectively contrast inside and outside. The walls of the dining room are deep red, providing a sense of lushness and interest inside not repeated in the somewhat haphazard and accidental landscape outside. Although this is in no way a forbidding landscape, even the tree seems frail and does not invite. The female figure outside is wearing a red dress (like the red of the dining room) and appears to belong to the interior rather than to the cool hues of the landscape. She leans on the windowsill looking inward. The comfortable rocking chair inside, inhabited by a kitten seems a safer place from which to view the environment as observer of the scene rather than as an actor in it. Nevertheless, the door to the room stands wide-open as does the window; it is a door with its four panes of glass constructed to let in the light and landscape and to create for the inhabitants of this room an interaction of their interior world with the rural landscape. In this painting, there is an intensely real sense of the relational influences of human behavior and environment.

American artist Edward Hopper portrays a different version of interior-exterior visual meaning and relationship. In his interior of a public place, "Sunlight in a Cafeteria" of 1958, (Figure 2-2). Hopper paints a door as an enigma. In Hopper's painting, a woman sits near the window highlighted against a wall slanted with bright sunlight. Her arms are bare and round. With an untouched coffee cup before her, she looks down, lost in thought. A green, spiky plant sits on the windowsill but does not catch the sun. The urban building outside is gray, anonymous and forbidding while sidewalk and stores seem empty of all human imprint. On the right side of the painting, in shadow, sits a man who may be looking at the woman or looking at the window; it is unclear. His back is to us and we see his profile. He holds a cigarette, but his hands seem ineffectual. There is no evidence of replenishing food in front of him. A shaft of sunlight strikes the wall near the figure, but it only serves to increase his gray, almost ghostlike appearance.

Figure 2-2. Edward Hopper's "Sunlight in a Cafeteria 1958," Yale University Art Gallery, Bequest of Stephen Carlton Clark, BA 1903. Reprinted with permission.

Compositionally, there are three doors in this painting and, because of their visual meaning, we have the feeling that not one of them can be opened nor threshold crossed. On the left, the window serves as a door closing off the ominous outside environment. This must be the cleanest window in the city because we have no feeling of it as glass or tangible reality. Paradoxically, this complete transparency serves to accentuate the effect of closure and separateness inside. It might as well be a brick wall! The boundary delineated by the sunlit wall, between the woman's row of tables and the man's becomes another impenetrable barrier prohibiting human interaction. The "actual" door of the painting, the revolving door, is tucked into the wall on the right side on the man's side of the picture. It seems too small in scale for the other structures. It is not clear that it is big enough for real people to maneuver through. The viewer cannot understand the relationship of this door to the outside landscape. It provides a formidable barrier in which one could apparently revolve forever. Size and ambiguity of interactional potential make this door seem false, tricky and intensely dangerous. The only air and life in Hopper's urban world are where the woman sits in the sun. Although she appears physically healthy, the viewer feels that time has stopped—the plant will not grow and the waitress will not bring lunch. In Hopper's world, people do not interact with each other or their surroundings. They sit suspended in a wax museum of architecture with no exit, into eternity. What is not allowed through this door is change.

Alice Neel was an individualistic New York painter who died some years ago at age 87 and who had become known for her honest and idiosyncratic portraits of well-known people. Elizabeth Layton, who died relatively recently, was a Kansas artist who began to draw at the age of 68 and through her artwork, mostly self portraits, found a way to come to terms with a difficult life and a 30-year struggle with depression. Both women married, raised children and grappled with the prevailing expectations and limitations of women in this culture. In looking through books of reproductions of the two artists' work, I was struck by doors only appearing in association with a particular subject—that of family.

Figure 2-3. Alice Neel's "Mother and child, 1967," Private Collection. © Estate of Alice Neel. Reprinted with permission.

Neel's artwork is direct and unencumbered. Her portraits seldom include background information of any kind. In reproductions of 179 of her works, there are merely seven doors, or shapes that could be construed as door, and most appear in paintings of Neel's family (Hills, 1983). In these family compositions, space around the figures deepens and becomes more complicated. Neel's are not doors to read as simply open or closed, as connecting interior to environment psychologically or physically; they are more complex than that. But that they exist at all in her family portraits leads me to speculate about the artist as mother and grandmother. I cannot help wondering if whatever ambivalences pervaded this role for Neel are not expressed through the image of the door: women bear children, raise them, love them and then let them go out the door to create their own life's adventures.

In *Through the Looking Glass: Drawings by Elizabeth Layton*, 36 drawings are reproduced (Mid-America Arts Alliance Program, 1984). Doors are included in only four compositions. Three of these appear in portraits of Layton's second husband Glen. Layton married her first husband in 1929 when she was 20 years old. After ten years she found herself with an unstable marriage and five children. She endured a series of separations for the next years divorcing her husband finally in 1953. Divorce then in a small Kansas town, was thought to be immoral.

Layton married Glen in 1957 shortly after undergoing 13 electroshock treatments. Layton's open doors speak of the comings and goings of a marriage, of reciprocal giving as love, and of the lack of privacy and the psychological and physical shrinkages of illness (Figure 2-4).

Figure 2-4. Elizabeth Layton's "Husband on Scales.'" Courtesy of Don Lambert, Topeka, Kansas. Reprinted with permission.

Bachelard described houses as

The places in which we have experienced *daydreaming* . . . it is because our memories of former dwelling places are relived as daydreams that these dwelling places of the past remain in us for all time. . . . We cover the universe with drawings we have lived. These drawings need not be exact. They need only to be tonalized on the mode of our inner space.

EXTERIORS AND THE EXPERIENCE OF SEPARATION

When we enter the surround—the outside environment—we may feel a sense of spaciousness, freedom, independence and a fear that we are outside our skin and alien to home. Naturally, our experience of exterior space, whether built or natural landscape, differs and carries meaning according to its own reality, our feeling response to it and the interaction between. Although both offer spatial and visual excitement, to walk in the skyscraper canyons of New York is a different sensation than to stroll the wild-flowered Headlands of Mendocino, near my home in Northern California, watching the wild ocean break over ancient rock formations. All behavior takes place in some sort of space and all behavior is an adaptation to a physical environment. Differing environments require dissimilar behavioral responses.

Winston Churchill said "We shape our buildings and thereafter they shape us." The relationship between the architectural environment and the individual is complex and shapes human mood and behavior. Some environmental psychologists propose an architectural determinism that forms people's behavior. This viewpoint ignores interaction influences, privacy and group formation. Other researchers suggest that an architectural environment presents us with opportunities wherein we are free to make individual choices. Obviously, the reality lies somewhere in between in that all architecture allows for choice, but also offers probabilities associated with specificities of design defining behavior. Built architecture represents an environment constructed by human hands interposed between people and the natural environment. We relate to the built environment experienced from the outside and it limits and bounds our sense of our self psychologically and physically. Are we caught once again in a dialectical labyrinth? In the exciting expansiveness and potentiality of the surround do we also feel cast out of intimacy and do we paradoxically yearn to "go home again"? Or do we eagerly seek to walk away to adventure, to find a separate context to escape the constraints of home? Doors by artists provide interesting definition to the meaning of being outside.

If Edward Hopper's interiors often convey feelings of loneliness and separation within the potential for intimacy and a dangerous world outside, his exteriors perpetuate his vision. In "Early Sunday Morning" (Figure 2-5) by removing all people and their activity, Hopper again creates an image of detachment and silence. Although this building clearly contains human activities and commerce, all are now suspended. The light falls on the upstairs windows where we guess people sleep. Downstairs, shops are empty and in shadow; their doorways deeply hidden within the structure, like eyes behind closed lids. Monday morning, the doorways and the stores will open again and people will move through them, but for today it would not do to go banging on these doors. As the viewer projects into the future of Monday morning, we imagine that, like a stage set, these buildings are shallow, will only allow for limited activity in space, and that people who enter and exit these doors will move slowly as in a dream.

Figure 2-5. Edward Hopper's "Early Sunday Morning, 1930." Collection of Whitney Museum of American Art, New York. Purchased with funds from Gertrude Vanderbilt Whitney. Reprinted with permission.

Hopper's "South Carolina Morning" (Figure 2-6) and "Summertime" each show a solitary female figure emerging through a door into the sunlight. Both women stand on the last step and seem to be considering whether to cross into the outside world. In Figure 2-6, sunlight assaults her and the woman bends backward to avoid sun and heat.

Window shutters are tightly shut. The house seems suspended above yellow grass, but not connected to it–substantial yet detached. In the distance is a hint of a cooling ocean but one cannot see a pathway through the grass to reach it.

The young woman in "Summertime" (she resembles the figure in the sunlit cafeteria) seems to be enjoying the sunlight. She has walked away from the cool and shadowy door, come down the steps and will soon walk into the street. We imagine she may be on her way to meet a friend. The possibility of human dialogue exists in this environment. Wind rustles curtains through an open window that conveys a sense of interaction between interior and exterior elements and hints at a door that permits free interchange of inside and outside. The threshold is a cocoon to protect the figure. But we infer the door behind the figure is closed and is a barrier. We speculate that the woman would go back inside if she could to the comforting cool and dark. Avoidant, she is thrust out alone into the unwelcoming elements.

Figure 2-6. Edward Hopper's "South Carolina Morning, 1955." Collection of Whitney Museum of American Art. Given in memory of Otto L. Spaeth by his family. Reprinted with permission.

In "East 12th Street" and "Book Shop: Hebrew Books, Holy Day Books," Ben Shahn portrays two conflicting versions of doorways in the urban scene. In "East 12th Street" three girls roller-skate up a sidewalk past hundreds of anonymous, unwelcoming doorways. Another series of doorways frames the opposite side of the empty street. These opposite doors have large round holes in them. The viewer experiences the doors as fortress, as thick barrier against what must be the fearful environment outside. The holes portray a kind of peephole through which the distrustful person inside can peer out unobserved. But the fortress doors are impenetrable. It seems impossible that any of the three people on the street would be able to open one of these doors to go inside. Streets are centers of social life and they are passageways. But Shahn's street through the lonely landscape is solely a passageway. His environment is stripped of trees and cars and empty of any signs of the litter and residue of human life. Is this a war zone after the rubble has been cleaned away? The girls' roller skates give a hint of play, but they may also simply be a way to speed more quickly than walking through the devastated desolate city toward the horizon line and the natural world of sky.

In "Book Shop," Shahn describes a more welcoming doorway. This bookstore door image connects the viewer to ethnicity and to the pleasures of a homogenous Jewish cultural group. We have an echo of an attachment/separation theme in the contrasting demands of the American immigrant experience of assimilation and differentiation within the dominant culture. In particular, the painting conveys values of the Jewish culture, with its emphasis on education and books as the repository and the carrier of tradition. Additionally, we gain a sense of the Jewish emphasis on family through the portrayal of mother and baby. The image conveys that there is not only past but future and that the ethnic/religious traditions of comfortable stability will be passed on.

Through his expressive line, Shahn emphasizes the architectural details of the building that are ordered, balanced and reminiscent of Roman architecture. The door itself is sheltered within an alcove and the woman stands against it with her baby. As doorway shelters the woman and her baby, so the bookstore shelters books. As far as the viewer can tell, it is a glass door. Unlike Hopper's window in Figure 2-2, this glass has substance and offers protection, but it also presents a comforting transparency. The eye can see through it to the inside and to the outside. That this store houses books, with all their information and potential odysseys for the imagination, offers interest and comfort (for those of us who love bookstores). And the sign in the window, "Basement," lets us know that this building has depths to discover (and perhaps bargains). Viewers bring their own associations to the picture, which creates an image in the mind of a familiar and inviting interior.

It is interesting to compare the relationship to its environment of Shahn's figure in the doorway with those of Hopper. Shahn's mother and child seem intimately connected to their surroundings. Perhaps they live in the store or building. They are protected by the entryway and compositionally by the shape of the door. This visual meaning is echoed in the way the mother protects and contains her baby with her shawl; but the baby's head is free to explore the world. The figures are not thrust out, nor held inertly within the door frame—there is individual choice in such a world—and we interpret a relaxed integration of intimate needs with the expectation of choiceful independent action through the urban environment.

Most of the examples in this section are from urban landscape and, in most, we sense the separation of the city dweller who, within the density, noise and stimulation of the urban world, feels alone. Outside the composed space of façade, in the external world, we are aware of an interior life inside the boundary of the door that may be comfortable, compelling, distanced or refuge. In these artists' paintings, the viewer experiences what it would feel like to go back and forth through the door and whether exterior is compatible with inner space. By removing evidence of human interaction and visible detritus of human behavior Hopper and Shahn create an exterior landscape stripped to basics, a silent world with all sound muffled in cotton, a world sucked clean of air, a world in which we feel alone. It is a world that exerts a strange fascination on the viewer because it is so alien to our day-to-day experience of urban life. The imagistic subtext is of the profound loneliness and isolation underlying much of urban life.

A different sense is conveyed by Hopper's "Summertime" and Shahn's "Book Shop" in that the possibility of human interaction and connection exists in these exteriors—of dialogue, diverse and homogenous, small group behavior and of community.

---

5. *Webster's Ninth New Collegiate Dictionary*, 1986.

THROUGH THE DOOR AND BEYOND: TRANSCENDENCE

Dictionary definitions of transcendence are "exceeding usual limits," "extending or lying beyond the limits of ordinary experience." In Kantian terms, they are "beyond the limits of all possible experience and knowledge," and "transcending the universe or material existence."[5] Transcendence implies the going beyond ordinary material reality and boundaries of thought and feeling. In a dream, we open a door and find ourselves transformed within a spatial, psychological experience that did not exist until we dreamed it. Out of the paraphernalia of daily life and events, out of all that we know and are, though an act of transformative imagination in our dreams, we create a new existence unencumbered by laws of gravity or demands of a real world. Some artists through the creative act have portrayed a visual imagery of transcendence that communicates to the viewer and promotes a perceptual dialogue that can take one into new realms of being. Bachelard wrote: "The poet speaks on the threshold of being" (1964).

Abstract Expressionist painter Mark Rothko paints transcendence in art. To experience his rectangles of fluctuating color is to enter metaphoric doorways through which viewers pass and are transformed. The intensity of the physical reality of Rothko's paintings cannot be understood by looking at reproductions. But standing in front of one of his huge paintings (or a wall of them) in a museum, viewers find themselves drawn past the outer boundaries of the canvas into a fascinating world of color and feeling, through which one passes as if in a dream. If viewers allow the called-for fusion with the image, they *become* for a moment the image and cannot return unchanged. Huge expanses of color juxtapositions create a psychological and physical reaction in viewers. The paintings seem to breathe and hover. Art historian and Rothko's biographer, Dore Ashton wrote:

> He knew how to stage a moment of stasis full of promise. I can remember entering the Janis Gallery and stopping in the center of the room. It was much as if I had entered a remote forest on a still day with nothing stirring, and heard, or imagined I heard, a single faint rustle somewhere. In [Rothko's] paintings there was always some all but invisible movement that I could never quite locate but that seemed to pervade the whole . . . it was this very equivocation that gave back so much that had been banished from painting—a chance for metaphor, a chance for indeterminate feeling, a chance for mystery. (1983)

Abstractions, relying on universal, archetypal forms and colors, Rothko's paintings speak of another place and of a hidden world beyond, beneath the surface that is apparently visible but easily vanishes as we move into the picture. Ashton wrote:

> [Rothko] discovered that a painting sufficiently large so that when you stand close, the edges are grayed off to one's peripheral vision, takes on a kind of presence in its surface that renders internal relationships irrelevant . . . [it] is like opening a door into an internal realm. (1983)[6]

Rothko could have been describing the experience of transcendence when he said about the process of creating his paintings that ideas at the beginning were merely the doorway through which one could leave the world. Within Rothko's compelling vision, viewers are invited through the doorway of the canvas frame, into a resonating enigmatic and obscure environment of the mind and heart beyond anything known or seen. Rothko had said he wanted to paint the finite and the infinite. The paintings from his last years, after a serious aneurysm, were dark and foreboding. Inserted in them was a decisive line separating two rectangles. Mark Rothko committed suicide in 1970 at the age of 67.

CONCLUSIONS

Within a sociodynamic perspective as an art psychotherapist, I have explored images of doors by twentieth century painters. Some dimensions of the human being's relationship to environment have been illuminated as I have speculated about balance, intimacy, separation, limits, and boundaries. This exploration was based on the assumption that—like the client's creative work in art therapy—the artist's visual topology in paintings represents an externalization of an internal psychic world and can be seen as metaphor, a doorway in this case, through which to plum deeper levels of meaning beneath the surface to what is hidden. Since the invention of photography, artists have been untied from necessity to create image as a substitute for a visually perceived reality. Artists as they paint are architects of a space evolving from their own psychology. In this investigation, spatial relationships in artwork were seen to represent a glimpse of the artist's

---

6. Ashton quotations used with permissions of Oxford University Press, Ltd.

sense of self in the world and the vicissitudes and struggles that lie within those relationships. So too, client-created artwork in the art psychotherapy process provides a particular set of formal spatial relationships from which client and therapist together learn. Through the power of an imagination that does not pass through the demands of the natural world, on the canvas the artist creates a world that has never existed before. Metaphor is the bridge to memory and the artist's and the client's invented world is informed by perceptions, memories and dreams and the experience of living in a particular place, time and culture.

> Space that has been seized upon by the imagination cannot remain indifferent space. . . . It has been lived in . . . with all the partiality of the imagination. . . . It nearly always exercises attraction for it concentrates being within limits that protect. (Bachelard, 1964)

This inquiry suggests that information from diverse sources and disciplines may offer us knowledge about the essences of relationship between humans and the natural and built environment, and that we can look to artists for how we have lived, how we might live and for insights about our work and lives. What artists teach is that in our perceived world, as in the realm of the imagination, there exists no true dichotomy between self and surround except by artificially drawn boundaries. These artificial boundaries, all too often, are perceived as limitations and barriers by our clients instead of flexible doors that can be opened and used in a variety of ways. These barriers can inhibit the free play between inside and outside, wall off and create stereotypical and problem thinking and acting instead of permitting in the light and air of change. Poet Rainer Maria Rilke wrote:

> Works of art always spring from those who have faced the danger, gone to the very end of an experience, to the point beyond which no human being goes. The further one dares to go, the more decent, the more personal, the more unique a life becomes. (1963)[7]

Artists teach that the environment and human beings are not only *interdependent,* but inseparable like form and content, and this suggests that what is needed are bridging models and descriptive theories. Fi-

---

7. From *Letters to a Young Poet* by Rainer Maria Rilke, translated by M.D. Herter Norton, original copyright 1934, 1954 by W.W. Norton & Company, Inc., renewed © 1962, 1982 by M.D. Herter Norton. Used with permission of W.W. Norton & Company, Inc.

nally, what artists tell us is to look beneath the surface of our external landscape to fresh ways of seeing, to recognize our assumptions, to be supported, but not bound by them and to search for enhancing and creative new ways of visioning our relationships. As the therapy clients' artwork provides the doorway to an inner world not accessed through words, so artists on canvas open their interior psychic space to us and invite us in to understand its meaning.

REFERENCES

Ashton, D. (1983). *About Rothko.* New York: Oxford University Press.

Bachelard, G. (1964). *The poetics of space.* Trans, Maria Jolas. New York: Orion Press Original copyright © 1958 by Presses Universitaires de France.

Cooper, C. (1976). The house as symbol of self. In Proshansky, H., Itelson, W. & Rivlin, L. (Eds.) *Environmental psychology* (2nd Edition). New York: Holt/Rinehart/Winston.

Eliade, M. (1959). *The sacred and the profane: The nature of religion.* New York: Harcourt.

Hills, P. (1983). *Alice Neel.* New York: Harry N. Abrams.

Greenbie, B. (1981). *Spaces: Dimensions of the human landscape.* New Haven, CT: Yale University Press.

Jung, C. (1969). *Memories, dreams and reflections.* London: Fontana Library Series.

Michelson, W. (1968). "Most people don't want what architects want." *Transactions,* 5: 37–43.

Mid-America Arts Alliance Program, (1984). *Through the looking glass: Drawings by Elizabeth Layton.* Kansas City, MO: The Lowell Press.

O'Keeffe, G. (1976). *Georgia O'Keeffe.* New York: A Studio Book of the Viking Press.

Rilke, R. (1963). (M. Herter Norton, Trans.) *Letters to a young poet.* New York: The Norton Library, W.W. Norton.

Chapter 3

GEORGIA O'KEEFFE:
ATTACHMENT AND SEPARATION, THEMES
AND RESONANCES

In this essay with an art therapist's viewpoint, I explore a repetitive theme reflected in the life and imagery of the remarkable and iconic female figure who has been a tacit mentor for many women–the twentieth century, painter Georgia O'Keeffe. From a feminist perspective, I focus on the psychological implications of separation and individuation and speculate about O'Keeffe's *midlife crisis* revolving around these issues and visible in her artwork. I suggest that in spite of O'Keeffe's presumed unconventionality and avowed refusal to live the "normal" woman's life of the time, her particular separation struggles nevertheless were typical of difficulties with the ongoing cultural milieu and sex role definitions for women in this country. Exploration of this struggle is the content of this essay.

I should mention that O'Keeffe hated and denied any psychological interpretations of her work.[1] While I respect her reluctance, obviously, this interpretation of her life and work and their interrelationship is my own and I "own" it as such: I present it because it has fascinated me and to encourage further questions and thinking about this important and remarkable woman in American art. We have created myth from O'Keeffe's life and art: reproductions of her artwork are everywhere and along with Van Goghs are hung in many undergraduate dormitory rooms and we visit her last home at Ghost Ranch in New

---

1. In fact, I was denied permission to publish O'Keeffe's images in this chapter by her estate for this reason.

Mexico almost as a shrine. But I believe there may be here a far more interesting story here than the myth-laden story. This narrative has significant implications for all women and all artists today.

DEVELOPMENTAL THEORIES

Erik Erikson enlarging on and adapting Freud's work, delineated a pattern of development based on the identification of *conflict* in each development phase as the harbinger of growth and change within the human life cycle. According to Erikson, dialectical and paradoxical possibilities exist at each stage which, through their resolution, offer both a heightened and dangerous vulnerability for the individual and a new opportunity for increased, emergent strength.

Erikson has been much criticized by feminists for his notion that female and male development is considerably different in adolescence and young adulthood. Erikson argues that the adolescent female must hold her identity formation in abeyance in order to remain more open to intimacy, which he defines as the task of the next stage. Outdated though it seems now, Erikson wrote that the female must find the man who will give her his name, define her status and rescue her from emptiness by filling, in Erikson's terms her "inner space." (With very little change, this concept still pervades action and thought for many men and women today.) Erikson asserts that the man must achieve a sense of identity *first* before attempting intimacy. If this idea seems old hat and sexist, it is because it is. But as the *zeitgeist* was influenced by this paradigm of development and still pervades the thinking of many today, so Georgia O'Keeffe grew up in a culture which believed Freud's and Erikson's ideas. Thus for a woman, according to Erikson, identity is fused with attachment and she is known by and through her relationships, while a man is known through his separateness.

Gilligan in her groundbreaking study *A Different Voice* (first published in 1982,) criticized Erikson's developmental views as defined and colored by male experience and focused on separation as the normative value. Gilligan writes that Erikson splits love and work, relegating expressive capacities to women and instrumental to men. Attachment was assessed as an *impediment* in the development of women. Gilligan persuasively argued that this stereotype of adulthood was seriously out of balance: what was presented by Erikson and others, she said, were *stereotypes* in which women were seen as ideally expressive and men as instrumental. Within this frame, separation and autonomy were desired as "normal."

For many, Gilligan's groundbreaking reappraisal opened their eyes and redefined both female and male development. According to Gilligan in her classic book, the relational experience in women must be reinterpreted not as deficient and abnormal, but as *different*. O'Keeffe's life history in this essay is based on information from Lisle's (1980) *Portrait of an Artist, a Biography of Georgia O'Keeffe* and Robinson's 1989 book *Georgia O'Keeffe, A Life*. For images of her artwork, I refer the reader to O'Keeffe, (1976) *Georgia O'Keeffe*.

O'Keeffe lived to be 98. During her almost 100 years she committed her life to the making of art and was a legend long before her death. She is without question one of the most important artists the United States has ever produced and is easily the most significant woman artist. Her compelling imagery as well as a life apparently lived in the singular pursuit of her art without the usual accoutrements of womanhood caused her to become a matron saint of feminists and of women artists.

I suggest that O'Keeffe's life and artwork in her clear and expressive manner provide a *mirror of woman in relationship*. I believe her long life and body of work in their relationship to each other reveal a vivid and courageous developmental struggle centered around the conflict between separation/individuation and attachment and intimacy. Not surprisingly, it is in her childhood growing up on a Wisconsin farm, that we find the roots of O'Keeffe's impulse to create. In her history grow the distant events which will become a resonating theme and the paradigm from which her adult creative intuitions evolved. O'Keeffe's first memories juxtapose intimacy and pleasant attachment with emptiness and separation.

The historical context for women and women painters was dismal. It was not until the twentieth century with the growth of technology and urbanism that suffrage became a central issue and in 1920 American women finally gained the right to vote. Another important cultural happening during this salient time was the publication of Freud's dream book which opened a climate of thought and discussion of the subconscious, sexuality and the role of women. Artwork by women artists in the last part of the nineteenth century generally centered on still-life and miniature painting, and sculpture. At the beginning of the twentieth century, woman began to paint the human form and took up portraiture tending toward scenes of home life, including sympathetic and sometimes sentimental portraits of children and family life. Previous to O'Keeffe, most artistic representation of the so-called "feminine experience" was focused on prettiness, delicacy and daintiness. O'Keeffe's artwork throughout her life is remarkably consistent in style and it is anything but pretty, delicate or dainty, although at first she was focused on as a *woman* painter. One critic of the times wrote: "Much of her work showed a womanly preoccupation with sex . . . O'Keeffe was being a woman and only secondarily an artist" (Kootz in Lisle, 1980). I believe, she should be acknowledged, not as a woman painter, but as an important American painter.

O'KEEFFE'S LIFE

Georgia O'Keeffe was born in 1887, the second child of seven and the first daughter in Sun Prairie, Wisconsin. Her yard, in the prairie-wheat country of southern Wisconsin, looked out on 600 acres of farmland extending on all sides to what O'Keeffe would find again in her adulthood, a landscape of wind and emptiness. From her father, a dairy farmer, she learned an enthusiasm and affinity for the land that would remain central in her life and painting. O'Keeffe's mother was very interested in education and education for women was a family tradition. But O'Keeffe preferred her father's love of land to her mother's world of learning. She was a solitary child always able to amuse herself. She spent much of her time alone reading and nurturing her imagination. But she was also a child who wanted to be different, thus drawing attention to her hidden self. At the age of 12 she announced she was going to be a great artist.

Apart from her relationship with the land, the central relationship in O'Keeffe's life was with Alfred Stieglitz. Stieglitz was an American-born photographer who had studied in Germany. An advocate for photography, he intended to make it as legitimate as painting and sculpture. With the photographer Edward Steichen, he opened "The Little Galleries" in 1905. Later this became known as "291" because of its street address in New York City. Stieglitz was an established artist and at his gallery showed the European Modernists Picasso, Matisse, Braque and Brancusi for the first time in the United States. In 1929, he moved the gallery to a new site calling it "An American Place." He was a prime mover of American art, discovering and showing Arthur Dove, John Marin, Marsden Hartley and Max Weber.

O'Keeffe first saw Stieglitz in 1907 while studying at the Art Students League in New York. When she was 22 years old, she attended an exhibit of Rodin watercolors at his gallery. (It is said that she liked Stieglitz but not Rodin.) But the first conversation she had with Stieglitz was in 1916 and was due to O'Keeffe's rage: He had taken her drawings and displayed them without her permission and under the name "Virginia O'Keefe" [sic]. When O'Keeffe met Stieglitz she was a painter, commercial artist and art teacher in Texas and South Carolina.

Stieglitz left his wife who would not give him a divorce for O'Keeffe and they began living together in 1916. They married in 1924. She was 37 and he was 61, three weeks older than O'Keeffe's mother. Soon after the marriage, O'Keeffe painted her first enormous flower. Stieglitz gave O'Keeffe her first show at his gallery in 1917 and she had yearly shows after that. Under his tutelage her art thrived. She wanted to have a baby, but he refused and convinced her that her art was her children. Here we first encounter O'Keeffe's attachment theme: She attached herself to Stieglitz, a vastly older man, perhaps a father figure, who nurtured her and her art and presented her to the world in his gallery and in photographs. Paradoxically, she envisioned a rather traditional female family role for herself.

Only four years after they married, in 1928 Stieglitz had a serious heart attack. O'Keeffe cared for him through his convalescence and the winter afterward became depressed. Stieglitz encouraged her to go alone for a summer trip to New Mexico. By the time she went to New Mexico they were having serious marital difficulties. O'Keeffe's four-month visit to New Mexico was the first time she had been apart from Stieglitz since they had begun living together in 1916 when she was 30. Now she was 42 and the central love affair of her life—hers alone—with the New Mexico landscape began. She wrote at the time that something in her life was ending and another beginning. While she returned to New York and spent time at Lake George, Maine, where the Stieglitz family had a house and where she took care of Stieglitz, typically spending her time entertaining and relating to his family, O'Keeffe's deep romance with New Mexico and her own independence will not end until her death.

In 1930–31 there was more difficulty between the two. Stieglitz grew interested in 21-year-old Dorothy Norman, an assistant in his gallery, who became pregnant by him. Norman took over a "wifely" role that by this time, O'Keeffe was moving away from. Norman helped Stieglitz in the gallery by organizing the business and fund-raising so that he could open "An American Place."

In New Mexico, O'Keeffe bought a black Model A Ford and for the first time, learned to drive. She sent a barrel of bleached bones she had collected back to New York. This was the period of the famous skull paintings. Although she was going to New Mexico by herself, and grappling with her creative independence, when she returned to New York, O'Keeffe struggled with depressions. It was said that she felt drained and despondent. She had severe headaches, was hypersensitive to noise, insomniac, anorexic and in a deep depression. An additional condition of her depression was her inability to walk. O'Keeffe was psychiatrically hospitalized for seven weeks in 1932. In New Mexico she had searched for and achieved her creative independence as a solitary woman, but it was at the cost of her marriage and of whatever dreams she may have nurtured about marriage, children and family.

Stieglitz died in 1946. After settling the estate O'Keeffe moved permanently to New Mexico. In 1953, at age 65, she set out to see Europe and its art for the first time. In 1970 (O'Keeffe was 83) there were retrospectives of her work at the Art Institute of Chicago and the Whitney Museum of American Art. Up to this point, no book had been published about her or her work. Georgia O'Keeffe died in 1986 at the age of 98.

INTERPRETATION

Camus, the great French philosopher and writer said: "The work is nothing else than the long journeying through the labyrinth of art to find again the two or three simple and great images upon which the heart first opened" (*L'Envers Et l'edroit (Betwixt and Between)* 1967).

Twenty years after her death, Georgia O'Keeffe would hate my "psychologizing," I make the assumption that artwork is reflective of the artist's psychic life and that the artist's life is reflective of the artwork. We can learn by putting a frame around both and trying to see the repetitive themes. It is clear, that one's look at any person's work and life is not objective. This essay is an invitation to the reader to explore with me in a fresh manner some of O'Keeffe's work. As art therapists, we are privileged to be invited into people's lives and imagery and I believe that the way people invent themselves, live their lives and create images are the most interesting things in the world.

In this essay, I suggest that O'Keeffe's depression and hospitalization and her artworks of the period provide a behavioral and visual metaphor for a midlife crisis concerning separation and individuation. O'Keeffe's relationship with Stieglitz provides her with a fatherly yet sexual mentor. Refusing to father her children, he helps her birth and parent her art convincing her that her *art is* her children. Despite apparently caring little for convention, O'Keeffe, to a large extent, allows Steiglitz to nurture her art, while she takes care of him, particularly in their summers at Lake George, Maine where the Stieglitz family had a house and where she makes little art, but instead entertains guests and family. With his heart attack, the threatened loss of Steiglitz, and increasing difficulties in their relationship, O'Keeffe struggles with depression. With his encouragement, she goes to New Mexico alone for the first time, learns to drive and feels an attachment to the New Mexico light and landscape that will compel her for the rest of her life. Finally, O'Keeffe's passion is for landscape.

Stieglitz has an affair with a young woman assistant and takes photographs of her, as he had O'Keeffe. Photographs of the two women are even displayed together. Stieglitz's relationship is a replay of the earlier mentoring father/daughter relationship with O'Keeffe. Upon her return to New York and Stieglitz, O'Keeffe grows deeply depressed and is hospitalized. Ironically, a symptom of her depression is her inability to walk. She was able to "walk away" to her independence in New Mexico, but upon her return to New York and her difficult relationship with Stieglitz, perhaps she unconsciously punishes herself and expresses the dynamics of her separation conflicts with the symptomatic metaphor of not being able to walk.

From its beginnings through her life, O'Keeffe's artwork maintains an unusual consistency of style and form which provides the art therapist an opportunity to trace ongoing themes and the twists and turns of encountered change. Replying to critics who saw "womanly" sexuality suggested in her work, particularly in the large flower forms, she denied any interest in sexual imagery or in exploring the unconscious. She continued her stance of refusing to explain her art throughout her life and thus helped create a more mysterious milieu within which to view her work. At first glance, O'Keeffe's art seems simple and direct.

But within the apparent simplicity there are visible complications and significant psychological implications.

O'Keeffe's paintings are essentially paradoxical, and like all really superb art, essentially unknowable. They appear frontal and accessible and have a sharp photographic focus. But instead of revealing they conceal, acting as masks for unusual and often contradictory messages and subtexts. Edges come up against space. Negative space and positive space relate to each other; they come together and they stay apart. We see the difficulty in finding a way to relate shapes, the pleasure in finding a way to relate, and the pleasure of finding a way to stay separate. O'Keeffe said "I was most interested in the holes in the [pelvic] bones (O'Keeffe, 1976).

One is aware of the conflict between O'Keeffe's exhibitionism and her distance: She creates huge scale and boldness in her work apparently wanting to be seen. Yet at the same time there is an essential remoteness resulting in a feeling of passion combined with detachment in the viewer. In a way O'Keeffe in her paintings hardens her heart against being known. She invites in, but finally defeats the viewer's understanding. I am reminded of the door at Abiquiu which O'Keeffe found, painted again and again, and declared herself irrevocably connected to. She said "It was something I had to have." She described her compulsive connection to that door as an illness and a curse (O'Keeffe, 1976). Her desire for and desperate fear of intimacy coexist simultaneously. I propose that this can be seen in her artwork, in which O'Keeffe is concerned formally with boundaries and the edges of things. How objects can come together and yet remain apart and the spaces in between are focused on almost as content. This formal repeat could be viewed, in Freudian language, as a "repetition compulsion" in which O'Keeffe attempts again and again to grapple with attachment/separation issues for once trying to make them come out right. I believe that the vicissitudes of these paradoxes in O'Keeffe's work, both formal and psychological can be viewed as her underlying and courageous struggle with issues of separation and independence and attachment and loss.

In O'Keeffe's artwork objects are whole. There are no fragmented forms. She is consistently concerned with how whole objects can come together and how they can be apart. Her art is about fullness and emptiness, closeness and distance, simplicity and complexity, grandiosity and the diminutive, the visionary or psychological versus observed physical reality, landscape as human figure, the mask and the Self. All speak of the essential paradoxes of life. Her art, in its formal concern with edges, boundaries and the spaces in between, portrays the varieties of these *paradoxes of relationship* with their opportunity for pleasant intimacy and attachment juxtaposed against the felt threat of fusion and even death. O'Keeffe's art in its ongoing attempt at mastery of these themes presents to the viewer a tension and an emotional intensity locked within a kind of cool formal distance that is tremendously compelling and often unsettling. I speculate that through O'Keeffe's language of forms, what we feel is the edge between relationship and isolation, consciousness and unconscious, sanity and insanity, life and death.

As has been mentioned, it is well-known that O'Keeffe refused to attribute any validity to psychological interpretations of her work and thus, as art therapists, we arrive at the ultimate paradox: *Her silence.* Through O'Keeffe's silence, the viewer is bound even more closely and irrevocably to the work. We look not from a distance, but through our own attached and intimate relationship to the painting, we begin to understand the treacherous and ambiguous territory between the self and the world in which the artist works and makes meaning. It is there, out of what is known and what cannot be known, that a whole new thing may be created, which through our experience of it, has the power to transform our understanding of ourselves and of the essential nature of reality. Let us remember O'Keeffe's obsession with the door at Abiquiu which she painted for 30 years. I view it as a metaphor for her need and her difficulties in stepping over the threshold, to perhaps finally know the unknown and the possibility of attachment within individuation. Paradoxically, I view the image of the door as O'Keeffe's recognition that to step across that boundary and to walk away is to potentially destroy meaning, experience loss, and ultimately lose the mystery.

DOOR AT ABIQUIU–NOVEMBER 25, 1986[2]

She thought sometimes
She no longer lived within the confines
   of her own skin.

---

7. This poem, which I wrote, was first published in *Art Therapy: Journal of the American Art Therapy Association,* March 1988. Used with permission.

But in some never-never land of betwixt
  and between.
Permeable boundaries
Of yes/no, where/why
Being born and dying.

Lately: upon approaching the ends
Of sidewalks, she noticed she could not
Step forward into the street
to cross with the light
without a palpable wave of panic.

Edges of paper or of feeling
newly attracted her
and she found herself leaving broad white margins,
watching
the lines and forms and colors of the evolving image
huddle together in an immaculate
safe space bounded on all sides by emptiness.

She remembered Georgia O'Keeffe's
obsession with the black door
in the house at Abiquiu
which she painted again and again.
And she thought O'Keeffe had also
struggled with the
beckoning paradox of threshold as
the invisible line between before and after
the knife edge between
relationship and isolation, fullness in the void,
symbol and mystery, known and unknown,
sanity and insanity.

In the prolonged act of noncompletion
  there is the promise.
In the prolonged act of noncompletion
  there is the beginning.
In the prolonged act of noncompletion
  there is the constancy.
In the prolonged act of noncompletion
  there is the going on.

Though bound to that doorway,
O'Keeffe would not cross over until the
day at age 98 in the warm spring of 1986
when she died.

In November, she awoke one night
after a dreamless, fitful sleep
and came downstairs at two a.m.
to sit at her littered desk amidst
the house's luminous silences and watched
as the black-felt-tip penned words flowed avidly
from her fingers like blood from a secret wound.
They sliced onto the yellow-lined pad and
were crossed out to start again.
And lines accumulated, one onto the next and the next until
moving slowly, slowly, finally, they filled the space
to its ends.
And she found no comfort in the act.

She took two valiums
round like yellow moons and
lapsed, into black sleep.

REFERENCES

Camus, A. (1967). *L'envers et l'endroit (Betwixt and between)*. Philip Thody (Trans.) In *Albert Camus: Lyrical and critical.* London: Hamish Hamilton.

Erikson, E. (1950). *Childhood and society.* New York: W.W. Norton & Co, Inc.

Gilligan, C. (1993 paperback). *In a different voice: Psychological theory and women's development.* Cambridge, MA: Harvard University Press.

Lisle, L. (1980). *Portrait of an artist, a biography of Georgia O'Keeffe.* New York: Washington Square Press, Simon & Schuster.

O'Keefe , G. (1976). *Georgia O'Keeffe.* New York: A Studio Book of the Viking Press.

Robinson, R. (1989). *Georgia O'Keeffe, a life.* New York: Harper & Row.

Part II
CREATIVITY

Chapter 4

CREATIVE REALITIES, A SYSTEMS APPROACH[1]

I believe that if it were left to artists to choose their own labels,
most would choose none.
—Ben Shahn, *The Shape of Content*

This essay is about alternative systems of creativity in the visual arts. While "creativity" is a central catchword for our time, description and definition of the motivation for, process of and results of the creative process, surprisingly, have remained at a cursory level. Theoretical conceptualizations have generally proven to be equally unconvincing in my judgment. A major thrust of the literature is that creativity is really one kind of "thing" but is too vast to encompass adequately. Within this conceptualization and across disciplines many varieties of creativity tend to be viewed as similar. Another viewpoint is that creativity is ultimately mysterious and deserves to be left that way in the hands of the gods and muses. Also, still prevalent, in spite of abundant research to the contrary, is the Freudian-based notion that creativity is akin to madness and a process of abnormality arising out of personality psychopathology.

Models of creativity typically have been unitary and reductionistic, attempting to limit to a simple theory creativity's multicolored threads. But to attempt to capture creativity in this way is to pursue the elusiveness of the fleeing dream in daylight, or to grasp at rainbow-hued

---

1. For a more expansive discussion of creativity and alternative realities with visual artists and writers, the reader is referred to my book, *Creative realities, the search for meanings* published in 1998 by University Press of America.

soap bubbles which burst as we touch them. Some theoreticians such as Howard Gardner (1982, 1983) are now looking at differences in creativity such as between visual arts and mathematics, and between intellectual and emotional intelligences, but, to my knowledge, there is no creativity inquiry or theory into different realities or world views.

Art therapists look hard and long at artwork made by clients, but there is little convincing research about created *meaning*. Some art therapists believe that it is the creative process itself that is healing but, again, there is little evidence other than anecdotal that shows this. Historically, psychoanalysts and psychologists have examined the *life course* of the artist, because they believe it is there they will find essential clues to and roots of creativity.

This essay is based on a typology of Alternative Realities[2] originated by LeShan (1976) and developed for business and organizations by McWhinney (1984, 1985, 1988a, b) From a paper written in 1989, to a doctoral study (1991) revised in a book and published in 1998, in my work I have expanded the alternative realities approach to the visual arts. My inquiry is based on the assumption that artwork itself in its form and content, not the life of the creator, can provide evidence of a distinctive reality approach to creativity and of the motivation, process and particular paradigmatic world view from which it arose. To experience a painting or a work of art, I believe, is to engage with the artist's reality at an intense level; as though the painted image becomes a rabbit hole through which we enter the painter's world that can merge with, expand, and transform our own. In this essay's systems observations, I attempt to broaden the lenses through which we view creativity and its products. I engage with creativity based in the idea that one can be creative in different ways and along different paths and that it may be useful and enriching to presuppose diversity rather than unity. As I pursue these many roads, my hope is that we will be able to see fresh elements about artistic creativity and ask different, perhaps more essential questions.

A STORY

I begin this essay with a story about a conflict of realities:

---

2. The words "reality" and "world view" are used interchangeably.

Once there was a professor in a middle-sized university on a bluff in a large sprawling city near the ocean. This professor was a woman which was unusual for a teacher in this school and she was of a different ethnic background than many of her colleagues and students. Moreover, the subject she taught was viewed as slightly suspect (even verging on inappropriate and bizarre) by administration in the tall building with the dark hallways. It was even questioned whether these subjects should be taught in the university as no one could understand what they were about anyway and why anyone would want to study them.

The woman professor was not unhappy in her position despite often feeling as if she were in a foreign country or was a foster child who could be sent back to the state authorities if she did not mind her manners sufficiently and eat her oatmeal and vegetables. She liked her students and she liked her teaching. And she tried to watch and abide by the university road signs and territorial markings that were often written in a foreign language. For her, there was a certain pleasure in treading carefully and successfully through rocks and shoals and land mines of life on the bluff. She thought she had managed to leave some deep footprints on the path along the way and that pleased her because she liked to make a difference. She had never been a "fitter inner" anyway.

One day in her eighth year atop the bluff she was invited by the people in the tall building with the dark hallways to apply for a sabbatical leave which would occur two years in the FUTURE. Although she was the kind of person who didn't know who she'd be when she woke up the next morning and could hardly envision two whole years away, she decided to request the leave.

The professor was not surprised at the university's approach to the FUTURE. Remember, she had been listening to the foreign tongue they spoke for a long time and was able to understand a good deal of it. She knew that the school worked as much as possible on the assumption that the earth would stay put in one place, not revolve around the sun even, and especially, unforeseen change would not occur if the earth's surface was covered with plans, route slips, post'ems and sticky, gigantic words on paper. She knew they thought that the earth would stay put if procedures of great importance were followed diligently by serious-minded men with lines in their foreheads and glasses on their noses. She sometimes laughed to herself about this delusion promoted by the DEMONS OF CONTROL that men (and some others) enjoyed that the sun would come up every morning and that things and people would stay put and that the world would be safe and predictable. She laughed because she knew about volcanoes, earthquakes, hurricanes and about love and that no matter how well you kept any of it clean and in order and plastered down, it didn't stay put!

To apply for her sabbatical two years in the FUTURE, the people in the tall building with the dark hallways told her to write a proposal composed of nine parts and answering NINE BIG QUESTIONS and to submit it to the Sabbatical Judges who would ponder and think and question and decide its merits. The professor was no dope and she recognized that in order for the judges to understand what she wanted to do, she would have to do her best to speak to them in their own language, still foreign to her though it was.

So the professor screwed up her forehead and her brain and she worked and she worked. From sunup to sundown, she worked. First, she wrote in her own language. Then she carefully translated the words and their meanings. (This was not easy as the words kept slipping off the paper and flying out the window on the breeze.)

But when she was done, she was pleased at what she had accomplished. Words on paper are good, she thought. I can see them and touch them, unlike the bands of dreamlike light that flit around my brain and often disappear before I can catch them. Words on paper are good, she decided even if they don't have much to do with what I am trying to say. She felt a little bit of the DELUSION OF SAFETY offered by the CONTROL DEMONS, and in a deeper way, she could understand its attractions. She even felt herself longing to believe in THEIR WAY, although she knew to write such a document was a lie because if you don't know who you'll be when you wake up each morning you can't know what you'll want to do two years in the FUTURE, after all.

As she carefully folded the words-on-paper into the proper envelope and carefully sealed it in just the right way and carefully addressed it in her best handwriting, and carefully delivered it to the room in the tall building with the dark hallways from whence it would be sent out to the cave of the Sabbatical Judges, she experienced satisfaction. Then she awaited their response. For months she patiently awaited their response for she knew they were busy judges. And she waited and waited and waited.

Finally, on a bright morning in March, the professor received the envelope. It was a very proper envelope from the room in the tall building with the dark hallways. It was very properly addressed and very properly typed and properly official. The letter inside wished to communicate, it said, what the Sabbatical Judges had communicated: The Sabbatical Judges, try as they might, were unable to make their decision, the letter said, because they had not received enough BIG INFORMATION. Along with the NINE BIG QUESTIONS, there were riddles to be answered, they said. That you, Ms Professor, did not recognize these hidden riddles indicates that you do not really understand our language and our ways. Your language is foreign to us and thus your proposed endeavor a waste. As we understand it, it is unlikely to provide the sticky paper and miasmas of words needed to keep the skittish planet in its place so that it, and we, can be in OUR place and know in our scholarly brains the SAFETY OF CONTROL. Thus of what use is it? (Her heart sank into her shoes.) The letter went on: However, since we are kindly Sabbatical Judges (along with being ultimately wise,) we will give you one more chance to answer satisfactorily the great riddles of DEFINITION and METHODOLOGY.

The poor professor didn't know what to do. Because, you see, her proposed project had been about the subject of Creativity, and she knew well there the difficulties of definition and methodology. Her project was intended to come at the subject in a new and different way, a way that might more closely touch the volcanoes and earthquakes and hurricanes and love inherent in true creativity. Her project was intended to touch the transforming experience of creativity which she knew words on paper written in the language of DEFINITION and METHODOLOGY so seldom even approximated.

Then the professor was invited to sit before the CEO Sabbatical Judge to receive help from him. He asked her questions in a very deep voice: "Has anyone ever done this project before?" he asked. "No!" she said, feeling good and proud. "Have REAL scholars proven this can be done?" She began to feel herself shrinking, like Alice drinking the potion, and he was becoming huge. "Is there a large body of IMPORTANT literature describing THIS approach to creativity?" he boomed. "No" she said feeling smaller and smaller. The Sabbatical Judge sat up in his huge brown seat and puffed himself up like an immense green frog: "Then WHY," his voice boomed, "do YOU want to do it?" She felt like laughing at the absurdity of his question but she knew this was how they talked in the university and to laugh would mean death. So she put on her most serious, grown-up, biggest voice and she said: "Exactly that! It is exactly that it has not been done before that I want to do it!" (For some reason the CEO Sabbatical Judge was beginning to look more human and less like a puffed-up frog.) The professor spoke further, gaining strength and power as she talked: "I LIKE to do difficult things. And I HATE to do things that have already been done before." The CEO Sabbatical Judge looked at her in astonishment. He batted his eyes five times, took three deep breaths, placed his hands under his chin and said: "Oh." The professor began to breathe again. The CEO Sabbatical Judge, looking somewhat embarrassed, gathered his great robes around him, rose from the chair till he touched the ceiling, pushed her out the door into the dark hallway and roared: "Well remember, you have two days to answer the great questions of DEFINITION and METHOD-OLOGY and they'd better be right or else!"

As we already know, the professor, in actuality, was no dope. And she kept in her pocket for such times of need a small black patent-leather purse filled with absurdities, stupidities, assaninities, and varieties of meaningless clap-trap useful in the university, called "policies and procedures," "strategic planning," "jargon," "psychological language" and "bullshit." Usually she tried to keep the clasp of the purse tightly closed against escaping stupidities, but being no dope (as we know,) the professor was also a realist. As such, she recognized that some people feel more Comfortable and Safe and In Control when they hear and see familiar, usually meaningless, forms of stupidities floating around in the air. And she recognized that many (but thankfully not all) of the people at the university on the bluff needed to feel comfortable and safe and in control. Certainly the Sabbatical Judges did and the CEO Sabbatical Judge did, and the people who inhabited the rooms in the tall building with the dark hallways did. So she opened her black patent-leather purse and using exactly as many stupidities as she needed and no more, completed her answers to the ultimate riddles of DEFINITION and METHODOLOGY about Creativity. Then she wrote her stupid answers on very proper white paper, folded it properly into the proper envelope, carefully sealed the envelope in just the right way, carefully addressed it in her best handwriting and ran across the fields of the bluff and in and out of buildings tall and otherwise until she came to the cave of the CEO Sabbatical Judge.

Considerably out of breath, she rapped on his door which opened quietly. The Judge was not in his robes and looked rather small for a change. "Oh, it's you" he said. The professor handed the Sabbatical Judge the envelope with its stupid answers to the ultimate riddles of DEFINITION and METHODOLOGY about creativity. As he took the envelope, he surprised her by winking. "Ho, ho, ho," he laughed. "Well, I guess you won't be coming around talking to any of us Sabbatical Judges about creativity on your sabbatical will you? I guess we've proved we're too UNCREATIVE to understand it!"

The professor was still breathing hard from her run to the cave and she had to take a few deep breaths in order to respond. Thus it was, luckily, that she had the opportunity to quickly snap shut the clasp on the black patent-leather purse before a giant stupidity could escape from her mouth. The stupidity that was just on the edge of her tongue but, luckily, did not escape was "At least you're goddamned right about that!" (Some stupidities, are true, you know.)

As she walked back across the campus, the professor thought about the Sabbatical Judge's last remark and decided that perhaps they had been able to speak each other's Language a little after all and she took pleasure in that understanding. One month later, the professor received through proper channels and by proper procedures, approval of her sabbatical and two years later when it finally came, she lived happily and creatively ever after.

THE ALTERNATIVE REALITIES MODEL AND FOUR MODES OF CREATIVITY

The Alternative Realities Model is an hypothesis that (within Western cultures, at least) people hold different beliefs about reality. Although we don't know their origin, these beliefs may in part be genetic emerging from a person's unique physiology and psychology. Additionally, any culture promotes its own belief system or systems with which the individual interacts. Our belief system indicates our deep and basic convictions about the world and the self. But from one person to the next, these beliefs may be quite dissimilar. Our belief system limits the way we see reality, defines the questions we ask and the answers we find and largely determines our behavior and relationships. It is the spyglass through which we see and provides the language of our vision through which we understand and communicate meaning.

LeShan conceptualized four views of reality. McWhinney organized and modified this conceptualization with a two-dimensional model separating and relating the four realities. McWhinney's realities represent a field of paradoxes. One or two realities may be dominant, but a person may also move between different world views. When a single world view is adopted, the paradoxical opposite is evoked. The classification scheme is based on two paradoxical dimensions (Figure 4-1). The first dimension is one of *difference–monism to pluralism*. The second paradoxical dimension is that of *determinism versus free will*.

Monistic ← → Pluralistic

	Monistic	Pluralistic
Determined	UNITARY	SENSORY
Free Will	MYTHIC	SOCIAL

Figure 4-1. "Alternative Realities, McWhinney's Model."

DEFINITIONS OF THE FOUR ALTERNATIVE CONCEPTS OF REALITY AND MODES OF CREATIVITY

Unitary Reality

The Unitary person believes that reality is the "Whole" or "Oneness" as a manifestation of God or the spirit or perhaps of one's village or culture. In the pure monistic, there is no separateness, no duality, no distinctions and no need for an explanation. There is only the pure undifferentiation of community. The person's role is to reflect God on earth. From outside, this appears to be an authoritarian world. But from within, the concept of authority lacks meaning because there are *no alternatives* and no options. A Unitary world view is monistic and ultimately determined. There is no change since everything that will be is already there. We might label Unitary people as patriots, bureaucrats, "true believers." Some professions which attract the Unitary are the legal practice, priesthood, accountancy and pure mathematics. Mathematics, as the unfolding of logical propositions and Arabic and Moslem art, in the elaboration over and over again of design themes are examples. Bach probably fits in here as well.

McWhinney suggests the possibility that there is a "dis-integrated" version of the Unitary world view which he calls the "Dialectic" in which the person standing outside the system, denies the truth of the system and works against it (McWhinney, 1988b.) People who are able to leave cults are examples.

Creativity within the Unitary world view is the unfolding of previously created ideas and images. The Unitary believes that the world and everything in it is preordained by God, a supreme being or natural laws. Therefore, there is no invention that is not directly evoked and forecast by first causes. Creativity as the creation of something out of nothing is not possible in this mode because there is no freedom of choice. The Unitary assumes one truth and one logic. Rules by which "truth" is interpreted are a given. This is monism at its purest: I am one with God and God is one with me and God speaks through me in a common language.

The Unitary reality is authoritarian and hierarchical—creativity within the world view of the superego. Unitary artists, sometimes through proscribed rituals, try to prepare to receive what God gives. They take the gift from God, embellish it, and elaborate on it—as in elaborating on an idea or theme. These elaborations, no matter how far afield they may appear, are always within the proscribed constraints and limits of the given "truth." Creativity within this world view is *received* and *transmitted.* It adds to the greater glory of God or the spirit; it is predictable, orderly and controlled. Unitary creativity is to come in tune with the spiritual nature of things, to be responsive to it and to reflect back the spiritual. Thereby, I lose my sense of separateness in the spiritual unity and become one with it.

The Dialectic Unitary creator stands outside the truth system and calls it into question. This may be simply an anti-authoritarian stance, but it negates and brings errors into the light and suggests and acts out alternatives. The strength and lack of ambiguity inherent in the Unitary world view, by definition, offers no pluralistic possibility of dialogue or negation. It provides the convenient wholistic structure to hit against, even attempt to topple. This form of creativity is creativity from rebellion against the establishment (or parents or God's norms and truths) which in itself is a cry for a new Unitary position.

The painter, Mark Rothko, is a contemporary example of the Unitary creator. Rothko's large canvases pulsate with flickering color. Huge expanses of color create physical and psychological resonances in the viewer. As we stand before a Rothko, we are deeply stirred. The viewer is drawn into a fascinating transcendent world. We long to pierce the obscure façade, to encounter the other. At the abstract level of careful, balanced, universal forms and colors, we find a hidden place beyond the surface. Rothko's paintings with their cloudlike forms do not limit or define the world beyond; they make it visible, felt and whole.

In Western art, early Christian art and architecture and sculpture in the service of the church are examples. They were the visible symbols of God on earth. With a didactic purpose, they provided illustration of the Word of God through symbolic representation. Anyone who has entered a Gothic cathedral has experienced space as a unity with God. Illuminations in religious books are examples, as are the plethora of great paintings with religious subjects.

The Italian fresco painter Giotto's art provides a particularly arresting view because he is a transitional figure. While his work falls clearly within the Unitary world view, Giotto was also interested in the natural world. He gave visual form to the shifting paradigms of the medieval world which would give way to the Renaissance and a Sensory-Humanistic reality. Both paradigms are evident in his artwork.

Like every form of human life, during the late Middle Ages, art was permeated by questions of relationship to God. It began to transform itself as a symptom of an emerging world view. Religious painting before had been flat, decorative, symbolic. During this period it began to approach a more naturalistic realism. Still, within the unifying Christian mission, it portrayed God and the person's relationship to God. A more realistic art was created to enhance a sympathetic vision of sacred images, the Madonnas and saints, to make it possible for the viewer to identify. Eventually, spiritual painting was created in a new manner, moving away from flat ornamentation with its other-worldly quality and giving material, three-dimensional substance to people and things to enable the viewer to "feel" about the painting instead of just "reading it" or learning from it. This new way of painting, such as that of Giotto, might fall into McWhinney's definition of the Dialectic, for it created a fatal split within the Unitary world view, giving voice to the distinction between spiritual and material reality and the worldly and the other-worldly.

MOTIVATION:	Express the word of God, supreme being or natural laws Make visible the transcendent spiritual Make visible the common language Express truth The more I reflect back, the more responsive I can be to God

Figure 4-2. "Works of Art in the Unitary Mode." Adapted from Junge (1989).

Figure 4-2 (Continued)

FORM:	Form proceeds from first causes; no creation of anything new as such–expression of what is given by God Elaboration, ornamentation, embellishment, rhythm Symbolism → abstraction 　Modeling of objects & processes Symbolism & metaphor of the Word of God Dualism only in the service of increased unity Unity: In the many is the WHOLE Elaboration through series such as storytelling of Christian and medieval art Process: entrainment with the transcendent Form implies "other-worldliness." Flat, unnatural Naturalism implies attachment to the Sensory world (may appear as a Dialectic within the Unitary)
CONTENT:	Understood limits & constraints Hierarchical Authoritarian/cult/disciples The existence of something beyond Comforting Constraining Didactic Instructive Storytelling Simplification Meditative, contemplative
VIEWER RESPONSE:	In the presence of something greater I understand the TRUTH/ I am the truth of the spiritual There is something which transcends my world. I can know it by coming in tune with it I become ONE with God I feel continuity I feel one with the Unity within the Whole, within community I receive Insight into God as ultimate Simplicity and order Awe & love

Sensory Reality

The sensory concept of reality is the dominant notion of Western thought. It is a belief in a predictable linear physical reality all preceding from first causes. The environment is the source of all knowledge and rational, objective questions about "what makes it work" are central. Reality is expressed in distinguishable physical objects according to mass, size, color and other visible physical characteristics. We know this reality by measuring it. Sensories are scientists, engineers, empiricists, environmentalists, sensualists. For the most part, the American public school system is now and historically has been, *Sensory*. Sensory creativity may be an illustration or a painting tied to the visible physical world or it may be an Abstract Expressionist work representing the direct sensual experience of paint and its physical action. Creativity within the Sensory mode is often demonstrated through the recognition of nature as stimulus and as objective. It is assumed the "real world" provides *information* about the look, feel, smell, touch and sound of "things." The more responsive the Sensory artist can be to nature, the more it can be reflected. The Sensory artist recognizes the distinctness of things and looks for ways to connect them. Three apples and a pear on a table provide stimulus for the painter of still life to transform a representation of what is seen to a two-dimensional surface. It is the artist's task to find color, brush strokes, texture and shape to reflect back on the canvas the "true" nature of things. Within this mode, human beings are objects in nature. Sometimes, with the truly great artist, the work transcends the visible reality of the observable world, to portray a deeper sense of the underlying "truth" and energies of nature and environment.

While much of Sensory creativity moves toward pictorial realism, it is by no means all that way. Great designers and pattern-makers such as Henri Matisse are Sensory creators. Their patterns portray a metaphorical representation of the picture plane of natural laws and organization principles. There are few unexpected surprises. The images are "right," logical and in their painted relationships to each other, there is often a comforting vision of the orderly "rightness of the universe." Conceptual artists are Sensory as are Abstract Expressionists who in their sensate enjoyment of the physical properties of paint and what it can do, exhibit a sensual, possibly hedonistic pleasure in the process.

I propose that David Hockney is a Sensory artist. His approach to the natural world (as were Seurat's, Monet's and other Impressionists) is to take it apart and to reassemble it in such a way that it becomes more immediately realistic. His photographs are a good example. One is able to sense the reality beneath the reality and to see the vision that we do not ordinarily see deeply buried within the natural environment. Hockney's artwork reminds us that there are many possibilities beyond the formidable outer layer and that we should not allow ourselves to stop short of looking clearly at what is in front of us and beneath surface reality.

MOTIVATION:	To nature The external world provides information for artistic production Sensory discrimination: Color, shape, line, texture The more responsive I can be, the more I can reflect back Sensate enjoyment → Sensuality → Hedonism
FORM:	Surface outside reality is important Emphasis on senses Sometimes "super" realism → Form for form's sake and the pure enjoyment of pictorial elements Articulating Connecting things which are separate Toward Unitary: Design as metaphor for natural laws & patterning Illustration, scientific illustration, advertising → Great art
CONTENT:	Relationship emphasized in brush-strokes, line, shape, color, composition Connecting things which are separate Separating things which are connected, but which remind us of our CONNECTEDNESS Integration toward a values "message" Often subject matter is human beings, social events, class, socio-economic conditions, fallibilities of humans, inequities of the social order, war, illness Size: Small intimate objects to large wall murals (e.g., the Mexican muralists) and the AIDS Quilt.

Figure 4-3. "Works of Art in the Sensory Mode." Adapted from Junge (1989).

Figure 4-3 (Continued)

VIEWER RESPONSE:	Helping me to see Somewhat removed to detached, scientific objectivity Reasonable, interesting, observing, enjoyment of sensate emotions Seldom anger, outrage, passion Search for the truth of things Insight into what is real Great Sensory art transforms our vision about the realities of the natural world

Social Reality

Acting within this reality, the person believes the world essentially is a creation of *social interaction*. We are choosing, creating, imaging human beings together and, therefore, a social reality viewpoint is about *values*. Relationship is the drive and in and in and of itself is valued. Values are defined, evolve and are redefined through relationship. Creating is through the construction of a community's culture. The Social world view is dualistic and choiceful. It is primarily individualistic: There is me and there is you and we are separate but we decide to relate and experience shared pleasures and pains. Generally, people in the helping professions are in this category.

Creativity within the Social reality concerns the expression of values and raises value questions. It engages the viewer in an interpersonal response (as in Mary Cassatt) which sometimes invites to action (as in Picasso's "Guernica"). It can speak of love and warmth, anger, outrage and revolution. Its intention is to portray the feelings and values of the artist, the community, or the culture and it often seeks to invoke an impassioned response. The American AIDS Quilt is an example. We are separate but we choose to engage with each other through *empathy*.

MOTIVATION:	Communication of one to another, of values, feelings Interpersonal sharing of values so you will understand, act Relationship In relationship I know myself, I become larger Interpersonal relationship I expand by knowing you But we remain separate beings
FORM:	The GROUP as subject & object: Community as creator and creation in the service of community Relationship emphasized in brush-strokes, line, shape, color and composition Connecting things which are separate Separating things which are connected but which thereby remind us of our connectedness Integration toward a values "message" Values portrayed: Fairness/trust,
CONTENT:	sympathy (beauty) warmth/respect honesty, directness compassion Objectivity and reason as "law" eschewed Compassionate understanding of the human condition Satire, sarcasm, irony, outrage and the disasters of society, the social order and of human beings Empathy as the tool for communication, translation and transmittal of meaning and change
VIEWER RESPONSE:	Feelings portrayed, not values I feel Through empathy, I feel what you feel and take you in. Thereby, I change I feel sorrow, anguish, discomfort, anger Insight into what makes us human in the smallest most intimate sense Insight into people as ultimately good & ultimately evil Great Social art transforms our vision as to the essential nature of what it means to be human

Figure 4-4. "Works of Art in the Social Mode." Adapted from Junge (1989).

Painting within this mode tends to fall into two basic categories. First, it includes those works depicting the realm of human relationships as in home and family. Second, it focuses in the great art of social concern and protest. Style may range from realism to expressionism, but it is the deliverance of a values "message" about human beings and their relationships that is central. Examples are Cassatt, Munch and Daumier.

Mythic Reality

Believing that *they*, not God, a supreme being, or nature, *create reality*, the Mythic *is* God. The Mythic person creates new symbols and gives new meaning to experience. From what is known and unknown, the Mythic creator makes powerful original symbols which invent new meaning. Mythics strike at our familiar vision of the world, extend it, destroy it, turn it upside down and change it forever. We are engaged, charmed, seduced and even swindled. We come within the Mythic's persuasive vision and are changed and can never be the same again. Picasso is the obvious example in the variety and depth of his inventiveness.

Mythics take total responsibility for their acts as they are responsible for the whole world which they create and accept as real. Pure Mythics, if there were such a thing, are monistic. There is no possibility of another viewpoint or of discussing another's idea, since there is no possibility of any creation but their own. Unlike the monistic Unitary, free will is ultimate and enacted in creating and recreating the world all the time. The act of creation itself as *meaning-making* is all important. There are no social relationships as such because the Mythic creates the other as actor in their own play. Great leaders, charismatics and artists are Mythics as are megalomaniacs and visionaries. By definition they are our most creative people. They are loners, entrepreneurs and artists. Don Quixote was a mythic as were Van Gogh, Gauguin, Hemmingway and Gertrude Stein. Poet Paul Valery is an example of a Mythic when he wrote "I am the world which is in me." Contemporary writer Ray Bradbury titled a poem "I die, so dies the world." Much of great art is genuinely Mythic in that it reveals new and fresh forms of symbolization so the viewer "sees" differently than before and is transformed.

Mythics create for the sheer "livingness" of invention. Their form is the construction of reality, itself. They are the dreamers. Sometimes it is *the process of dreaming* that is enough. Action or the carrying-out of the dream may not seem necessary. For Mythics what they create is "truth" and they have total free choice. Play and the child within are inherent actors in the Mythic process, expressed through a rich array of metaphor and symbol. Since there is no dualism, others exist for the Mythic only within their created world and as envisioned by them. If you exist, at all, it is because they have created you. To try to argue a point with a strong Mythic is a frustrating experience because to allow two opinions, thus two realities, is a basic impossibility. The second opinion is just noise.

The Mythic envisions from deep primary process intuition. Mythics may have difficulty doing the usual work of the world because their extraordinary intuitive sense lends a metaphorical cast of meaning to everything, holds them in the metaphor and disinclines them to practical, mundane activities. After the dream is the expression of the dream in words or sounds, in paint, clay or stone. The mystery of the darkness within is made visible and assumes new order and meaning. Spanish painter, Francisco Goya was a great Mythic who also worked from a Social reality. His etching *The Sleep of Reason Produces Monsters*, in both its title and form, speaks of the process of the Mythic release of the frightening and pervasive ambiguities of the dream. It makes visible the powerful creative processes of the night within us all and reminds us that although we may keep these forces in check through reason, they only await their inherent opportunity to emerge into the light.

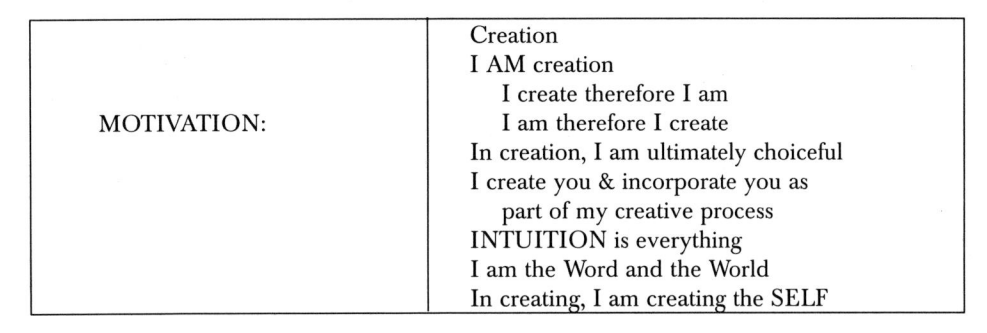

MOTIVATION:	Creation
	I AM creation
	   I create therefore I am
	   I am therefore I create
	In creation, I am ultimately choiceful
	I create you & incorporate you as
	   part of my creative process
	INTUITION is everything
	I am the Word and the World
	In creating, I am creating the SELF

Figure 4-5. "Works of Art in the Mythic Mode." Adapted from Junge (1989).

Figure 4-5 (Continued)

FORM:	Metaphor & symbol
	Abstractness: Away from specificity tied
	   to time, place, culture
	Archetypes
	The Universal
	The unexpected
	Paradox
	Subject matter from deep origins & mys-
	teries, myth, story, dreams–sometimes
	subject matter is irrelevant altogether
	PROCESS is what's important
	Invention of the new
	Line, shape, color in the service of
	   metaphor
	Unity and holism
	Many in the One/One in the many

CONTENT:	World above, below, around the surface
	   (surface only a disguise, does not exist)
	World deep within the UNCONSCIOUS
	Expression of my intuitive processes
	To the essential
	Evocation
	Play
	Play on words, play on images
	Mysteries & ambiguities
	Paradox
	Complete, compelling vision in which
	   mysteries remain
	Self-affirming
	Process as content
	Universals which I create and which are
	   infinite

VIEWER RESPONSE:	I am in the presence of something larger
	   than life
	I feel taken into, one with, sometimes
	   engulfed
	From within the system I can know the
	   mysteries which paradoxically will
	   also remain ultimately mysterious
	I "see" within: I understand, I do not
	   understand
	I am lost
	I am enlarged

Continued on next page

Figure 4-5 (Continued)

	I disappear
	I cannot differ, I cannot argue
	Creativity demanding that I unite with it
	Power, that I fear
	Power, that I long for
VIEWER RESPONSE:	Creativity as metaphor for all life, all being, all knowing, all unknowing
	Awe
	Love
	I am transformed

CONCLUSIONS

In this essay, I have explored an alternative realities systems approach differentiating realities in paintings by visual artists. My intention has been to introduce a journey that might yield new insights and definitions of creativity with the interactive potential to encourage a richer theoretical model about creativity than has been thus far put forth. I have hoped to encourage the viewer to "see" through the lens of the created art product to the world view of the artist, represented within the work. I have argued that the particular characteristics of the artwork in its form as the "shape of content" may provide a rich vein of clues to lead us to diverse motivations and processes. These territorial markings along the road can tell us about the artist's pathway and inform us about our own. Through the expressive image, artwork which represents the painter's belief system, can also act as a mirror of a specific reality system. As we look into the mirror, we may experience the possibilities of double or multiple images enhancing our core abilities to "see," and to create. As we look into the mirror we may be surprised as our vision expands and transforms.

Artists "study" creativity each time they undertake a project, seek to understand something, the world, God or themselves and communicate their vision. As ubiquitous creativity in our clients inspires us as art therapists, so I believe that creative people and their works are the ones who can teach us and the closer theoreticians stay to the freshness and immediacy of this raw data, the better. Creativity is too serious a subject to be left in the hands and brains of the uncreative to instruct us about creativity. What is needed are people who can *play* at serious theory building, who can risk the loneliness of being out there on the tightrope without a safety net. What is needed are *artists* of theory, who along with their skills at reasoned inquiry can, in this scientific and technological age of the twenty-first century remind us and help us believe again in the profound artistry of the poetry of the heart to teach.

REFERENCES

Gardner, H. (1982). *Art, mind and brain: A cognitive approach to creativity.* New York: Basic Books.

Gardner, H. (1983). *Frames of mind: The theory of multiple intelligences.* New York: Basic Books.

Junge, M. (1989). An inquiry into systems of creativity: An alternative realities approach. Unpublished Paper.

Junge, M. (1991). Creative realities, the search for meanings. Unpublished Doctoral Dissertation. Santa Barbara, CA: Fielding Graduate University.

Junge, M. (1998). *Creative realities, the search for meanings.* Lanham, New York, Oxford: University Press of America, Ltd.

LeShan, L. (1976). *Alternative realities.* New York: Ballantine.

McWhinney, W. (1984). Alternative realities: Implications for leadership. *Journal of Humanistic Psychology, 4.*

McWhinney, W. (1985). Alternative forms of creativity and particular training for their use. Unpublished Paper.

McWhinney, W. (1987) Meta-praxis. Unpublished Manuscript Draft.

McWhinney, W. (1988a). Alternative realities and worldviews. Unpublished Paper.

McWhinney, W. (1988b). All creative people are not alike. Unpublished Paper.

Chapter 5

WOMEN AND CREATIVITY WITH TWO CASE STUDIES OF THE ARTISTS FRIDA KAHLO AND DIANE ARBUS[1]

Using a psychodynamic lens, this essay investigates women's creativity with case studies of Mexican painter Frida Kahlo and American photographer Diane Arbus. Conventional wisdom in art therapy says that making artwork and engaging in the creative process are always helpful to the artist and often healing. In this essay, I question this central assumption and hypothesize that Arbus' artwork contributed to the shattering of her personality and to her eventual suicide. Originally published in 1988, as I have revised the article in 2007, it strikes me how little has changed about women and creativity.

I had been thinking of writing about women and creativity since I stood in the sculpture garden of Barbara Hepworth's house in St. Ives on the Cornwall coast of England. Her garden is connected to the house and studio in which she lived and worked for twenty-five years and in which she died in a fire in 1974. Hepworth's work in reproduction seems monumental because of its simplicity and abstractness of shape and form. Standing in her garden, I was struck by the surprisingly intimate scale of Hepworth's work and of her environment–almost a miniature, silent and secret garden, distinctly British, disengaged from the world behind its high enclosing white walls. To a Cali-

1. This essay is reprinted with changes from Junge, M. (1988). An inquiry into women and creativity including two case studies of the artists Frida Kahlo and Diane Arbus. *Art Therapy, Journal of the American Art Therapy Association, 5*, 79–93. Used with permission.

fornian used to the openness and accessibility of space of the coastal areas, there was the temptation to define the scale of Hepworth's personal miniature British world as "female."

Visiting someone's house we feel we know them in some essential inner way and as I wandered alone in Hepworth's house and garden on that bright fall afternoon, I felt intensely connected to her and moved by her creative vision and by the visible signs and symbols of the daily life she led. Also, possibly hovering about my consciousness that day, was the matron saint of women and creativity, Virginia Woolf, who lived and worked just a few blocks away in the house high on the hill overlooking St. Ives harbor.

Since early adolescence, when I came forcefully in touch with my own powers of creativity in the visual arts and the potential ability of the creative process to aid in the development of my own identity, I have read about creativity with dissatisfaction. Most of what I read seemed to offer little explanation, information, nor finally to pierce the essential mystery. Too much literature insisted on counting creativity. This I knew as a silly and meaningless exercise. For my generation, "creativity" became a catchword—e.g., cooking is "creative"—with any potential for capturing its qualities and essence apparently lost in the inability of words to describe such elusiveness. As a visual artist obsessed with the power of imagery, I felt a profound mistrust for mere words.

An early and precious memory is of accompanying my father on one of his weekend painting trips. We would drive to downtown Los Angeles and on Broadway or Main Street stop to paint. The sweetness of that memory of our shared closeness of the creative process remains a precious treasure and a continuing touchstone of definition in my life. Barbara Hepworth speaks also of car trips with her father as a powerful impetus to creativity:

> All my early memories are of forms and shapes and textures. Moving through the West Riding landscape with my father in the car, the hills were sculptures; the roads defined the form. Above all, there was the sensation of moving physically over the contours of fullnesses and concavities, through hollows and over peaks—feeling, touching, seeing through mind and hand and eye. The sensation has never left me. . . . Perhaps what one wants to say is formed in childhood and the rest of one's life is spent in trying to say it. (Bowness, 1977)

With circular reasoning, the dearth of great and recognized women artists throughout history has been used to explain the dearth of recognized women artists and their supposed inadequate creativity in all but the realm of home and hearth–the creativity of anatomy. Gratefully, times have changed somewhat. But women who attempted to be an artist historically suffered and still often suffer today, deeply ambivalent parental and cultural messages. Psychologically introjected, these messages may be injurious and potentially crippling. Thankfully, that sexism exists is no longer news. But given powerful cultural edicts, we must marvel at the strength of creative expression continuing to exist, against overwhelming tides, in some women's lives. And we must be thankful that for women there are more opportunities, awareness and support today.[2]

A series of books in which women talk about their lives and work exists today. Examples of this genre are Rudick and Daniels (1977), Gilbert and Moore, (1981). and Miller and Swensen (1981). The shift in attention is exemplified by Ghiselin's 1952 classic *The Creative Process.* Surveying 38 artists living and dead, only four were women–three writers and a dancer. More recent "integrated" compendiums have not significantly altered this typical non-representation and women artist's stories remain "ghettoized" in books and art histories specifically about women, largely written by women and, I suspect, read primarily by other women who are rightfully hungry for models. We are still at the necessary stage of the documentation of creative women's lives (judge by the increasing numbers of biographies,) but feminism notwithstanding we have yet to reach a time when we have much in the way of satisfactory theory.

No matter how much in ill repute Freud (1961) may be currently held, I believe many of his notions about the sources, motivations and transformative energy of creativity and even that the creative urge is ultimately akin to psychopathology, still pervade current thinking about art and artists and thus warrant a fresh look. Secondly, psychoanalytic methods have provided us with important tools with which to understand the artistic personality and its vicissitudes. Additionally, I have been an art psychotherapist for many years and believe that all art is a reflection of the artist, the environment and of the relationship between them. Thus, I thought it would be interesting to look into the lives and artwork of two visual artists, the American photographer

---

2. As I write this in 2007, I remember that Judy Chicago's "The Dinner Party," an important feminist work was relegated to a warehouse for many years and, recently, was to be destroyed by the artist because it had not found a home. Fortunately, it did.

Diane Arbus and the Mexican painter, Frida Kahlo and within an undeniably psychodynamic (though not strictly Freudian) perspective, explore questions about the genesis, meaning and uses of creativity in these two artist's personalities and lives. I felt these elements could come together to provide a useful way to proceed that might lead to the asking of provocative questions.

In the following section, I present a working definition of creativity and describe some basic ideas about the subject as it pertains to women. In the last section of the paper, Arbus and Kahlo are used as psychodynamic case studies for an inquiry into the role of creativity in their lives and personality development.

IDEAS OF WOMEN AND CREATIVITY FROM LITERATURE

A Working Definition of Creativity

The word "creativity" is used with an easy familiarity suggestive of universal understanding and has been defined from a variety of perspectives such as the psychological, the historic, the aesthetic and the behavioral. In reality it is not easy to arrive at a generally accepted definition of creativity. *Webster's Ninth New Collegiate Dictionary* states: "Creativity–the quality of being creative" and "Creative" as "marked by the ability or power to create." At least one author suggests that there are four recognizable and alternative forms of creativity and that there should be specifically differential training for their use (McWhinney, 1985.)

Creativity is the domain of human beings, (stories of chimpanzees and elephants making paintings notwithstanding) and it differentiates us from animals. We have evidence of its continuing existence even in the most extreme and devastating situations such as the Nazi concentration camps where in the face of an unbearable reality we are reminded of the best that is human. Arieti (1976) cites the importance of distinguishing creativity from spontaneity and originality which, he says, are feelings, ideas and images emerging from unconscious processes, experienced and sometimes acted upon, but which remain relatively unchanged and untransformed. He goes on to describe creativity as "a desirable enlargement of human experience":

[A creative work] establishes an additional bond between the world and human existence . . . [and] thus may be seen to have a dual role: At the same time as it enlarges the universe by adding or uncovering new dimensions, it also enlarges the universe and expands man [sic] . . . It is committed not just to the visible . . . but to the invisible as well.

Distinguishing between "ordinary" and great creativity, Arieti (1976) postulates a "magic synthesis from which the new, the unexpected, and the desirable emerge." For the purposes of this essay, Arieti's definition is accepted in its delineation of creativity arising out of the raw matter of the interrelationship between the person and the context, and through a special transformation something new is created which is positive and which expands the relationship between the person and the environment.

Ideas on Women and Creativity

The idea of the innate inferiority of women as creative beings has been mentioned previously. This is an idea held for centuries and still believed by many (e.g., Hillary Clinton's run for President of the United States in which being a woman may be a crucial issue). Patriarchal society in which the woman was relegated to the functions of motherhood and home, often as "property" to father or husband perpetuated the notion that women had no inclination toward creativity. Later, psychoanalytic theory suggested that the motivation in women to create is typically (and normally) sublimated into the creation of children. Neo-Freudian Karen Horney favorably (if unconvincingly) reframes men's creativity as a kind of *womb envy*. She substantially holds to traditional psychoanalytic thinking about women by suggesting that Freud's concept of *penis envy*, in women is transformed into the wish for a husband and a child and is therefore an unsatisfactory sublimation process.

Researchers, basing their models on prevailing patriarchal assumptions, evolved interpretations to support their assumptions. Cattell early in the twentieth century studied men of science in the United States (1903, 1906). In two articles published in 1910, he noted that between 1903 and 1910 *women in science* had not increased in number nor improved their standing. He concluded there was no cultural intolerance toward women but obviously women were "sexually disqualified." Cattell's misguided interpretation of data in which the effects of the social mileu are not even seen within the frame and thus the only explanation is biological inheritance is typical.

In 1913, Cora Sutton Castle followed Cattell's method and made a list of 868 eminent women (including politicians, mothers, mistresses and rulers) through 26 centuries and from 42 countries. She noted a marked tendency for eminent women to acquire prominence in the same field as their fathers and that they had not been particularly successful as wives. Castle could not decide whether the small numbers meant that women are innately inferior or had a lack of opportunity. She did not recognize the fact that two-thirds of the women on her list lived in the eighteenth and nineteenth centuries; she should have shown that environment influences statistics.

Tamar Cohen (1983) in her persuasive article, essentially grounded in Humanistic personality theory, "The Woman Artist: A Struggle for Self-Realization," postulates a conceptual framework based on a developmental model. Cohen, a psychotherapist who treated artists in her practice, points out an essential theme of the creative process: the artist's strong urge to create—both as a means of self expression and as a continuing marker of experience. Cohen (1983) quotes Miriam Shapiro, a well-known contemporary feminist artist, who said that as a child, teenager, and college student, all she wanted to do was be an artist. Somehow, she was able to push through her overbearing self doubt to paint images that had meaning. Shapiro describes her desire to make art as strong as that of food and sex. Her powerful desire led to her ability to overcome self doubt and to paint.

It was exactly this urge to create, to witness, to mark and to last, which compelled the artists of the concentration camps. Cohen (1983) argues that if a woman feels a strong drive to make art, it can create a conflict between this desire and her internalized women's role. She suggests that, like other women, the woman artist, initially internalizes the cultural myths about *woman's role*. As she struggles with her feelings about a perceived and/or actual role definition of wife and mother, her creative gifts and urges become additional burden for her and may even pose a threat to her evolving personality.

Cohen (1983) conceives of the woman artist's process as occurring in a three-stage developmental progression during which specific conflicts are dealt with. Each stage is characterized by the attitude the woman artist shows toward her work. In the first stage, conflict is avoided either by the woman accepting her social role or by consciously or unconsciously avoiding it. Feminist artist Judy Chicago (1982[3]) describes the latter position: she decided to be considered a serious artist and to make progress in the art world, she needed to stay unmarried, have no children and live in a large loft.

According to Cohen, in the first stage, the woman artist must repress or deny her needs and straddle the fence of ambivalence. In the second stage, conflict is displaced onto her female role. But a commitment to the work, Cohen writes, may render her confidence as a woman uncertain. For example, Georgia O'Keeffe wanted children with Alfred Steiglitz, but he refused and succeeded in convincing her that her art was her children. It was a life tragedy for her that Frida Kahlo could not carry a child to term. Diane Arbus had two daughters and eventually became a single mother.

Pervasive questions about the value of her work, feelings of self doubt and lack of self confidence often hinder the woman artist's ability to work productively. Her lack of productivity leads to further doubting and Cohen suggests that a typical result is often difficulties with commitment to her artwork. At this stage, the woman may talk of "other demands" which take her away from her art.

In the third stage of resolution, the woman artist begins to consciously, if painfully confront both her commitment to her work and her emotional needs. In her artwork, she feels new self confidence and experiences deep pleasure and a sense of fulfillment. Cohen states that it is during this stage, that the woman artist along with her immense pleasure which comes from accomplishing the work, knows the pain that accompanies growth.

In the third stage, the woman artist works productively and adds personal content and meaning to her work. Using the analogy of a mother allowing separation from her now-grown child, Cohen (1983) finds that the woman artist is now separate from her artwork. She may begin to exhibit her work, opening herself to criticism. Finally, Cohen suggests a social action role for the woman artist: Through communicating her reality in her art, the woman artist can help others confront the stereotypes and hindrances with which she has grappled.

---

3. First published in 1975.

CASE STUDIES OF TWO VISUAL ARTISTS, FRIDA KAHLO AND DIANE ARBUS

This section is composed of case studies of two visual artists, the Mexican painter Frida Kahlo, and Diane Arbus, the American photographer. These artists were chosen basically because their work is of interest to me. Additionally, there exist well-documented and complete biographies of the two. An assumption I make is that artistic creativity springs from and is innately related to the artist's life and that the artist's creativity profoundly influences roads taken and choices made in the artist's life. Further, the cultural, social and psychological milieu of the times are internalized and integrally intertwined with the artist and her life. The two women artists here are not formally compared although there is some attempt to highlight what may be important congruencies within their "stories." Each case study includes, first, the basic sources used and a description of the outlines of the artist's life. Next, discussion is centered around cultural, social and psychological questions designed to elicit information within an essentially psychodynamic framework. I seek to provide an in-depth exploration of the origins and uses of creativity in these women's lives and work and in the development of their personalities. The lives of both Kahlo and Arbus represent cultural edicts of time and place in which women were normally dedicated to husband and children and which intense creative expression for women, if it could exist at all, was usually relegated to "a hobby." That the flame still burned and the rock still stood is a credit to these important women artists.

Frida Kahlo

Sources

Life history information for this essay is taken from Hayden Herrera's 1983 book *Frida, A Biography of Frida Kahlo.*[4] Herrera's book

---

4. It is only relatively recently that Frida Kahlo has become an important figure, even a cult figure, to women. The Herrera biography was the first, I believe, and her work had only begun to be exhibited in this country at the time this essay was first published in 1988 (I remember seeing her major exhibit, hidden away, in East Los Angeles at La Raza. Today, with much fanfare, it would be at the Los Angeles Art Museum.) When I was a child, few knew her work, I remember my Father saying that she was a much better painter than her husband Diego Rivera. Although my parents owned a small Rivera drawing, I remember my Father wishing he had a Kahlo instead.

includes as sources excerpts from Wolfe's 1963 biography of Kahlo's husband, the Mexican muralist Diego Rivera, *The Fabulous Life of Diego Rivera*, and quotations from Rivera's *My Art, My Life: An Autobiography*.

Frida Kahlo's Life

One year before her death in 1954 at the age of forty-seven, Frida Kahlo's paintings were presented in a one-woman exhibition (Arbus committed suicide at age 48). This was her first major exhibit in her native land of Mexico. Kahlo was born on July 6, 1907 in Mexico City the third daughter of Guillermo and Matilde Kahlo. Her father was a German Jewish atheist who had immigrated to Mexico at the age of 19. He had been a promising scholar in Germany but suffered a brain injury and thereafter experienced epileptic seizures. Kahlo's Mexican mother was attractive, uneducated and a pious Catholic. At the time of Frida's birth, her father was a successful photographer. It was said that she inherited from him her eyebrow that connected across her nose and her intensity of gaze. After Frida's birth, her mother became ill and she was suckled by a wet nurse, an indigenous Indian woman.

The Mexican revolution broke out when Kahlo was three years old. Her father lost much of his photography work which had been commissioned by the government; he became depressed and distant. At age six, Frida developed polio. She spent nine months recovering in her bedroom during which time she invented an imaginary friend. Emerging from polio with a withered right leg, she would be bothered both physically and emotionally all her life; she covered her leg with the long skirts of Mexican folk costumes that became her trademark and her mask. After her illness, because of her leg Frida was teased and left out by friends. It is said that she became solitary and introverted.

At the age of 15, so the story goes, Frida first met the famous muralist Diego Rivera who was painting a mural at her school. Rivera was 36 years old when Frida fell in love with him. She married him seven years later against her parents' wishes and they stayed together, despite a divorce and remarriage and affairs on both sides, until her death.

At age 18 Frida experienced an accident which would transform her life. She was riding on a bus that was hit by a streetcar. Among her other injuries, her spine was broken in three places, her right leg crushed and an iron rod went totally through her at the level of her pelvis. As a result of the accident, she would never be able to have children and would endure 32 operations on her spine and foot. After the accident, neither of her parents came to the hospital. During her long recovery and her loneliness she began to paint—at first portraits of her friends. Then she did a series of paintings of herself.

After her recuperation, Frida took her artwork to show Rivera who was painting frescoes at the Ministry of Education. Despite Rivera's continuing liaisons with other women, their attraction grew and they were married in 1929. He was a famous 41-year- old Communist artist. She was 22. Shortly after, she became pregnant, but had a therapeutic abortion, the first of more abortions and three miscarriages. They spent four years in the United States where Rivera had mural commissions but returned to Mexico because of Frida's urging. Their tempestuous marriage continued. They were divorced for two years and then remarried. During the divorce, Kahlo remained emotionally tied to Rivera, focused her life on him and, in fact, took care of his bills and correspondence. She had periodic love affairs with both women and men. Leon Trotsky and Isamu Noguchi the sculptor were two of the men.

Although she played herself down as a painter in favor of her commitment to Rivera, Frida continued her artistic development. Through the years, she endured multiple operations which included many encasements in torso-length plaster casts and she continued painting. She died in 1954. From entries in her written and drawn diary there is a hint that she committed suicide. The cause of her death is listed as "pulmonary embolism."

Roots of Creativity in Frida Kahlo's Early Life

There appear to be three central themes that provide clues to the sources of Kahlo's artistic creativity and productiveness. They are: early family dynamics and Frida's attachment to her father, her illness with polio at age six, and the role of illness in the family dynamics and the development of Kahlo's personality.

Family Dynamics and Frida's Attachment to Her Father

Kahlo's mother was uneducated—she did not know how to read or write—and a religious woman who became ill after the birth of her third daughter. I speculate a period, perhaps a lengthy period, of postpartum depression. Although she taught her daughters housewifely skills, it is known that Frida was largely cared for by older sisters. At midlife, Frida's mother began suffering from "seizures" or "attacks" that resembled her husband's epileptic seizures.

Frida's father, a successful photographer until the Mexican Revolution, afterward was a man of silences. In spite of his depressive nature, Guillermo Kahlo was most attached to Frida of anyone in the family, thought her to be like him and encouraged her intellectual adventurousness. She resembled him physically and he considered her the most intelligent of his children. He lent her books from his library and encouraged her to share his passion for nature. He was an amateur watercolor painter and she would accompany him on his trips, collecting stones and leaves to bring home and observe under a microscope. Of their relationship, Herrerra (1983) writes:

> When she was old enough . . . her father taught her to use a camera and to develop, retouch and color photographs . . . her father's fastidiousness, his concern for minute surface detail would later appear in her own paintings. . . . Frida once said that her paintings were like the photographs that her father did . . . only instead of painting outer reality, she painted the [images] that were inside her head.

Eleven years after her father's death and two years before her own, she painted Guillermo's portrait from a photograph he took of himself. In the painting, Frida painted cells as if through a microscope. It may be speculated that this imagery reflects her looking through the microscope after collecting trips with her father, her profound and sexual attachment to her father and perhaps her sense of him as a source of primal energy. The inscription in the painting reflects both Kahlo's love and her use of him as a model for her own life of artwork created in spite of illness and suffering.

There are other examples in art history of women artists encouraged by artist fathers and there has been research to suggest that achievement in women may be dependent in part on their relationships with their fathers. Along with Kahlo, Tintoretto's daughter, Marietta Robusti was one woman artist with an artist father and Diane Arbus is another.

Kahlo's Illness with Polio at Age Six

Kahlo's nine months spent convalescing in her room at a period when the intelligent and active child would have spent time outside with friends expanding her world, resulted in loneliness and withdrawal into her own imagination. She invented an imaginary friend who was happy, understanding, physically agile and free. Frida's illness connected her even more strongly to her father and to his experience of illness. Afterwards, she was ashamed of her withered right leg and overcompensated by becoming a daring tomboy. Some of her descriptions of treatments during that time echo a fascination with the details of sickness and suffering which would be a predominant theme in the imagery of her paintings.

Illness and the Family Dynamics: It's Role in Kahlo's Personality Development

Because of Guillermo's epileptic episodes, this was a family intimately familiar with illness. Frida would often accompany her father on photography trips in case he needed aid. She learned to help him with his attacks in the street and also to make sure his camera equipment wasn't stolen. In addition, there were Frida's mother's illnesses, probably depressions, her own bout with polio and her later devastating accident at age eighteen.

Kahlo's early life engendered an "upclose" relationship to illness with its ramifications that would continue throughout her life. Her fascination with clinical details was an ongoing fact of her life and art. Illness' use to bring the secondary gains of attention and specialness would be essential in her relationship to Diego Rivera—her illnesses often had the power to attract him back to her when she had no other means. That she was a hypochondriac is well-known. There is no question that she had immense physical problems but there is also substantial doubt as to whether she actually required 32 operations or whether she had come to need illness and surgery as a way to be in the world. If she was something of a masochist who may have had surgeries she didn't need, who can blame her?

I speculate that, as a young child, she must have been rendered terrified, insecure and vulnerable by her parents' illnesses and by her own. In her evolving personality, this resulted in a clinical attraction as a means of mastering and controlling her fears. Frida intended to pursue medical school and had the accident not occurred probably would have. (According to psychoanalytic theory, to be a doctor is (sometimes) a defense mechanism against one's own feelings of vulnerability.) Later, when Frida began to paint, she would find another way to cope with her profound feelings of illness and suffering within the form and content of her artwork.

Frida Kahlo's Artwork: Her Creative Vision and Its Relationship to Her Life

Frida Kahlo's paintings are a kind of autobiography of memory and reality. They are physically small, super realistic and formal in style. Although content–predominantly self portraits–is often bloody, violent and masochistic, the paintings' connection to Mexican primitive folklore and their binding of emotionality through the restraint of hard-edged formal qualities provide the viewer with a welcome aesthetic distance. Concern with women, family, the land, suffering and death are uniquely Kahlo's subjects and seem ultimately rooted in the paradoxical nature of Mexican culture and the role of the Mexican woman of that time.

In "The Broken Column" painted in 1944 soon after one of her surgeries (Figure 5-1) Kahlo is confined in an apparatus such as many she was made to wear to allow spinal healing. She paints a jagged, bloody opening in the body, a crevice resembling an earthquake fissure; within, one can see a broken Greek column. Nails pierce flesh and tears fall from eyes. The orthopedic corset is both prison and necessary support. Without it, the body would fall apart. But within its rigid structures, Frida's breasts are contrastingly delicate and vulnerable. The figure is set alone in a barren landscape with cuts and crevices providing a metaphor for the broken body. At the horizon, is a strip of ocean with its possibility of comfort; but it is too far away to reach.

Kahlo's suffering and her strength, recurrent and dominant themes in her artwork, are evident in this painting. The subject matter is of almost unbearable anguish; but formal stylization gives a sense of solidity and permanence and also provides enough distance so the viewer can bear to look. The figure, though wrenched apart and in a stance of enforced passivity, stands upright and strong. The face is turned slightly to the side. Suffering is signaled by tears on the cheeks, but the face is mask-like and impassive and the eyes connect directly with the viewer. Schjedahl (2007) argues that "she makes eye contact not with the viewer but with herself–watching herself watch herself, in an extended but closed loop." In spite of wounds and tears, there is a sense of dignity and stoicism here. Colors are muted except in the flesh which appears distinctly alive and enduring. Shapes are solid, almost classically balanced and in their dimensionality imply durability. The painting is at once a poignant cry for attention and a heroic example of survival.

Figure 5-1. "Frida Kahlo's 'The Broken Column, 1944, Fundación Dolores Olmedo, photo by Schalkwijk/Art Resource, NY,© 2008 Banco de México Diego Rivera & Frida Kahlo Museums Trust. Av. Cinco de Mayo No.2, Col. Centro Del. Cuauhtémoc 06059, México, D.F.

Kahlo is the most personal of painters. She never attempted any subject without intense meaning for her and they were all filtered through the lens of the self and the imagination of a confined invalid. She was an exhibitionist of her feelings in a stylized, theatrical form. Herrera (1983) calls her paintings Kahlo's form of "psychological surgery."

Interplay Between Conflicts Engendered by Women's Social Urge Role and the Creative Urge

Until the last years of her life, Frida Kahlo presented herself as a semi-serious painter. In part, this was a pose that enabled her to keep her painting strictly for her own uses and not submit to the suggestions and criticisms inherent in exhibits and sales. Diego Rivera created large public paintings. Hers were small and private (and non-competitive with his). Since her school-girl days when she had first met Rivera, she put his needs first and adapted herself to them. Rivera's biographer, Bertram Wolfe, wrote that to Rivera, Frida came after art and his creation of his life as a series of legends, but to her, Rivera was first, before her painting.

Kahlo understood that being Diego's wife was a full-time job. Through much of her life, she painted only sporadically, at times completing only one or two works a year. She kept house, cooked what Rivera liked and tried to anticipate his needs. When he was working on a mural she would usually carry his lunch to him in a basket, stopping to do this even when engaged in her own painting. In sorrow, she did not immediately turn to her artwork for solace but to her "house-wifely" pleasures. In 1932, the two were in Detroit while Diego worked on commissioned murals. There, a newspaper article was written about Frida under the title "Wife of the Master Mural Painter Gleefully Dabbles in Works of Art," indicative of her general attitude toward her work (and also of the writer's attitude toward women).

Kahlo's abortions, miscarriages and inability to have children are indirectly and directly reflected in her art and were a tremendous source of suffering for her. After one early miscarriage, she painted a picture of her own birth. She was fond of dolls, pets and others' children and recognized them as the substitutes they were. Sorrow at her childlessness resulted in nostalgia for her lost childhood, as she identified herself with the child she could not have.

Another element of Frida's adherence to a female role was her interest in clothes and how she looked. In her life and art, clothes as costume, as theater, as metaphor and as mask, are of essential importance. She covered her withered leg with long skirts and liked wearing native Mexican costumes both because they covered and because they represented her solidarity with indigenous Mexico. Separated from Rivera, she cut off her long hair which he loved. She painted herself with short hair, in a man's suit with her shorn hair lying around her on the ground, as if she were divesting herself of her sexuality. Frida's clothes reflected a kind of visual language of her inner self. Herrera sees Kahlo's costuming as both a mask and a frame which defined the wearer's identity and provided a boundary to distract from inner pain. Schjedahl (2007) mentions contents and décor of Frida's house "La Casa Azul" in the Coyocán section of Mexico City, where she grew up, lived and died "as vibrant" as she was.

The question of female role expectations conflicting with the urge for creative self-expression is an especially interesting one with Kahlo. We may speculate that if she had been able to bear and raise children and had a more easy time with Rivera, she might have been satisfied to displace her creative urges onto his career and her children. If she had not been so physically restricted, often isolated and in a dependency which she hated, I wonder would she have so desperately needed to express her sense of herself as a functioning, separate, enduring and imagining human being? We can only guess that a woman of Kahlo's intelligence, vibrancy and creativity would have needed to find some way toward visual expression. But these are, of course, essentially unanswerable questions.

What we *can* know is that Frida herself, in her writings, expressed both sides of the conflict. On the one hand, she denigrated her work and said that anybody who bought her work had done so because he was in love with her. Expressing the other side of her ambivalence, she wrote of the accident irrevocably changing her life and keeping her from "normal" things: Her lack of "fulfillment" as a woman was fulfilled in her paintings, primarily self-portraits.

Psychological Significance of Kahlo's Art to Her Personality

As a young girl Frida Kahlo's intellectual pursuits and her observation of nature had been encouraged by a close relationship with her artist father. Polio at age six and her lonely nine-month convalescence had plunged her into the transcending pleasures of her imagination. Throughout her childhood she faced and coped with the mystery and unpredictability of her father's epilepsy and her mother's depression. After the terrible bus accident at age 18, during the period of her invalidism, she began to paint which provided her with the pleasures of the creative process, enabled her to continue interpersonal relationships through her portraits, kept her company, and finally brought her to Diego Rivera.

Throughout her life, Kahlo would associate suffering with creativity and for her, physical suffering was intimately connected to psychological suffering. In her artwork physical suffering would express deep psychic wounds and both would be presented unflinchingly—with dignity, control, almost objectivity. She denied that she was a Surrealist and insisted that she painted her own reality, which seems right to me. Artwork provided her with tools to tame—for awhile—her difficult inner and outer realities. Kahlo could escape into the healing potential of her imagination and express in paint a visual catharsis. Her paintings were small, personal, symbolic, primitive in style, controlled in form and color and in their careful brush strokes reminiscent of the photographic retouching techniques taught to her as a child by her father. To paint probably contained for Kahlo the comforting memory of her father's attentiveness and encouragement.

But it was through her use of form that she could forcefully and symbolically control and contain her pain, bind overwhelming feelings, ward off terrible vulnerability and fears of death and provide for herself the sense of psychic distance that enabled her to survive one more day. Kahlo's particular brand of primitivism conceals and reveals—the small scale, fantasy and bright color distance viewer and artist from intensely painful content. Kahlo's art is a metaphorical representation of two important aspects of her personality: her clinical fascination with and attraction to pain; and her dignity and courage in the face of it.

Diane Arbus

Sources

Much of the biographic material in this study is based on Patricia Bosworth's *Diane Arbus* published in 1984. An additional source is:

Diane Arbus (1972), an Aperture monograph edited by Doon Arbus (Diane's daughter) and Marvin Israel which includes reproductions of Arbus' photographs and quotations from some of Arbus' interviews, writings and text from tape recordings made at a series of photography classes she taught in 1971. The photograph discussed in this essay was taken from this book and serves as its cover. Also used for source material is *Diane Arbus' Magazine Work* which Doon Arbus and Marvin Israel published in 1984. This is a chronological presentation of the work Arbus did for magazine publication between 1960 and 1971.

Description of Diane Arbus' Life

Diane Arbus (pronounced Dee-Ann) was born in New York City March 14, 1923. She was the middle child and the first girl of a privileged Jewish family. Her father owned a 5th Avenue, New York, department store called Russek's. Her mother, beautiful and distant left the care of the children primarily in the hands of nannies. The family milieu was one of separateness and silences within the privileged but protected environment of the very rich.

Diane and her older brother Howard[5] developed an exceptionally close relationship. As young children they were recognized as gifted, imaginative and of a particular intelligence. During her school years she showed talent in painting and had a special interest in the work of George Grosz, a painter of grotesques.

Like Kahlo with Rivera, Diane met and fell in love with Allan Arbus when she was very young, 14 years old. She wanted to marry him right away but her parents insisted she wait. Against her parents' wishes, she married Arbus a month after her high school graduation in 1941; she was 18. Just before this, in her senior year at school, she had denounced all her paintings as "no good" and destroyed them, stating that all she wanted was to become Mrs. Allan Arbus. She said she wanted "to live under the wing of a man (Bosworth, 1984). Despite their wealth, Diane received no money from her parents after her marriage. She was, however, sometimes invited to come down to Russek's and pick out clothes. At times, particularly in her later years alone after her divorce, making a living was a major problem for her.

In 1943, during World War II, Allan joined the Signal Corps and learned photography which he later taught to Diane. With Allan away,

---

5. Diane's brother is the well-known American poet Howard Nemerov.

Diane moved back with her parents. She discovered she was pregnant and her daughter Doon was born in 1945. Diane refused to let her mother or sister accompany her to the hospital. She believed she had to be alone to truly experience something.

When Allan came home, the two became fashion photographers. Diane's father gave them their first account photographing fashions and furs for newspaper ads for his store, and for the next ten years or so they worked very closely, symbiotically together turning out photographs for newspapers and for most major fashion magazines in the United States. Usually he took the pictures and she tended to the model's clothes, the props, and so forth.

Like Kahlo, for Diane, marriage and her role as a housewife and mother were the important things. Nevertheless, in the postwar 1950s era of the housewife heroine, she remained a working woman. Allan longed to be an actor instead of a fashion photographer. In 1954, their second baby, another daughter, was born.

In the 1950s the photojournalism of *Life* magazine was dominant and in 1955 there was a huge exhibit of photography at the Museum of Modern Art organized by Edward Steichen–"The Family of Man." The overall concept of the show was a romantic, benevolent view of humanity. In contrast to this more sentimental approach favored at the time, when her Grandmother died in 1956 Diane took photographs of her in her coffin.

Diane suffered from recurrent depressions. It was said that she could sit for hours silently staring. According to Bosworth (1984) "terror aroused her and made her feel." In 1957, Diane and Allan dissolved their professional partnership and began to do things independently of each other. They agreed that Allan would continue to run the photography business and Diane would take photographs or work as she wished. They hoped that the new arrangement would help alleviate Diane's depressions. But the couple became estranged. Also in 1957, Arbus' father retired, sold his business, and with his wife, moved to Florida where he took up painting full time and exhibited his paintings.

In 1959, Diane studied with Lisette Model who became her mentor and her artistic role model and offered her a kind of mother-daughter relationship that she had never had. Model took pictures which were considered revolutionary at the time in terms of their size (16 x 20 prints) and their subject matter–drunks, beggars, ordinary people and the ugly—which she called "extremes" and "exaggerations." Model encouraged Arbus to pursue her own work and to photograph what she had been previously afraid to confront—ugliness, loneliness, freaks and oddities. Arbus began to prowl Manhattan at all hours to search out subjects. She said: "Freaks was a thing I photographed a lot. . . . Most people go through life dreading they'll have a traumatic experience. Freaks were born with their trauma. They've already passed their test in life" (Arbus, quoted in Arbus and Israel, 1972). She was devastated over the breakup of her marriage.

In 1963, Arbus' father died and she photographed him dead. He had been the first to encourage her talent. During the 1960s she continued to obsessively pursue her photography "of the forbidden" while she struggled with the demands of life as a single mother. She endured continuing depressive episodes and hepatitis. She was treated by psychotherapists and took antidepressant medication which seemed to do little to ease her depressions. She published some of her work in magazines such as *Esquire*, but much of it was considered too bizarre and confrontive for the mass media. She received two Guggenheim fellowships and in 1967 her photographs were exhibited at the Museum of Modern Art in a show called "New Documents" representing three photographers. Her work was gaining her much recognition which she didn't enjoy.

By the late sixties with both daughters increasingly away from the house, Diane was left alone. In 1969, she and Allan were finally divorced. She photographed, participated in peace marches and took portraits of feminists for the London *Sunday Times*. Although she was recognized as an artist she still couldn't make a living as a photographer. In 1971, she taught photography and took pictures of retarded people which she was dissatisfied with. She told friends she didn't think she could go on. Diane Arbus committed suicide on July 26, 1971, at the age of 48. In 1972, she became the first American photographer to be exhibited at the Venice Biennale.

Roots of Creativity in Diane Arbus' Early Life

The impetus for virtually all the themes in Diane Arbus' photography is found in her early life and particularly in her family's dynamics. Her work can be seen as a direct result of those dynamics and a kind of obsessive repetition compulsion of early feelings and patterns of behavior. What Arbus could not repress in her early years, she attempted to sublimate and master through her controlled life as Allan's "perfect wife" and her daughters' mother. As those demands fell away, in spite of continuous terror, in her artwork she plunged into the out-of-control, dark excessive world of her sexual and aggressive impulses that was both dangerous and exciting. That world finally killed her.

Diane could not resolve or integrate her conflictual urges, nor did she receive much support, resulting in multiple depressions. For many years she carried her cameras with her at all times and called them a "shield" against danger. A camera and the creative process became for Diane Arbus a transitional safety zone against harm. She said: "There's a kind of power thing about the camera. . . . This person could be approaching with a gun . . . and I'd have my eyes glued to the finder" (Arbus quoted in Arbus & Israel, 1972).

I speculate that even as a child, Diane showed schizoid characteristics. She was extremely sensitive and emotional, moody and uncommunicative and would lapse into remote silences which intimidated her parents. Her adulthood probably contained numerous unnamed schizophrenic episodes. But if her creative process contained within it the seeds of her destruction, for Diane it was clearly a courageous attempt at mastery and survival. If in the end her art failed her, it should nevertheless not be construed as mere visual pathology.

The Dynamics of the Nemerov Family

According to Diane's sister, the Nemerov family was one "of silences." Diane's beautiful mother Gertrude was not affectionate toward nor attentive with her children; it was said she was always busy looking in the mirror. (Years later, Diane would repeat this pattern in her photographs when she could not help looking into "the mirror" of herself and others.) Her businessman father was gone most of the time and also showed little warmth or interest in his children.

For the first seven years of her life, Diane was brought up by a nanny who was cool and undemonstrative but who almost never left her alone. In her privileged overprotection, Arbus developed many fears and from an early age, a sense of "unreality." Since childhood, she said, she had felt unreal and immune from adversity; her immunity was painful for her. Recounting her sense of isolation, she told a friend of an experience in summer camp: All her friends had been bitten by leeches and she wasn't. She felt an outsider. It was her feelings of isolation and unreality that later caused Diane to search out and confront any experience that could make her *feel*. She was preoccupied with anything physical, including her menstrual cycle and its blood; it was the physical that could make her believe she was alive.

The lack of an adequate bonding relationship with a parent caused Diane and her older brother Howard to cling to each other and they developed a symbiotic relationship. At times they would refuse to talk with anyone but each other. Howard who would become a well-known poet was all intellect it was said, and Diane all emotion. The symbiotic qualities of this relationship would be repeated in Diane's life with Allan and with her daughter Doon (1983). Later, this exchange of secrets would characterize much of her art. Her struggles to understand and cope with her feelings about attachment and separation and the challenge of establishing a separate identity would be a central theme of her life and would be played out, most particularly, in her photographic obsession with twins.

Diane's Relationship with Her Father

In spite of his lack of interest generally in his children, like Kahlo and her father, Diane was her father's favorite child and through her ambivalent attachment to him, she gained some sense of the energy of the outside world. Although he was not home much, as a child, Diane would often be taken to visit him at his store. He was a businessman fascinated by drama, richness and excess. Even when he was having financial problems, he spent lavishly to provide the visual *accoutrements*–the mask of wealth and excitement. His sexuality and sensual nature were openly acknowledged. He said that he wanted his store to be one where men could buy expensive presents for their mistresses and the fact that he had mistresses himself was apparently accepted by his wife.

And he dreamed of becoming an artist. When he went to Europe to see the fashion collections, Diane's father always took a sketchbook along. When he sold his store in 1957, retired, and moved with Gertrude to Florida, he became a full-time painter, exhibiting regularly and selling his work. His messages to Diane about artistic achievement when she was young were characteristically ambivalent. He encouraged her but dismissed her art as a hobby. Her real goal, her father said, was "to live under the wing of a man" (Bosworth, 1984).

According to psychoanalytic theory, the adolescent reworks the unfinished tasks of the earlier Oedipal stage. At age fourteen, the height of her threatening sexual feelings toward her father, Diane "safely" fell in love with Allan and thereafter for almost twenty years, displaced her incestuous wishes and her needs for intimacy onto her relationship with him. Ironically at 18 when she married Allan, Diane believed she was creating an independent life for herself.

The Compulsion to Confront the Forbidden

With her extreme sensitivity, Diane must have been continuously aware of hidden nuances under the surface. It was this awareness which allowed her to feel the pain of her isolation as a child and her sense of separateness. Within the unspoken and secret subtexts of the Nemerov family, she lived in ambiguity. For a young child, the mystery beneath the mask that cannot be spoken becomes something full of terror—bad and evil and forbidden. Unexpressed rage and sexual impulses go underground, and tend to become projected onto the world causing it to seem a fearful place. The forbidden side of Diane was not able to be completely denied or repressed, although she tried. Diane said that she lived with overwhelming fear every day of her life.

In 1957, Arbus studied photography with Lisette Model. The first photos she brought in, according to Model, were fragile and mundane. She told Model that she couldn't photograph what she wanted, because she considered it *evil*. Model urged her to photograph what she wanted—evil or not. With Model's encouragement, Arbus began photographing people and places she had been afraid to confront: She went to Coney Island, the Wax Museum, a traveling circus, photographed tattooed people and became obsessed with freaks. Bosworth (1984) describes:

> Gazing at the human skeleton or the bearded lady, she was reminded of a dark, unnatural, hidden self. As a little girl she had been forbidden to look at anything "abnormal." . . . Forbidden to look, Diane had stared all the more and developed an intense sympathy for any human oddity.

Diane Arbus' Photography and Its Relationship to Her Life

Arbus' photographic portrait of identical twins will be examined (see first reference, Arbus, D. and Israel, M., cover print). Two little girls about eight years old stand awkwardly together in front of a white cement wall. They wear smocked dresses. They have dark hair and bangs. One twin has a faint smile. The other holds her lips tightly together with a strained look. They peer directly at the viewer. Their faces are framed by identical white headbands held on with two identical bobby pins and by their dresses' jagged white collars. On their legs are white lace stockings with patterns that are not identical, as if their mother who tried to dress them alike had run out of steam. They stand on a brick wall splattered with white paint spots.

This is anything but a relaxed, pleasant portrait of two innocent children. The psychological complexity of the photograph makes the viewer feel that they have never really seen twins before (or, for that matter, children). One twin stands slightly in front of the other. The effect is of strangely connected Siamese twins or of a multiple ink blot made from folded paper. They are mirror images and yet different— two parts of a whole, but separate and individualistic. Their intimacy and inseparableness is palatable. They share secrets between them that no one can know. The viewer is drawn into the intensity of their relationship to each other and to the photographer. The feeling is of accidentally stumbling on something hidden; one cannot look away. Arbus said she never arranged her subjects, but simply arranged herself. The subject matter of the photograph appears innocent enough, but the frontality, objectivity and confrontive quality of the form along with the stark black and white shapes seem almost shocking. The white headbands, collars, cuffs and stockings appear to this writer reminiscent of the orthopedic corset in Kahlo's "The Broken Column." They structure, support and cruelly imprison. The effect is of control, order and quiet. However, the dissimilar stockings on the girls and the accidental drops of white paint on the bricks hint at an underlying psychic chaos.

The artwork of Arbus and Kahlo is not unlike, but Kahlo's primitive style provides the viewer with some distance with which to observe horrible suffering. While the viewer empathizes with the manifested suffering, because of Kahlo's painting's theatricality and exhibitionism, one cannot forget that it is Kahlo, specifically, who suffers. The super realism of Arbus' work and its psychological complexity along with the realistic immediacy of the photographic image reveals the universal dark side of human nature and intensely involves the viewer. With Arbus' work, the artist is not in the forefront but is an intrinsic part nevertheless. This photograph of twins alters and enlarges our view forever. Arbus is a dual artistic vision arising out of the splitting in her own personality between the masking normality of surface and the hidden terror beneath. (This can be equated to a co-existing super-ego and id without the mediating integration of the ego.) This photograph like much of her photography, reveals the abnormal in the normal.

Interplay Between Conflicts Engendered by Women's Social Role and the Creative Urge

Diane Arbus grew up in the years before World War II when the women of her mother's privileged class centered their lives around their husband. In spite of Diane's restless, creative spirit she always envisioned her life attached like a twin, to a man. At age fourteen, when she fell in love with Allan, she thought she had found the crucial relationship to define her life and that they would love each other forever echoing the romantic notions of the times. He was her mentor, her teacher, her reason for being. She called him "Swami" and he called her "girl." Like her symbiotic relationship with her brother, Diane was all emotion and she used Allan's cool perfectionistic control as a balance wheel. Although her parents disapproved, by marrying Allan, ironically, Diane hoped to achieve a life independent of her family, to win her father's approval and enjoy the pleasures of being the "good girl." She was brought up to please. But always crippling ambivalence was her constant companion; she described her own remoteness and depressive episodes, defining them as a defense against creativity. Certainly, Diane attempted to close her eyes to awareness. In high school when she began to say she hated her painting and that it had been a giant pretense, one of her friends speculated that Diane was frightened of her own huge talent because it made her feel isolated from others.

After marriage, Diane concentrated on being Allan's wife. During the war years, while he was away, she moved back in with her family where she was treated as a little girl and told how to dress. When her own daughter was born in 1945, she refused to allow her mother or sister to accompany her to the hospital because she thought that she had to be alone in order to feel. When she brought her daughter home, her mother had hired a nurse and, against Arbus' will, insisted that the baby be bottle-fed. Diane and Allan continued to come regularly to Friday night dinners at the Nemerovs. Nevertheless, in the postwar era of the housewife as the essence of femininity and normality, Diane was a working woman and must have felt constantly torn because of it.

In the late '50s, Arbus began to finally explore the parameters of her artistic vision that would consume her in just more than ten years; she was 38 years old. Her marriage had recently broken up, her parents had retired and moved to Florida and she struggled to sustain life as a single mother. She could no longer escape or sublimate the challenge of establishing an independent life for herself. It terrified her and she endured severe depressions. Arbus' descent into the depths of the physically and psychologically dangerous world of her art must be seen as an attempt to conquer her fears and save herself. Arbus said "I was terrified most of the time." Bosworth (1984) writes: "But terror aroused her and made her feel."

For Diane Arbus, conflict between the expected female role and her creative urge consistently existed; to achieve a balance was, for her, an impossibility. But the demands of her life as a wife and mother must be viewed as a positive personality dynamic: They did not make her happy, but they provided her with structure, order and the comfort of close relationships and thus aided in the survival of her fragile personality. At midlife, during the experimental permissiveness of the decade of the sixties, as roles of daughter, wife and mother fell away from her and Arbus explored the depths of her creativity, she plunged into an abyss of chaos, unbridled sexuality and loneliness that would finally engulf her life.

Psychological Significance of Arbus' Art to Her Personality

Diane Arbus' identity as an artist existed from an early age. As a child, her talents and giftedness explained and excused her strange, remote behavior. In an artist much "weirdness" is acceptable. She was special and she knew it but it made her feel painfully insulated from others. In adolescence, her strong urges and sensitivities were sublimated into her art and her relationships. Through the artistic imagination she could explore the forbidden territories that existed outside the limits of safety and thus still remain safe. For this fearful personality, her art would provide a counter-phobic and socially acceptable means to attempt to master her fears. Attracted to freaks, she saw them as being born with their trauma, whereas, she said, most people spend their life worrying about having a traumatic experience.

If in the end her art failed to save her, it should nevertheless not be construed as mere visual pathology. In her photographs, Diane Arbus transcends confrontation with the dark night of the soul to give a sense of meaning to that profound experience that resides in the depths of us all. Finally, she claimed that photography "no longer worked" for her and she killed herself.

Through her imagination, the isolated, protected youngster could prick her finger, smell the blood and know that she existed. And her feelings could be expressed and contained on paper and thus garner for a time for a measure of control.

The Question of Arbus' Artwork as Positive to her Personality

There is an important question here that has been alluded to before. We must ask whether in the little more than ten years of her individual work, Arbus' creativity was, overall, of positive benefit to her fragile personality? In the opinion of this writer, it was not. As Arbus' creative urgency loosened the ego's frail constraints and plunged her deeper and deeper into her unconscious processes, her personality shattered.

That her photography offered her a structured medium with surrounding craft and technique through which to approach and express the hidden parts of herself was certainly helpful. With her camera as transitional object, it provided her a psychological safety net in her interactions with the world. But one is led to wonder whether what we observe in the work is the cathartic and helpful reflection of Arbus' underlying aggressive hostility. After being photographed by her, writer Norman Mailer said: "Giving a camera to Diane Arbus is like giving a hand grenade to a baby." In my view what we see in the photographs is not rage, but an unflinchingly honest reporting of a very private reality. Hers is a vision of a reality seen without sentimentality or judgment or scorn. Arbus' subjects look directly at her and, unlike most people, she cannot bear to look away. It is this act of direct, human collaboration—in relationship—that gives the works their dignity.

On the negative side, her photographic work increasingly drove her into psychologically dangerous territory. Diane's obsession with freaks and oddities perhaps reminded her too closely of her own "freakishness." A drawing or a photograph of difficult emotional material is an image with an intensely confrontive impact of its own and is impossible to ignore. Words, once spoken, can float away dissipating their impact. Written words can be closed off within the covers of a book. Language is an abstract, symbolic representation of a distinctly distant reality. On the other hand, visual images speak directly to our most essential psychological and unconscious processes and often spring from the deepest parts of the self. (All art therapists know this.) Visual imagery such as Arbus' remains permanent over time and continues to demand attention. With such imagery, one cannot hide or deny or distance within socially acceptable "civilized" conventions. That primitive people thought the camera was able to steal the soul from the person and capture it in the image was for good reason.

If Arbus' medium had been words, she might have been able to adequately distance. As it was, I suggest that she became increasingly mired in a circular process from which, finally, there was no escape: the more she photographed, the more she confronted her own forbidden secret self. And the product of her creative process, the immediacy and intensity of the image, as she worked on the pictures in the darkroom, looked at them, thought about them and showed them to others, constantly caused her to return to the deepest, most hidden and painful parts of herself.

This circularity poses an interesting dilemma for a psychotherapist, for in Arbus' life and creative work, there is implied the possibility of choice between the preservation of her life and her essential creative vision. Could she have retained both? It is my hypothesis that in order to preserve the integrity and survival of her personality (and of her life) a psychotherapist treating Arbus would have needed to discourage her unique, obsessional subject matter and help her displace and sublimate her primary process material into a structured, cognitive framework and an overall more distant secondary process orientation. Additionally, the therapist might have helped Arbus achieve a less chaotic social environment perhaps out of the stresses of New York City, with its anti-traditional, promiscuous and acting-out art world of the 1960's. The doing of photography might have been discouraged altogether. If this could have been accomplished (and it is a big "if"), Arbus' life might have been saved. But without her artistic identity and creative artistry could she have survived at all?

CONCLUSIONS

With Freud, I believe that we are all prisoners and products of our life histories. There is no question that for Kahlo, her art was healing. When she was confined to bed much of the time, in the prison of orthopedic devices, she could paint when she could do nothing else. (I am reminded of the artist Henri Matisse who, in his last years, sick and in bed, was said to have demanded "tie a pencil to my hand.") When Kahlo was required to lie immobile and passive, through painting she could regain an active stance and the independence of creative choice. She could slip the bondage of her suffering physical self and escape through the open windows of her vital imagination.

If Frida Kahlo's paintings helped her cope with her difficult reality and possibly lengthened her life, so it may be possible that Diane Arbus' photographs offered her the same surcease from despair at least for a time. Through time and her increasing periods of depression, she roused herself to photograph and thus continued on. If her relentless explorations devastated her in the end, she left a legacy of meaning which will endure. She changed the direction of photography in the United States and those who look upon her pictures never see the world, nor our hidden selves, in the same way again.

The artist works within the ambiguous and treacherous territories between the self and the world and there, makes *meaning*. Out of what is known and what cannot be known a whole new thing is created which, when we experience it, transforms our understanding of ourselves and of the essential nature of reality. Arbus' creative power to make meaning is what the fictional painter Gulley Jimson in Joyce Cary's *The Horse's Mouth* is talking about when asked why he became an artist. He describes walking by a shop window in London and catching a glimpse of a Manet painting. "Manet," Jimson says, "skinned my eyes for me." We can only be grateful that through their creative vision, Frida Kahlo and Diane Arbus skin our eyes and help us to see.

REFERENCES

Arbus, D. & Israel, M. (Eds.) (1972). *Diane Arbus, An Aperture Monograph.* (Copyright by Doon Arbus and the Estate of Diane Arbus.) New York: Aperture Foundation.

Arbus, D. & Israel, M. (Eds.) (1984). *Diane Arbus' magazine work.* New York: Aperture Foundation.

Arieti, S. (1976). *Creativity, the magic synthesis.* New York: Basic Books.

Bosworth, P. (1984). *Diane Arbus.* New York: Alfred A. Knopf.

Bowness, A. (1977). *Some statements by Barbara Hepworth.* St. Ives, England: Barbara Hepworth Museum.

Cary, J. (1944). *The horse's mouth.* New York: Perennial Library, Harp-er & Row

Castle, C. (1913). A statistical study of eminent women. *Columbia University, Contributions to Philosophy and Psychology, 22.* New York: Science Press.

Cattell, J. (1903). A statistical study of eminent men. *Popular Science Monthly, 52,* 359–377.

Cattell, J. (1906). A statistical study of American men of science. *Science, 24,* 658–665.

Cattell, J. (1910a). A further statistical study of American men of science I. *Science, 32,* 633–648.

Cattell, J. (1910b). A further statistical study of American men of science II. *Science, 32,* 672–688.

Chicago, J. (1982). (Originally published in 1975.) *Through the flower, my struggle as a woman artist.* New York: Anchor Books.

Cohen, T. (1983). The woman artist: A struggle for self-realization. *Women & Therapy, 2.* New York: The Haworth Press.

Freud, S. (1961). *The standard edition of the complete psychological works of Sigmund Freud.* Strachey, J. (Ed. & translator). London: The Hogarth Press.

Gilbert, L. & Moore, G. (1981). *Particular passions.* New York: Clarkson N. Potter.

Ghiselin, B. (1955). *The creative process.* New York: Mentor Books.

Herrera, H. (1983). *Frida: A biography of Frida Kahlo.* New York: Harper & Row.

McWhinney, W. (1985). Alternative forms of creativity and particular training for their use. Unpublished Paper.

Merriam-Webster (1986). *Webster's ninth new collegiate dictionary.* Springfield, MA: Merriam-Webster Inc.

Miller, L. & Swenson, S. (1981). *Lives and works, talks with women artists.* New Jersey: The Scarecrow Press.

Rivera, D. (1960). *My art, my life: An autobiography.* New York: Citadel Press.

Ruddick, S. & Daniels, P. (1977). *Working it out.* New York: Pantheon Books.

Schjedahl, P. (2007). All souls, the Frida Kahlo cult. *The New Yorker,* November 5.

Wolfe, B. (1963). *The fabulous life of Diego Rivera.* New York: Stein & Day.

Chapter 6

FEMININE IMAGERY AND A YOUNG WOMAN'S SEARCH FOR IDENTITY[1]

This essay follows Erik Erickson's developmental stages and crises through ten years of a woman's artwork during adolescence and young adulthood. Erikson's notion that an individual's quest for identity is the essential and continuing theme of life speaks to our age as have few ideas before or since. From his first formulation, terms such as the *search for identity* and *identity crisis* have become so integral a part of our cultural milieu as to appear as if they have always been with us. Erikson (1950) recognized identity as the central problem of the twentieth century, like the study and expression of sexuality had been in Freud's time. According to Erikson (1974,) a sense of identity is the feeling of being at one with oneself. As identity develops, it becomes the connection with the person's history as well as their future.

Although the formation of a coherent identity is the developmental task of adolescence when it presents a special crisis, Erikson (1968) viewed the question of *who am I to be?* as the continual undercurrent and subtext in the process of human development. For Erikson himself, identity was a crucial concern. As an adopted child, a wandering young person and an American immigrant, he was a professor who, though distinguished, was not traditionally academic. Erikson lived with the need to establish an identity. He spoke of the loss of his defining landscape and his first language (Evans, 1967).

---

1. This essay is reprinted with changes from Junge, M. (1987). Feminine imagery and a young woman's search for identity. *The Arts in Psychotherapy, 14*, 121–133. Used with permission.

Although Erikson postulated his framework of developmental tasks through the life cycle more than 55 years ago, and in spite of increased interest and research in recent years in adult developmental processes, much of feminine development remains an uncharted wilderness. Further, the role of spontaneous images in the creative process and their use as visual developmental touchstones through adolescence and young adulthood has yet to be carefully addressed. In this essay I examine a young woman's individuation process and search for identity from adolescence through young adulthood with her use of feminine imagery in spontaneous artwork and personal art journals. Artwork shown and described is chronological and using her artwork, Yvonne can be seen pushing forward developmentally. The artwork covers a period of ten years from age 14 tough 24; it provides a rare visual record of the vicissitudes of a developmental journey which, though personally unique, contains the broader implications of universal lifespan processes. In Yvonne's artwork we also have the unusual opportunity to observe the relationship of psychology and traumatic stress to the artistic personality as it unfolds.

On a year's sabbatical from my university job, I was living in Mendocino, a small town on the northern California coast. I met Yvonne in a life drawing class. As we talked, I told her I was an art psychotherapist. She had never heard of art therapy before. She said that she felt she had done art therapy on herself and invited me to see her work. When we met for lunch in her studio apartment, Yvonne pulled drawings out from under her bed. Later I learned that this was the first time she had shared her artwork with anyone.

After giving a brief life history, I will discuss examples of Yvonne's artwork using her own words as description. The focus here is on the interplay between two main themes: (1) the evolution of a personal use of symbols into a coherent feminine imagery representative of underlying psychological and developmental processes; and (2) the use of media and imagery symbolic of milestones of a developmental journey. Finally, implications for mental health professionals are suggested. Throughout this essay, the subtext is the crucial and enhancing role of the creative process in Yvonne's search for identity.

HISTORY

Yvonne is the oldest child of three of middle-class Midwestern Catholic parents. The family was living on the West coast when the father, who was his firm's highest-rated salesman, suffered a nervous breakdown, was hospitalized, and died in his sleep of an apparent heart attack. Yvonne was nine years old. Shortly thereafter, her mother moved with the children to live in Minnesota. Yvonne remembers that first year in Minnesota: "Nobody talked about death. My mother was real strong."[2] Although she had never been an allergic child, in Minnesota, Yvonne became allergic to everything, even her favorite dog which had to be "put to sleep." After this, Yvonne grew depressed and withdrawn; she stopped eating, was often sick, and spent most of her time alone.

In the summer of Yvonne's 13th year, her mother began experiencing angina pains and spent much of her time in bed. Yvonne became the household's mother preparing meals and caring for her younger brother and sister. That winter her mother was operated on for open-heart surgery, lapsed into a coma, and died three days later. Yvonne was 14 years old.

After her mother's death, Yvonne and her siblings lived—usually separately—in a series of foster homes across the state. Yvonne began to show signs of serious pathology. She became withdrawn and stopped attending school. She drank a good deal, took drugs and was sexually promiscuous. Because of her acting out, Yvonne was taken to psychotherapists and psychiatrists, but she refused to attend sessions or allow a relationship to develop. It was during this time that she began to draw, first on scraps of school notebook paper, later in journals she called "art books."

Erikson (1950) sees the play of children as one of the mechanisms of human development. Through play, emotions are expressed, the future is imagined, past situations are recreated and mastered, and problems are solved. It is through play that change and development can occur. Erikson cites art as a form of play. He wrote that, like play, it is *through creativity*, that special individuals can find resolution of their difficulties.

---

2. Yvonne's words throughout this essay are from interviews I conducted with her in 1985 and 1986.

Yvonne's artwork provided for her a safe container for difficult thoughts, feelings, and questions and a means of communication, clarification and expression for this virtually non-verbal teenager. Importantly, her artwork gave Yvonne a visual, permanent record confirming that *she existed* in what had become, with the death of her parents and the dissolution of her family, an all too unstable and impermanent world. Yvonne said: "I just started to put my feelings down; every time I'd feel emotional, I'd draw. I was still very withdrawn and art was the only way I communicated." In her artwork, Yvonne could grieve and thus finally she found a way to proceed with the difficult process of her separation and individuation as she became a young adult. In her artwork, themes of loss and death coexist with creativity and renascence as she developed a moving vocabulary of imagery in her search for self.

Now, Yvonne is a professional artist and writer. She is an art teacher and has taught art to children for many years. During the time of these drawings, she innovated a program for the elderly to work with teenagers on art projects. Completing her Bachelor's degree at age 27, she married and earned her Ph.D. Currently, she teaches art in a women's college in Kuwait and exhibits her artwork. She continues her art journals.

ARTWORK

Erikson (1963) postulates that the developmental stage (Stage 5) of adolescence concerns the dialectic resolution of the tasks of Identity versus Role Confusion moving the young person toward young adulthood and the stage of Intimacy versus Isolation. Two sections of Yvonne's artwork will be shown, from ages 14–16 and 17–20 that coincide with Erickson's Stage 5 of adolescence, as well as Yvonne's work from ages 21–24, representative of her moving toward Stage 6 of young adulthood. The artwork and events of Yvonne's life are assessed within Erikson's framework of adolescent and young-adult development and the evolution of a personal aesthetic and imagery. Artwork has been selected to exemplify developmental themes and processes and is chronological, but it should be recognized that the illustrations shown are examples from a larger body of work.

The 5th Stage of Erikson's blueprint for development is Identity versus Identity Diffusion. The coming of puberty signals the end of childhood. The young person enters the long period of adolescence. In this developmental stage, childhood issues re-emerge to be worked on and mastered; continuities relied upon are questioned. An integrated ego identity must be gradually formed so that the young person is ready to face the challenges of adulthood. The danger inherent in this Stage is role confusion and identity diffusion, and at no other point in the life cycle are the promise of finding oneself and the threat of losing oneself so closely connected (Erikson, 1963).

Ages 14-16

Yvonne remembers:

> I was fourteen. My mother had just died. I had moved from my house, the house I had spent most of my life in, to live with different people. I was disoriented and depressed, suicidally depressed, so I started to draw. I started to draw these little people with things happening to them. They're all about a lot of pain. The images would just come. I would sit down with a pen and I'd feel better.

In artwork from this period, we see the beginning of an evolving range of imagery: Yvonne's ungrounded "Little People" are floating, burning or drowning (Figure 6-1). Passive-appearing circular blobs, they have no specific fingers or toes and no sexual characteristics. Some have no eyes at all or eyes that are empty and frightened. Their tiny ineffectual mouths seem unable to speak, even to cry or rage and they are in obvious pain.

Figure 6-2 might be said to visually portray the negative side of Erikson's dialectical conflict of Stage 5, that of Identity Diffusion. The figure grown older now seems trapped in a desolate landscape. Its head is attached only by strings to a still-sexless body and lies caught in a road strewn with heads. Ambiguous dead tree-like shapes—perhaps fissures—inhabit this desert landscape and a dark and ominous sun hangs above.

With an inheritance from her mother, Yvonne leaves the Midwest and drives to Oregon where she buys land and, virtually by herself, builds a cabin. Of this period, she says:

Figure 6-1. "Little Person."

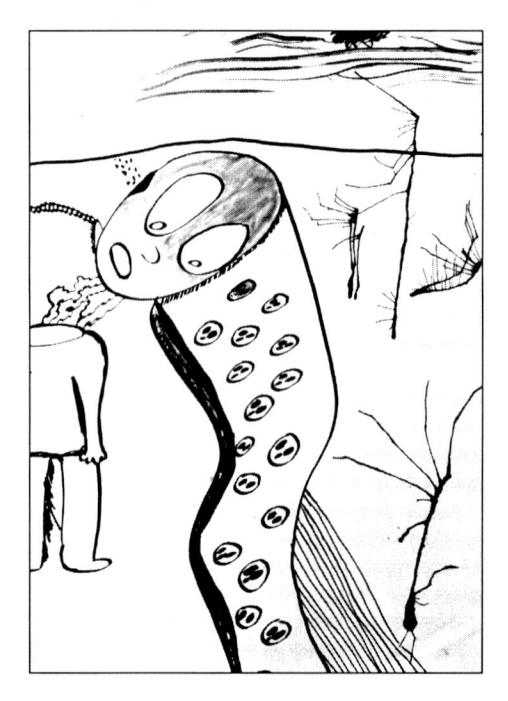

Figure 6-2. "Little Person Grown Older, Age 17–20."

As a kid I always felt very connected to nature and the earth. I spent a lot of time alone there. When I was up in the mountains after my mother died, I started to go out and be alone and walked the land a lot to find solace, the nurturance I needed there. I moved into the mountains because I had to go. I found my mother in the earth. I found this body that would give me what I needed. She wasn't all the time real easy on me, but she taught me a lot.

Threatened with disassociation and destruction by her losses, using her mother's supportive inheritance, Yvonne seeks a more nurturing home for herself in Oregon. She creates her own protective shelter, a cabin, and achieves an almost mystical connection to the land that enables her to begin to grow again. Eventually she leaves Oregon to enroll in a nearby college, but unable to integrate still another loss of home, she cannot concentrate, grows depressed and drops out to return to the mountains.

Figure 6-3. "Split between the Rural Environment and the Hostile City."

Figure 6-3 shows Yvonne's land and cabin in Oregon and reflects her felt split between the hostile city and the supportive rural landscape. The city appears in a frame in the top of the drawing. In the city, anonymous buildings without windows stand in a road. Above the buildings, lightning strikes; a lightning reminiscent in shape of the trees in Figure 6-2. On a hill in the foreground stands a tree. A tree is typically seen as a self symbol (Buck, 1978), and although this one seems strong in trunk and branches, it is a leafless winter tree cut off from its intricate root system; it is thus unable to derive sustenance and is in danger of dying. In the tree, the back of a female head can be seen, with long hair tenuously held by a branch. In this series of drawings, for the first time, Yvonne's figures take on a gender orientation perhaps reflecting her growing sense of female identity. The head looks toward the city buildings and the hair is entwined around the frame, but the buildings face away. Yvonne's reality and home remain the country.

Drawings done during this period are typically in ink with strong contrasts of black and light; they give the impression of separation of form; they are cold and stark. Primarily, in the tree and cabin, black and white seem to blend more easily to produce a softer, more integrated effect.

A house drawing can be viewed as an indicator of a person's associations concerning home and the interpersonal relationships with those living there (Buck, 1978). Yvonne's cabin is in the middle ground of the picture, giving the viewer a sense of distance from it. It is sturdy and well-built with a sheltering front porch; it is built on a foundation of stilts and does not touch the ground. This treatment of the cabin echoes the theme of the tree detached from its root system and could be construed as both a reflection of Yvonne's sense of separateness from her "roots," and also as a defensive mechanism of self-protection. Instead of any open indication of interpersonal relationships inside, we cannot see into this fortress-like house. However, it is interesting to note that the cabin's one dark window, high up, faces toward the tree and that the lowest branch of the tree touches the house revealing the strongly felt relationship between the two.

In a later drawing from this period (Figure 6-4) Yvonne illustrates for the first time what will be an important recurrent theme: the integration of the female figure, now become an erotic figure, with the landscape. Sometimes the landscape lies outside the figure, sometimes it is contained within (both are evident here), but from now on, it is as if Yvonne, in her art, attempts a fusion with the environment. It is an environment that may be nurturing and soft or wrenching and jagged but from here on, Yvonne's art speaks about the various relationships that the female body has with diverse interior and exterior landscapes.

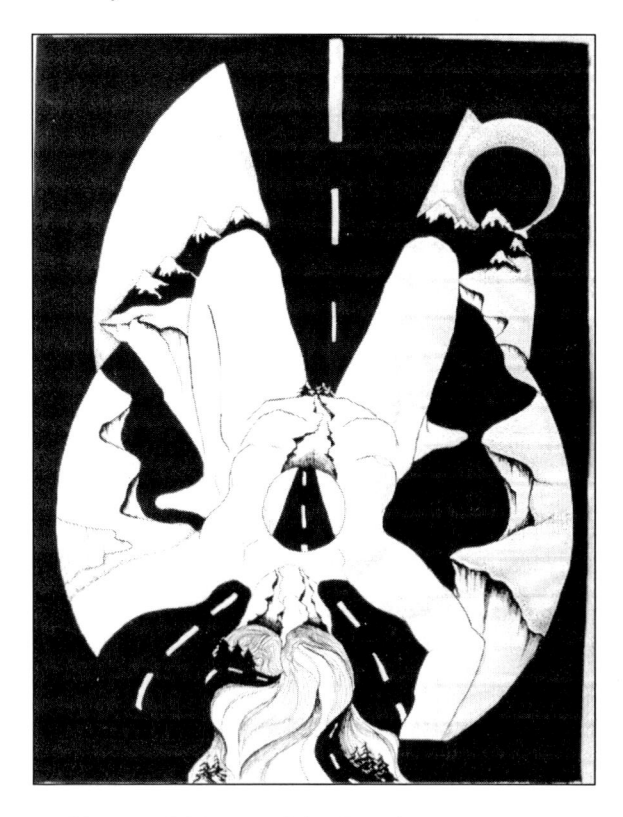

Figure 6-4, "The Road-Merger of the Female Figure with Environment."

The female body in Figure 6-4 both lies in the road and the road goes through her; she *is* the road. At her sides, the ground, like earthquake fissures, seems torn away from the figure by some violent force. At her center, breasts become hills as road penetrates womb. The figure is contained by a circular shape. This containing, healing circle will prove to be an important and repetitive image in Yvonne's artwork—a key motif that can become both egg and womb, and that can hold within its totality conflicting aspects of the psyche.

The achievement of identity is both an individual and a communal issue and represents overcoming a sense of identity diffusion that is the polarity of this developmental phase. At one side of the crisis is the urge toward integration and synthesis of the inner self with one's environment. On the other side is diffusion, leading to a sense of instability and discontinuity in the midst of many confusing and oppositional inner and outer demands. As she ends her adolescent years, though not this developmental stage, Yvonne seems very much an immigrant in a strange landscape who must strive to redefine and develop new reference points in order to create a wholistic and coherent sense of identity for herself.

Ages 21-24

For her 21st birthday, Yvonne is given a Japanese accordion book which she begins to use as an art diary. Hereafter, she will use this kind of book for her most personal art work. It is noteworthy that, before her marriage, Yvonne's mother had worked as a photographer for a time in Japan and that the book was a gift from a woman approximately her mother's age. In a Japanese accordion book all the pages are attached to each other, with the first page attached to the front of the book and the last to the back. A fold, not a cut, marks the end of a page and the beginning of another and all the pages fold in against each other within the covers. Through the symbolism of such a book, Yvonne could experience a permanent, connected stable container of her personal imagery and of her self. Here would begin the symbolic exploration of the boundaries where things come together and where they end, and thus the process of her separation/individuation process could move forward. Selections from four books will be shown and discussed.

Book 1

Yvonne titles this book *Walking Dry Minnesota Memory Fields* and reveals: "It is about my starting to come from the darkness toward the light." She takes a major first step from the adolescent's projection of hostility onto the outside world, as in her city/country drawings, to the acknowledgement of rageful feelings within herself, thus indicating a developmental shift and progression. She says:

> I was feeling all this earthquake energy. I filled up my truck with food and water and my sleeping bag all ready to head out when the earthquake came. I went over to my friend's house and said "There's going to be an earthquake": and she said, "Silly, the earthquake's not outside—it's inside you"—and it was.

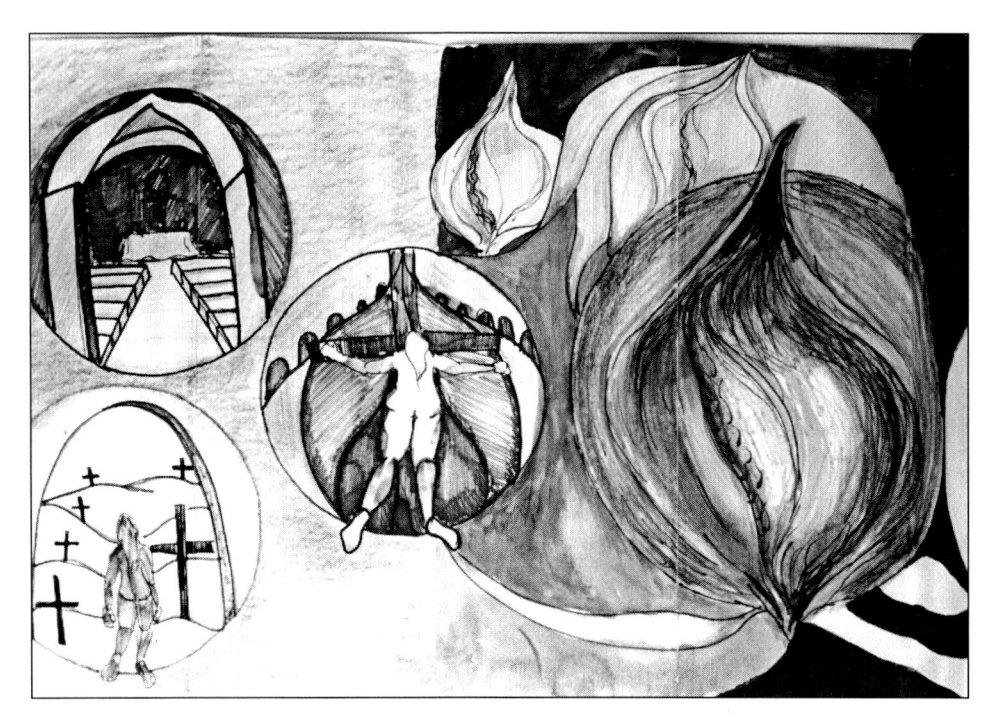

Figure 6-5. "Walking Dry Minnesota Memory Fields."

Seven years after her mother's death, she returns to Minnesota. Yvonne remembers:

> Actually it was my mother's birthday. They had a birthday Mass in the same church where I was baptized, where my parents were married, my parents were buried. I went to the graveyard on that day looking for her stone. It was like the floodgates opened. I began to cry. I hadn't cried until then. I lay on the grass and felt my mother under there, felt the mother earth. I found my mother in the earth. The seed pods in Minnesota in the fall dry up to a hard shell and burst like I did.

The book *Walking Dry Minnesota Memory Fields* visually describes Yvonne's renewed experience of her family's home and history and her acknowledgment of her devastating losses. As she remembers, she begins to feel again and as she feels, she remembers. Years after the actual events, now she can express her grief within the safe confines of her art journal. In it, she displays her memories and dreams and suggests a theme of death and resurrection. Unlike the stark black and white of her earlier drawings, images in Yvonne's first art book (Book 1) are colorful, explosive, and the forms more plastic with less distinct boundaries (Figure 6-5). Circles repeat themselves throughout as landscape intermingles with figure. Initially in the book, imagery becomes more lush and suggestive of the sexual organs of the female body. However, the last drawing of this book is a dried-up field with dead wheat stalks and empty pods. A leafless tree and the grey of the rendering reveal the renewed onset and severity of Yvonne's depression.

Book 2

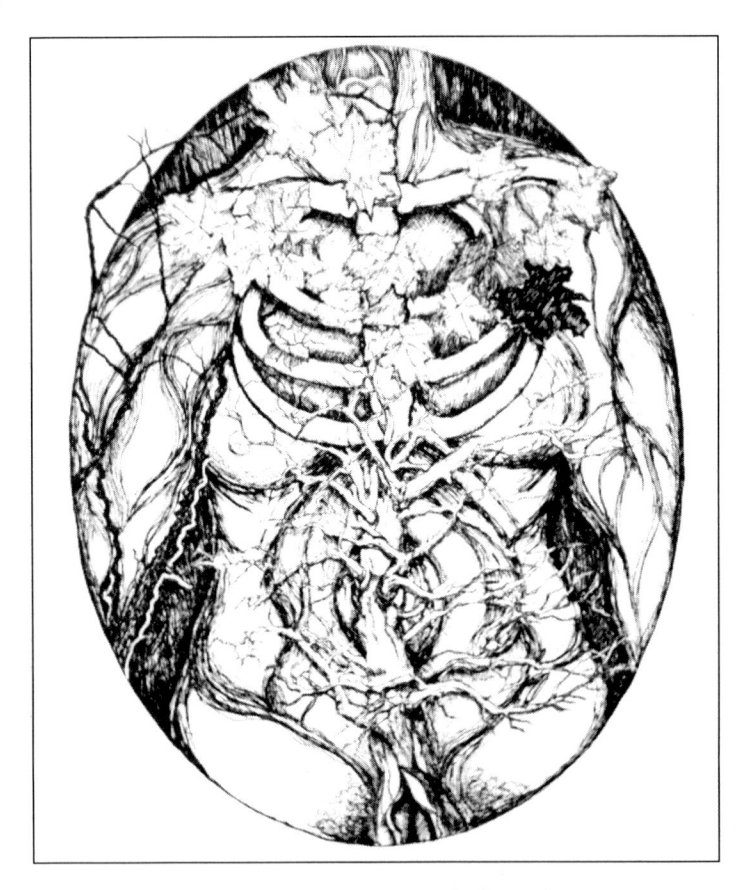

Figure 6-6. "December Sadness."

Of this book, Yvonne says: "It was done at Christmas time. I was feeling this very great sadness in my body, a heavy sadness, the kind of sadness where it's hard to breathe." We may speculate that with the symbolic psychological containment provided by the process and product of her artwork and with her gradually evolving identity, seven years after her mother's death, regression in the service of the ego could occur to finally allow normal grieving.

Book 2 begins with a series of female torsos within circles. They have no heads, no arms, no legs. They seem to represent a tearing and a wrenching apart within and appear unlikely to be contained (Fig. 6-

6). As the book progresses, black increases and threatens to engulf all imagery. Finally, in the last pages of the book, the white shape of a girl or young woman in fetal position emerges (see Figure 6-9, right bottom, for example of a fetal figure). This adolescent figure appeared, for the first time, in Book 1 under moon shapes outside a circle where other people warmed themselves around a fire. Here, the fetal girl is encased under the breasts of a mature female figure.

Although Book 2 is clearly a representation of extreme depression, it is important to note that if depressed persons can make even a mark on paper, they have moved into an active rather than a passive mode. Thus it can be speculated that Yvonne's drawings both helped her maintain a hold on her sense of her reality continuing in the world and also gave her an important tool with which to alleviate her depression.

Book 3

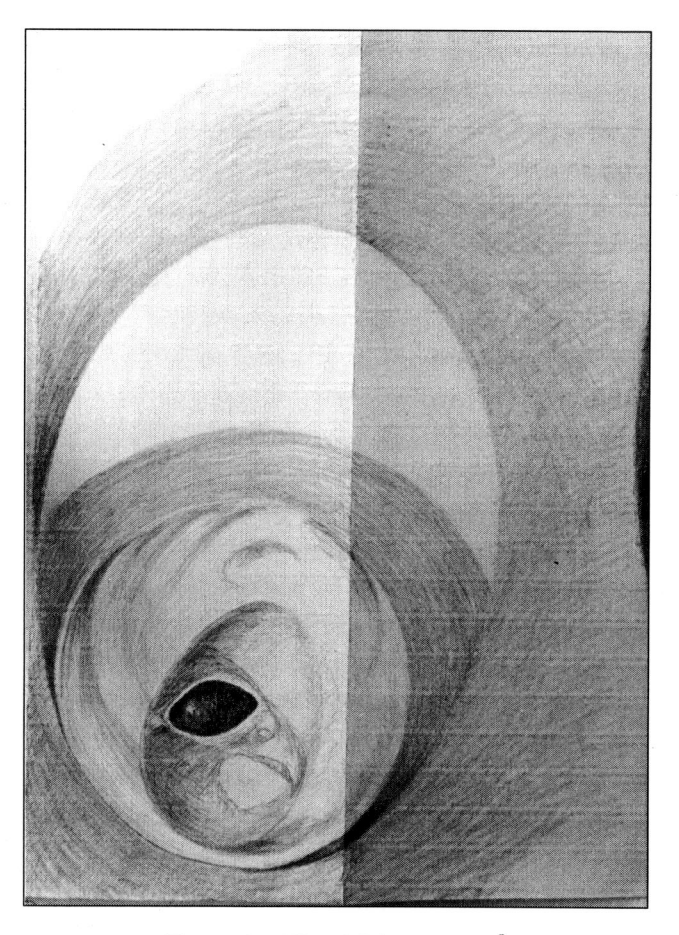

Figure 6-7. "Egg Within Torso."[3]

3. Note: Shading of half the picture in Figures 6-7 to 6-10 indicates the fold of the page. It is a result of photography and is not in the original artwork.

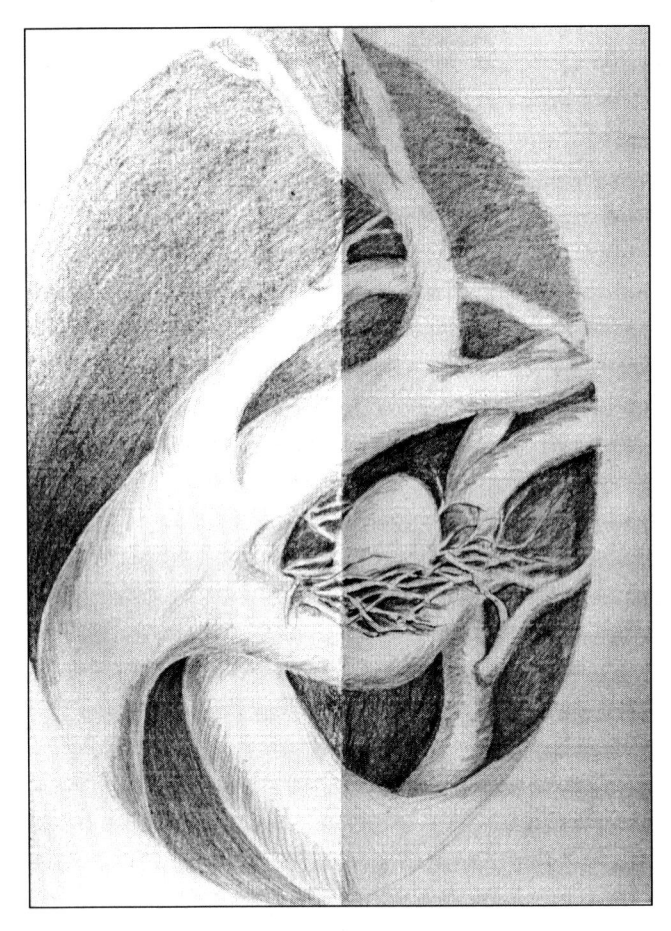

Figure 6-8. "Egg Within Tree."

This book, which Yvonne calls her *Process of Individuation,* is the longest one of the series. She begins by drawing in pencil, an impermanent medium easily erased. She draws an egg with a deep tear (Fig. 6-7). The egg is nested in a tree with ambivalent branches which are perhaps protecting and perhaps dangerous. As the book progresses, the branches look increasingly female (Fig. 6-8). Finally, the still-injured egg rests on a mothering female body and then can be seen inside it. Next, a fetus is shown within an egg-shaped womb and contained within it is the faint shadow of another egg. The fetus peers out of the birth canal apparently undecided whether or not to be born. The drawing following is of a new baby, like a reprise of the "Little People," in a crib helpless and staring. In the next drawings, Yvonne, in a sense, *reparents* herself as she illustrates important childhood memories and her own parents' deaths (Fig. 6-9). The last drawing of the book, titled "Me All Alone," shows a small child on a porch. The child, drawn in black and reminiscent in shape of the "Little People," stands firmly. She is on a porch between two large windows and at the top of stairs. This picture is drawn across the fold of the book and with equal parts on each side, indicative of Yvonne's increased ability to acknowledge beginnings and endings and to continue on across them. "After this drawing," she remembers, "I felt I had worked something through." According to Erikson, (1954) a sense of identity assures the young person a definite place within her own niche in society. The sense of identity provides continuity between childhood and an anticipated future.

Figure 6-9. "Memories and My Parents' Deaths."

Book 4

In Book 4, Yvonne moves from using erasable pencil back to more permanent black ink as she states "I know I am beginning to grow." Book 4 is characterized throughout by experimentation and diversity of theme and technique. Media are used in a variety of ways as if the touch of the pen is at times intensely involved and at times tenuous and distant as it makes its mark. Toward the end of the book the images are created by combinations of small dots in Seurat-like fashion. The first drawing of the book in India ink is of a nude young woman arms outstretched in the cleansing rain. The second drawing shows the same young woman leaping joyously into the air. Each drawing is contained within an egg-shaped circle and crosses the page fold. The figures of this art journal are sometimes mature-appearing young women, sometimes more adult versions of the nebulous "Little People." Having achieved a reasonably well-integrated, if still damaged, identity (as represented in the egg imagery,) Yvonne is now able to experience isolation without feeling destroyed and thus can strive for the relationship and intimacy of Erikson's Stage 6 of Intimacy versus Isolation. Yvonne states:

> Sometimes I regress and am my egg self again. But more often now I feel close to other people. I do get scared; it's hard to come out again. but I do it. Sometimes to be alone in nature is comforting. I feel my mother in the earth. My egg self is surrounded by softness and protection.

Drawings are often indicative of inner growth processes or they may be predictive of growth to come. The final three drawings of the book portray what I believe is a visual rehearsal of Yvonne's separation/individuation process as she moves into Erikson's developmental Stage 6 of Young Adulthood. The first of the three drawings shows an encircling hand in which the egg lies as in a protective nest. In the next drawing, the egg has left the hand and rests on the earth. Two hands appear at left, one in faint shadow. They seem ready to guard the egg's safety and are not restricting but supporting. The egg can experience independence yet security. Is this drawing symbolic of the best kind of mother-daughter relationship of this life stage, in which the daughter is ready to leave and both mother and daughter know it and can allow the departure to occur? The final drawing of the book seems to bear out the speculation (Figure 6-10). The hand has opened and the egg has rolled away into the distance across the hills and valleys of a feminine landscape. The hand remains behind, open and available. In Yvonne's words: "I feel loved. I feel I can even leave and venture out toward the mountains. I believe my safety and security will stay with me and I can come back if I need to."

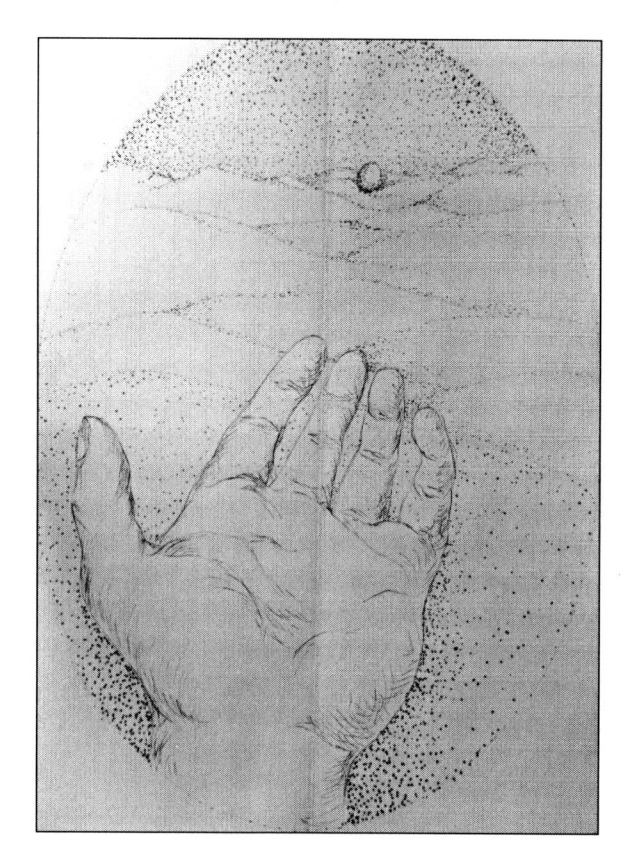

Figure 6-9. "Memories and My Parents' Deaths."

FROM A DEVELOPMENTAL PERSPECTIVE

Yvonne's journey to identity is longer than many because of her devastating losses that set her adrift and propelled her toward destruction. Nevertheless, it reflects Erikson's universal developmental sequence as a gradual, continuous dialectical process with a special crisis in adolescence. In looking at Yvonne's pictorial journey, we see her at ages 14 through 16 cut prematurely adrift from continuities of parents, family, and home. She is forced into independence too early.

Experiencing overwhelming identity diffusion, Yvonne exhibits delinquent behavior and apparently verges on psychosis, which Erikson (1954, 1956) views as the youngster's attempt to gain some mastery and coping. She draws herself in the "Little People" drawings drowning and in flames. With an inheritance from her mother, Yvonne buys land and, an immigrant in a strange landscape, achieves an almost mystical reconnection to a mothering environment as she begins to set out *new reference points for herself* on which to build an identity. She constructs her own house, a log cabin of strength and simplicity. She continues her artwork. Emotionally more anchored, she enters college in the city. However, her drawings from this period reveal that she experiences a feeling of forced and premature independence and she projects her anger onto the hostile and unnurturing environment of the city. Eventually she leaves college to return to her land in Oregon. For awhile Yvonne regresses and clings to the land. Finally, her regression takes her to Minnesota where she re-experiences her family's historical permanency and, as she visits her mother's grave, recognizes her own grief and despair. This trip is a touchstone for Yvonne's developmental processes as she then begins her first art journal, *Walking Dry Minnesota Memory Fields*, and uses her art to take an active role as she explores past memories and traumatic losses.

In Book 2, the *Winter* book of torsos without limbs or heads, she is deep in her depression and perhaps will become overwhelmed by grief. Yet she is apparently able to contain her sadness within the symbolic walls of the book. Perhaps she can move forward again. Book 3 is titled *My Process of Individuation.* This book of her early twenties, shows most dramatically Yvonne's separation/individuation struggles and her striving to establish continuity of meaning within a context that can lead to a confident sense of identity. She realizes that she must symbolically rebirth herself so that she can emerge as a separate human being in the world. At the end of the book Yvonne recognizes herself as alone but whole. Out of this recognition she can move toward Erikson's Stage 6 of Young Adulthood.

In the next book Yvonne takes responsibility for herself, develops social contacts and interactions and goes about creating support systems for herself as a young woman. She gathers her emerging identity to deal with the coming questions of this stage, of intimacy and isolation. Finally, in the hand drawings, we see a reprise of Yvonne's connection to the nurturing, female, mother landscape and thus her ability to freely move away and stand on her own. In her own way through her art, Yvonne successfully fights the battles of earlier years and the war within herself. She is ready to move forward.

EGG IMAGERY AND SYMBOLISM, EVOLUTION OF THE FEMININE

In her use of the egg, Yvonne's imagery grows from the silent and empty circles of the "Little People" drawings into the pod shapes of her first art journal. She draws a Minnesota seed pod that holds within it both death and rebirth: the pod must dry almost to dust in order to burst open with new seeds and new life for the coming seasons. This cycle of death and renewal tied to the process of the seasons speaks of an essential vision of nature as female. In Book 2 of the torsos the egg shape acts to contain. It encircles the black and white forms and provides a safe shell in which the depressed self can mourn and rage. In Book 3, as Yvonne's sense of identity grows, the egg becomes an actual object and actor. First damaged, it is passive and protected within a nest, then within the mother's body a fetus grows inside an egg-shaped uterus and, almost as if by choice, is born. Now it can actively search out and confront painful memories and losses. I speculate that the meaning of Yvonne's egg symbol, judging from the severe tear in its surface, is that the egg is deeply injured, but through caring and love it can still grow. Finally, in Book 4, Yvonne's sense of identity is consolidated and she moves toward young adulthood with its potential for intimacy. Here, the egg becomes a vehicle for social interaction: the "Little People" have grown into adults and friends who play, who protect, and who, like good parents when it is time, let go.

Yvonne's unconscious use of the egg symbol provides for the unfolding of multiple meanings in the process of her artwork. It is a uniquely female symbol that suggests the menstrual cycle with its monthly opportunity of ovulation and the cleansing flow of blood, or of fertilization, gestation, and birth. It speaks of lunar cycles and the cycles of the ebb and flow of seasons of the year. The egg's surface provides a smooth solidity that is a container for matter and thought. It offers a context for growth and change inside itself and in its relationship to its environment. Within, hidden things may actively exist, be protected, nurtured and transformed to finally emerge into the light when it is time. Although its shell is fragile, the egg holds within it the potential of life and birth and suggestions of immortality.

MEDIA AS MIRROR OF A DEVELOPMENTAL JOURNEY

A look at Yvonne's use of media as her artwork progresses provides further symbolic evidence of her continuous quest for identity. Her choices of pencil, pen, or brush and her use of color and line keenly reflect her affective states at the time, while a change of medium or technique tends to mirror a regressive shift or a potential gain in her psychological process and thus to provide additional visual milestones in her development.

The "Little People" drawings are primarily black and white. What color there is seems extrinsic, like a hand-colored photograph. Yvonne's drawings of ages 17–20 are stark black and white; negative and positive shapes remain separate and apart—polarities felt and seen. Few shades of gray, ambiguities, or integrations intrude. Line quality remains defensively strong and imposing. In the Minnesota book the reawakening of Yvonne's memories first evoke intense warm colors— red, yellow, gold—as she remembers a comforting past world. But as she begins to re-experience her tragic losses, the book loses its color and moves again toward black and white. In Book 2 of the torsos, black takes over, indicating a level of serious depression. Toward the end of this book, white increases to symbolically signal a lifting of depression. In Book 3 Yvonne changes to pencil, as if she feels now she does not exist, just as a pencil mark can be easily erased; and indeed, she lives only in egg form until in the central section of the book she is born. After this rebirth, lines become less tentative, stronger, darker, and are often in ink signifying an increased sense of permanency. In Book 4, as she moves out into the world, pen and ink are used again with tentative, pale color and, for the first time, Yvonne, begins to form some of her images by a series of dots. This imagery of dots is particularly interesting in that it appears to be yet another symbolic indication of a mastering and remastering process of separation/individuation and of a growing identity. In this stage, however, Yvonne can trust that if she separates the lines into dots, literally, they will not disappear (as *she* will not disappear) but can continue to exist independently. Moreover, she trusts that the dots can, and will, combine together to form a new whole. On her own, she has achieved a great deal of trust in herself and her environment.

Erikson (1950) writes that ego identity is the integration of experiences from childhood on but is more than the sum of them. It is a combination of the ego's ability to continuously integrate libido, genetics, and social role resources from the past resulting in a sense of gathering confidence. This integration reflects a similarity between internal confidence and the young adult's meaning for others.

IMPLICATIONS

Typically, the adolescent needs to retain a sense of personal immortality in order to forge an identity. If the young person is repeatedly assaulted by loss or death, that sense of immortality is destroyed. Yvonne's experience reminds us that despite severe trauma, a sense of unity and safety can be restored. She achieves this through her use of art. Along with a concrete, permanent record of development, her artwork becomes an active therapeutic agent. Within its protective boundaries, she puts her feelings into images to express the experience of her suffering. In art, she creates for herself an environment that enhances the mourning process and provides a positive way to understand and work out her deep sense of loss. In a sustaining *twinship*, Yvonne values her art as an extension of herself; she relates to it as her most significant other. From her first drawings, she saves her artwork and keeps it with her wherever she travels, deriving from it a kind of *cloak of safety*. I speculate that Yvonne's sense of self-worth begins to develop out of the self-mirroring fostering of her art. For many years, Yvonne recreates a sense of herself and her family's history through a kind of intensely personal and secret "photograph book." Eventually, she is able to share her visual experiences for the first time with this author and thus takes an essential step in her growth.

An additional therapeutic element that should be acknowledged is Yvonne's use of her art journals as a mourning rite. (I will comment further on the use of art books to enhance grief rituals in Chapter 13.) Although separated by loss from the comfortable rituals of family and religion, within *her artwork*, Yvonne creates her own symbolic objects, endows them with meaning, and carries them with her; they provide both focus and distance, a place for expression and the opportunity to master her losses. Yvonne progressed at her own pace as she opened and closed the pages of her books. Her artwork contains memories and the history of her family and gives them tangible importance and reality again within her world. As mourning rituals aid in the transition from one life stage to another, so Yvonne's artwork actuated a ritualizing approach that enabled her to continue to move forward.

Yvonne's relationship to her art mirrors the relationship that some troubled adolescents are lucky enough to have with a therapist, in that for her it was containing, supporting, facilitative, and provided an avenue of expression when she had no other and when, because of her degree of damage, she could not accept a close relationship with a caring adult. Ironically, it is the more healthy adolescent who can tolerate the inherent dependency of the therapeutic relationship. Yvonne could not. But she could allow a relationship to her art and in artwork, she could control and thus maintain her necessary sense of independence.

In our work as psychotherapists we often encounter young people who, because of their level of deprivation and basic lack of trust, cannot endure much intimacy and therefore cannot work well within a therapeutic relationship. Yvonne shows us that art for such an adolescent can provide a safe vehicle through which to affectively experience, explore and work on essential developmental tasks. Art for such an adolescent can be effective if the psychotherapist realizes that much healing is in the client's connection to their artwork and that art may, in fact, be a most essential tool in working with his age group.

Yvonne's artwork mirrors the sequential developmental stages suggested by Erik Erikson and thus supports his theory. As we might expect, however, she moved more slowly than Erikson predicts. As Yvonne moved along, she grappled with typical life tasks of adolescence and young adulthood. She lived out the stage of Identity versus Role Confusion and progressed toward the stage of Intimacy versus Isolation by the time she was 24 years of age. Yvonne's journey reflects that even with prescribed developmental stages, there exists an individual and personal timetable that may not coincide with any model. Because of our life experiences and environmental context, we may move more slowly than others in the unfolding process. Moving at our own pace, our sense of identity is in continuous formation and as Erikson recognized, evolves and changes throughout the life cycle.

Yvonne's compelling story proves that creativity and the art process can offer a unique therapeutic resolution to even the most difficult of life's developmental struggles and promote the evolution of an enhancing identity.

REFERENCES

Buck, J. (1978). *The House-Tree-Person Technique, Revised Manual.* Los Angeles: Western Psychological Services.

Erikson, E. (1950, 1963). *Childhood and Society.* New York: Norton.

Erikson, E. (1954). Wholeness and totality: A psychiatric contribution. In C. Friedrich (Ed.) *Totalitarianism. Proceedings of a Conference held at the American Academy of Arts and Sciences.* Cambridge, MA: Harvard University Press.

Erikson, E. (1956). The problem of ego identity. *Journal of American Psychoanalytic Association, 4,* 56–121.

Erikson, E. (1968). *Identity, Youth and Crisis.* New York: Norton

Erikson, E. (1974). *Dimensions of a New Identity.* New York: Norton.

Evans, R. (1967). *Dialogue With Erik Erikson.* New York: Harper & Row.

Part III
SOCIAL ACTION

Chapter 7

THE ART THERAPIST AS SOCIAL ACTIVIST: REFLECTIONS AND VISIONS[1] WITH JANISE FINN ALVAREZ, ANNE KELLOGG AND CHRISTINE VOLKER

I revise this essay in the week of the tragic killings at Virginia Tech. It is my hope that this terrible occurrence has provided an opening for conversation and debate for much-needed deep change in mental health resources that we may not have had before. The mental health system in the United States is clearly broken and has been for a long time. By allowing this devastation to flourish, our country has been seriously damaged by its own actions. The world we live in is unstable and potentially violent, and growing more so all the time. We have many complicated problems close on our own doorstep–hungry and dying children for example, but we talk of "global warming." Global warming may indeed pose a serious threat, but it is also a safe focus for people and the country to support because it is relatively "far away" and, in my opinion is a convenient denial of our many up-front problems.

From a systems perspective which includes family and world environments as having meaning to the individual, the role of the art therapist as social activist is discussed in this essay. Through our artists' identities, art therapists are natural agents of change. But often our education, typical training as individual therapists and strivings for

1. This essay is printed with changes from Junge, M., Alvarez, J., Kellogg, A. & Volker, C. (1993). The art therapist as social activist: Reflections and visions. *Art therapy, Journal of the American Art Therapy Association, 10,* 148–155. Used with permission.

professional acceptance mediate against our natural proclivities toward change.

Along with my own thoughts about activism, case examples of their experiences as change agents are presented by three art therapists: Anne Kellogg and Christine Volker write in dialogue about their participatory research project with Central American refugees and Janise Finn Alvarez describes her work as a trade union activist. While all-too-few clinical agencies are unionized, Janise uses her own employment life as the case example, with the ubiquitous issue of low salaries for creative arts therapists. As far as I know, Janise's brave account is the only one in which a union successfully sought to systemically examine, challenge and change therapists' working conditions. Janise gives a wonderful example of the power of the group and individual courage necessary to create change.

Substantial parts of this essay originally appeared as a journal article more than a decade ago. I have left much of it alone, and ask the reader to consider how much and how little times have changed.

ART THERAPISTS AND THE PARADOXICAL GIFT OF SIGHT

Maxine Borowsky Junge

Art therapists are particularly talented at seeing; it is our stock in trade. The dictionary states, seeing is "perceiving, coming to know, forming a mental picture of, and understanding the meaning of something."[2] Seeing, we come to profoundly understand our clients. Visible to us, in their art expression are the depths of their terrors, the joys of their inner worlds and a reflection of their efforts to change those worlds. The art therapist's and the client's engagement with the process of creativity as a method of inquiry and a way of knowing, pictorially reveals and externalizes reservoirs of memory and deeply felt implicit and tacit awarenesses hidden from consciousness.

Art expression takes us to unknown places that lie beneath the silence of words; it brings our darkest terrors into the light where they may be tamed. All human beings are paradoxically both cursed and blessed by the darkness of not seeing. What do we look at when we see? We cannot bear to look upon mountains of corpses, bodies and

---

2. *Webster's Ninth New Collegiate Dictionary* (1986).

faces from the Nazi Holocaust or images of the evil of African-American slavery and oppression. Such imagery assaults our eyes and threatens to burn them out. By seeing too much we go blind; we close our eyes to defend against our own powerlessness in the face of such unspeakable horror. By closing our eyes to shut off what is too terrible to know, we may go blind to what is straight in front of us.

What do we see when we look? Thirty-five thousand people die of starvation each day; the majority are children. Images of African children haunt us. The AIDS pandemic rages; already lost are many of our best and our brightest. Violence in the cities explodes daily, in particular against and within minority groups. There are many desperate realities in which people must live their life.

What do we see when we look? A decade of denial when we allowed ourselves to be lulled to sleep by a handsome, forgetful Hollywood actor and later, a President who wanted a "kinder, gentler, world" and never left his office. His son has taken us into horrors we could not have imagined. In America we see a country where in most places the sale of fireworks is illegal, but the sale of guns is not. In the Los Angeles rebellion or "riot" (as you may choose to call it,) we saw the faces of despair and desperate, encroaching poverty and racism. We saw the logics of pain unraveling identity. Katrina victims lodged uncomfortably in our vision. Since that cataclysmic event altered the consciousness of our nation, not enough has happened to rebuild. How can we come to know the truth in Krishnamurti's words: "You are the world and the world is on fire"? Images that lie before us are what we must see.

Artists as Those Who Help People See

We who come to the profession of art therapy embrace the tradition of artists as those who help people see. We resonate with the idea of the artist as outsider, observer, social critic. Imagine the images of Bosch, Goya, Daumier, Ben Shahn, Picasso's "Guernica," Maya Lin's Vietnam Veterans' War Memorial in Washington, her civil rights memorial in Montgomery, Alabama with Martin Luther King's words on it, "Until justice rolls down like water and righteousness like a mighty stream," and the AIDS Quilt. Let these images glide through your mind and speak their truths to your heart.

As these images move through you, you cannot avoid feeling the sweeping power of the arts for change—you *feel*. And it is that word, "feeling," that is the problem. Feeling requires that we open our eyes to break through our denial. It can lead to deep questioning about ourselves and our world; it can lead to intense discomfort, possibly despair and possibly joy. Feeling lets us know what we try hard not to see: that we do not have control over much. Feeling leads to opening the windows so that the unknown comes in and the winds of change blow through and we see.

The Role of Imagination

The great painter Goya told us "the sleep of reason produces monsters." The key to sight and beyond it to change, is the power of the imagination. To paraphrase Goya: The sleep of the imagination produces, even in life, death. *Imagination* is the bedrock and the touchstone of *hope*. Hope stirs the heart to offer possibilities of a better future; it is hope that opens the potentialities of change through a creative process. It was startling to me that the word "imagination" did not appear in many of the books about creativity written in the last 30 years. In our culture, prone to counting what is visibly evident, if "imagination" was not in our books, was it *real*? It was if imagination didn't exist. If "imagination" is not acknowledged, not "seen" as a potent force for change, how can change occur? If one cannot have a vision of something different, through human imagination, how can we strive toward difference and relish a better life? Dictionary definitions of imagination hold within them the intriguing duality of imagination as creative and change on the one hand, and, on the other, as something not quite real, devoid of truth, as in "imaginary."

For me, it is the act of imagination that offers a vision of something, different, better, and the resulting hope that can impel us to action. Without hope, there can be nothing better. The power of the imagination gave rise to the dream of democracy, at Tieneman in China for example, and the tumbling of the Berlin Wall. These examples prove that change seldom comes when or as we expect it to, nor in a necessarily orderly or predictable fashion. In my opinion, the concept of planned change is an oxymoron.

Psychotherapists, Art Therapists and Social Change

Psychotherapists, unlike artists, have not tended toward activism, but rather have been agents of social control. As the mental health system crumbles around us and our clients, we must wonder if our twin identities of artist/therapist—the artist awake to change and the therapist holding on to containment—forces us into some impossible double bind. At first, therapists thought about the individual and their intrapsychic problems, but seldom considered that there might be something important beyond the boundaries of the person's psychic skin. Most therapists sat in the protected havens of their offices and waited for clients to come and to work. A powerful conceptual leap occurred when therapists widened their view of the individual's struggles to also include the family system. Most therapists, however have not yet taken to the streets nor understood that to adequately treat our clients, our rightful territory must include community, society and the larger world environment. All too often therapists heal what is already wounded and do not attend to the milieu which wounds and re-wounds again and again and more deeply.

Suggested by Jung, Rank, and others, people project outwardly the dark parts of the Self that cannot be tolerated within. For example, in the twelfth and thirteenth centuries, an era of denial of the body, leprosariums isolated lepers so that they would not have to be seen and infect others with the awareness of bodily reality and mortality. At the beginning of the Renaissance, a time of renewed worldly sensuality and the birth of rationality, leprosy died out and the leprosarium buildings became insane asylums. Insanity became then the disavowed projection of the age of science and rationality necessary to be locked away from view.

Psychotherapists embraced the notion of themselves as scientists, objectivists, rationalists of the psyche. They focused on the examination of the individual mind, with social adaptation as a goal—let us not forget the era of lobotomies. Conformity to the culture was, and to a large extent still is, the norm within the white medical hierarchy; the labeling of deviance as psychopathology had as its intention the reification of control. If deviance and irrationality are imprisoned, they become invisible, and safety of the status quo can be maintained.

That our ideas are culturally and socially constructed is not news. Even in the short 35 years I have been in the mental health field I can remember when mothers were blamed for all problems in their children, particularly boys. (This mother-blaming era, of course, is not over yet!) Schizophrenia was thought to be caused by families, particularly schizophrenogenic mothers. Autistic children were a result of "ice box" or very distant parents. Father/daughter incest was not all that bad and could even be helpful for a girl. The dominance of women in single-parent black families was destroying black men and children, and a patient who was unable to get to the clinic with her six children because she could not afford bus fare was considered resistant to change. Although paradigms and pendulums shift, we retain within the new, habits of the old. Thus, many of these ideas remain today in barely disguised form.

O'Connor, in his article "Therapy for a Dying Planet" (1995), writes of an incident which occurred in Frieda Fromm-Reichmann's practice before she left Germany to come to the United States. Fromm-Reichman cured a young woman of her irrational fears through psychoanalysis. Soon after the therapy was successfully ended, the young woman, who was Jewish was sent to a concentration camp by the Gestapo. The message is obvious: In the words of a social psychologist friend, "Are we missing the forest for the clouds?" As art therapists are we too often helping people adjust to a destructive society? Are we ourselves co-opted by the status quo and understandably, yearning to be inside, do we adapt, make do, and continue to cope with a fatally injured mental health system?

Art Therapy Education and Activism

What about the art therapist's education as education for activism? Does our education help us see? Part of our history as art therapists which may impede us is that we have been trained as "appreciators" of art, as reflectors, supporters, explorers of the intrapsychic landscape. We have been trained in a passive stance, rather than to be activists and co-creators engaged together with our clients in their struggle, which is ultimately also our own. Typically, art therapists are not trained as advocates nor revolutionaries, not as social and cultural analysts or critics, but as those people who through the art therapy process help people cope and adapt.

As the former director of a Masters program for the education of art therapists at Loyola Marymount University in Los Angeles, I confess to you my belief that all too often education is not authentically or transformatively based. The process of professionalization itself initiates the student into the community through a series of formalistic rituals which may deaden the senses and overinflate thinking processes to the exclusion of feeling and imagination. Student art therapists learn many unforgettable lessons about change. But when they graduate into the professional world seeking to enter the ranks of employed and respected practitioners, unfortunately, all-too-often in the words of Pogo, "They see the enemy and the enemy they are us." Quite naturally, with student loans on our backs, we embrace the status quo, strive to climb the hierarchical ladder and forget everything we ever knew about the artist's mission to make waves.

As example, a few years ago our Masters program engaged in deep changes in the system which included not only the department, but also the university, the mental health community, and the state. On the face of it, a simple issue of licensing was the core. But we all are aware that nothing is as simple as it seems and political and economic tides arise out of complex struggles and exert enormous pressures on our lives. Themes of the artist, the arts, and therapy as outsiders in the academy and in the mental health professions were apparent along with art therapy emerging as the projected dark side of rational, scientific, behavioral psychology.

In this circumstance, people, particularly students, refused to accept the status quo. They found that the answers were in themselves which empowered them to action. Touching and acting on the strength in themselves, in my opinion, was education at its best, and in an extraordinary way helped them understand the meaning of empowering their clients as human beings. To grow, the art therapy profession needs this kind of systems observation, reflection, and social change, and we must willingly embrace the chances in front of us to create change with our eyes wide open to the possibilities. In our times, working with a client to adapt is not enough.

I propose that art therapists must make the leap to becoming activists. To begin we must recognize ourselves and those with whom we do therapy as deeply interrelated. To do good therapy is not simply psychic tinkering, but an intensely complex and serious matter. Next, we must acknowledge that we and our clients are part of larger systems in which life and work can go on or may end in despair. And we must see that struggle clearly and engage in it strategically and effectively beyond the artificial boundaries of office walls and the psychic limitations of our own consciousness, denial, and arrogance.

THREE STORIES, ART THERAPISTS AS ACTIVISTS

Following are the experiences of three art therapist/activists: Christine Volker and Anne Kellogg speak in a dialogue about their participatory research project with Central American refugees. Janise Finn Alvarez writes about her participation as a trade union activist.

A DIALOGUE

Christine Volker and Anne Kellogg

Christine Volker: I come from the tradition of the artist/activist. In art school I found myself drawn to the work of Käthe Kollwitz, the German Expressionist artist. Although Kollwitz's work was inspired by a great spirit of social activism, I had trouble making that leap in my own artwork. Prevalent in my art education was the axiom of the formalist school of painting, that one never mixed politics with art. As a result, I kept my political activism and my art separate throughout the 1980s. But I could not let go of such an essential part of myself.

Political activism eventually led me in 1986 to Nicaragua. I celebrated New Year's Eve with the *campesinos* of the state-run coffee farm cooperative where we had been picking coffee beans high up in the mountains. Later, I drank a toast with Luis, a *Commandante* of Sandanista troops stationed there to guard us from Contra attack. Our four-mile radius was protected, but nightly I heard the shooting and saw the helicopters flying the wounded to the hospital in nearby Matagalpa. I returned to the United States a changed person.

In 1987, I enrolled in the art therapy program at Loyola Marymount, where I was astonished to meet another social activist, Maxine Junge, who also happened to be the Director of the program. When I talked about my trip to Nicaragua, a fellow student, Anne Kellogg, stated "I feel very connected to you." From this connection began our joint clinical research project.

Anne Kellogg: When Chris and I discovered each other, we realized we had both been previously active in social justice work with the Central American community. We decided to integrate our past and our present, developing a project we called "Going Through the Journey with Central American Refugees," to explore the conditions of uprooting, migration, and relocation through family art therapy.

Our project examined the family drawings and dynamics of Salvadoran and Guatemalan refugees who migrated to the Los Angeles area because of serious problems, sometimes torture, in their own countries. Particular attention was paid to the psychological effects of pre-migration conditions, the migration process, and post-migration relocation in the United States.

CV: This work with refugees from El Salvador and Guatemala provided for us an integration of activism, art, and psychology. Our multiple "personae" have finally become one. This integration is partly what we hoped to accomplish with our interventions with refugees: An integration of their past identity in their country of origin with their present reality as they adjust to a new culture and country–an integration which involved an acceptance of self. For only in realizing our pain, can we heal.

AK: In the early eighties I became involved in housing Central American refugees as part of what was called "The Underground Railway." This movement helped to shelter, feed, and find work for Central Ameri-cans. As part of a church peace group, I became active in educating my parish about U.S. involvement in Central America and the conditions of refugee's experiences after their arrival in the United States. My parish supports a sanctuary house in Los Angeles called Casa Grande which gives short-term shelter to arriving Central Americans. More than one million Central American refugees have arrived in the United States in the last years, largely due to increasing violence and oppression in their own countries. While many received amnesty un-der the 1986 Immigration Control and Reform Act, hundreds of thousands have illegal status and, if returned to their country of origin, could be subject to political reprisal, torture or death.

CV: Our art therapy project was accepted by the committee at Casa Grande. The house is a temporary shelter which provides community for Central American refugees who have arrived in this country in the last one to five months. While staying in the house, refugees may apply for political asylum and search for work and more permanent living conditions.

AK: We hoped artwork would provide a safe place for containment of the multiple traumas experienced by these people during their uprooting, migration and relocation. We hoped the art process could facilitate grief and mourning, capitalize on family strengths, and begin to integrate past experiences with present reality. Perhaps most importantly, the art product could create an historical document to be used

as a touchstone marker in the defense of these people's human rights.
CV: We held two pre-session meetings with the families in the house before obtaining permission to do therapy. We found our values as "gringo" psychotherapists challenged. We were questioned and rightfully. "How could drawing pictures possibly help?" they asked "Didn't we realize that these were painful issues better left alone?"

AK: As we attempted to address their questions, we felt an overwhelming respect for these people who had gone through so many traumatic experiences to reach our country. We also knew that our own country was responsible for fueling much of the violence felt by these refugees with our military aid to El Salvador. We realized that this project was as much for our own healing as theirs. While it was difficult to establish trust and respect under these circumstances, we received approval to proceed with the group.

CV: The multifamily group consisted of twelve people, including two intact families. The others were single members of families who had come to the United States hoping to bring other members of their families later. Since families usually arrived in stages, many felt fragmented and experienced grief for absent members. Following are case examples of representative themes or issues which came up during therapy.[3]

The Chibarras are a reconstituted family consisting of Father Esteban, Mother Ana, two sons, Gustavo, nine and Rene, seven, and a daughter, Estrelita, three.

Esteban fled to a refugee camp in Honduras when his village in El Salvador was ambushed by government soldiers. But soldiers often came to the village looking for evidence of guerilla activity. When the soldiers came, the villagers would flee, taking specially prepared boxes of provisions to sustain them in their hiding places until a scout informed them that the soldiers were gone. On one such occasion, the returning villagers were met by a surprise ambush attack. A massacre ensued. Esteban was one of the returning villagers. He escaped the soldiers by diving into a lake to emerge behind a bush with just his nose and eyes above water. He watched from the water while his village was burned and his neighbors slaughtered. He watched while his four children were butchered. He watched while his wife was raped and then shot to death.

After the soldiers left, Esteban ran to the nearest refugee camp.

---

3. Names are changed to maintain confidentiality.

There he eventually met Ana who had lost her husband in similar circumstances. Together they reconstituted a family, migrated to the United States and found sanctuary at Casa Grande.

The artwork of this family depicts various intrusive themes–bombs, soldiers with guns, helicopters flying overhead machine-gunning the people below. One drawing shows four children and a wife sitting at a table eating. The father, Esteban, is pictured standing in the corner. Esteban explained that he had returned to his village from the refugee camp in Honduras to get a table left behind when he fled. Esteban had built this table for his original wife and children and retrieving it was important to him; it served as his transitional object. A border is drawn encircling the family, symbolically containing the anxiety stirred by this memory. Esteban said that the border represents a map of Honduras, yet [in the picture] he places himself outside the family. Esteban's present family with his new wife Ana has only three children; here were drawn four children. Could Esteban have unconsciously drawn the family he lost in the massacre?

In his drawing, Rene, age seven, shows two helicopters. One is black, he said, signifying the death helicopter shooting people on the ground below. A person is shown lying on the ground dead. Two donkeys look on, one with a black death head. Three trees are drawn, all uprooted from the ground. One of the trees, like the dead person, is lying on its side, perhaps also dead, maybe signifying that the life force itself was also dying. The house is depicted with people standing in the doorway, seen through the walls. Rene spoke about his drawing: "Here's the helicopter, here's the dead person, here's a fallen tree."

Rene was asked to draw something about the United States. He illustrated a helicopter shooting a figure holding a machine gun pointed upward outside Casa Grande in Los Angeles. People are inside the house, sitting at the table and two figures stand at the entrance to the house. The recurring theme of the shooting helicopter was seen in many of the children's drawings and seemed to symbolize the common trauma of war they had experienced. The children were also aware of helicopters in the skies over Los Angeles since on many evenings a helicopter could be heard flying over Casa Grande. For Rene, the black image of the shooting helicopter represented a threat not only from the past but also in the present. This is an example of the intrusion of thoughts and feelings associated with past traumas which are symptoms of post-traumatic stress disorder.

Esteban's and Ana's three-year-old daughter Estrelita used glue, pen, masking tape and collage to create what she called "La Bomba." She and the two other young boys in the group were the only ones who mentioned bombs. The adults did not talk about them. Children seemed to have more direct access to their memories of the traumas of war or were more willing to talk about them. Adults seldom referred directly to the conditions of the war relevant to their uprooting. Like Nazi Holocaust survivors, they preferred to forget the horror if they could.

A collage by Esteban illustrates the conditions in El Salvador. He portrays four images: two men riding horses signifying, as he said, life in the country; a scene of the desert representing the crisis in El Salvador; an old woman and her granddaughter, symbolizing love and respect for the elderly; and a perspiring boy with a thermometer in his mouth, representing the sick ones and perhaps the sickness of the country.

Predominant in the children's drawings are destructive weapons of warfare: The helicopters firing down, the man with the machine gun, and the bomb. These represent intrusion of the past traumas of war into their present reality. Floating houses, which we found in many of the drawings, symbolized the loss of home and country and current rootlessness.[4] Casa Grande was only a temporary shelter. Floating houses without any baseline represented the insecure existence of these refugees in a foreign country.

The floating house, the uprooted tree, and the running man occurred repeatedly in the artwork and seemed to symbolize the trauma of the uprooting, the migration, and the relocation. The multi-family art therapy group was brief crisis intervention work and did not allow for addressing the many losses in depth. But the project was a gesture of healing in the context of incomprehensible wounds.

AK: During our work at Casa Grande, we came to admire and respect the strength and courage of the men, women and children we met. Through the art process and product we tried to validate this strength and normalize the natural responses that come from going through such out-of-the-ordinary experiences, to contain the pain in the context of the art.

CV: From individual statements presented by the refugees at the final evaluation meeting, the art therapy process helped more than any

---

4. MBJ: I have often seen floating objects in the artwork of dying people.

other kind of therapy that had been done at Casa Grande. Visual imagery, they said, allowed for the confrontation of painful past events. The refugees told us this was not easy for them, but they said it was necessary.

AK: Creation of symbols to explore their past and present experience, offered these damaged people the opportunity to address traumas and to integrate them as much as possible. But monumental wounds continue. People arrive with living images of murder, rape, torture, and the loss of loved ones. When they first arrive, they are preoccupied with survival, but as time goes on the images return as nightmares. How can we provide healing in this overwhelming context? We believe the art helps: the people we have worked with say that it does.

THE ART THERAPIST AS UNION ACTIVIST

Janice Finn Alvarez

I am Central American in heritage–Central American and Irish. My mother comes from Nicaragua, and my father from Ireland. There aren't too many Central American art therapists around. And I am bilingual. I was born in Los Angeles, but Spanish was my first language; I learned English in school.

I feel a kinship with many of the Salvadorans since one of the groups most persecuted there are trade unionists. It's up there with being a Jesuit priest in terms of the mortality rate. As disheartened as I often am by the attitude in the United States toward labor unions, I think most people have been successfully brainwashed by the forces of major business which Ronald Reagan personified and to which George Bush [father] and George Bush [son] were handmaidens. It is powerful and deeply moving when I think of my trade unionist counterparts in El Salvador who are killed.

When I graduated from a Masters program in art therapy, I was thrilled and grateful to have a job, especially the job I wanted working with families in the Hispanic community in East Los Angeles. But I started to get a little uncomfortable about the fact that art therapists and dance therapists made lower salaries than other MA-level therapists. Being an activist is first, having pride. When you're a trade unionist, you have pride in your work. You feel you must be taken seriously and be listened to. I had a good sense of what I was and felt my training was good. I also believed that my specialty as an art therapist was very important and that I should actually be paid more than other therapists. But at first I didn't try to get that across to others.

I mentioned my sense of injustice about the situation, and someone suggested that I run for the union negotiating team because we had a contract coming up in the agency. So I did and was elected. It was an empowering experience to achieve what I wanted, which was equity. The sense of sitting down across the table from your employer as an equal was also empowering.

Suddenly, I had changed the job. I didn't beg for it. I didn't plead for it. We just sat down and got what we asked for. I thought this was really wonderful: People's lives change this way. I helped myself, but I was also helping others. My dance therapist sisters on the staff cried they were so excited with our success. They had all been beaten down with the idea that we were lucky just to have a job. "Creative arts therapy—what is that? You're so lucky to get what you can get—whatever little crumb—five dollars an hour, ten dollars an hour . . . hey you're doing well!"

That experience changed me. I went on and ran for President of the union chapter, and I continued to inform myself about labor history. (It certainly dispelled a lot of the myths that I had heard over the years.) I became the Treasurer of the Local, which was a state-wide Local, representing social service workers throughout the state of California.

I also had a wonderful experience when I attended a women's conference. For one week I was surrounded by other union women from all over the western United States—rural women, urban women, professionals, highly degreed women, and also sheet metal workers—all different colors, all different shapes. I'd never seen a less racist situation in my life. And we were all representing workers.

The strike that occurred at my agency was remarkable for me. After we resolved the strike, I went back to work at the clinic, and it was tough. I had to go back and deal with harassment and the things that make people afraid of being in a union. One of the most effective methods that employers have when they wage a campaign against a union organizing drive is to say that the workplace is going to be different—it's going to be non-adversarial. It *is* adversarial. It's not a question of morality. It's a question of each person looking out for his or her own interests and if you're not looking out for yours and you're thinking that your boss is doing it for you, you're really in a dangerous victimized situation. As a therapist, if you're leading your clients to believe that the world is basically okay and it will always take care of you because you believe that, you're leading them into some dangerous situations.

A strike is, of course, the most adversarial of situations. We went out on strike and stayed out for twelve weeks. Even though the economic issues were settled in a week, management wanted to keep every scab they'd hired. If we had accepted that contract and gone back to work, that would have been selling out so we stayed out for twelve weeks in solidarity. We were able to triumph. I'm very proud of that. It's a special moment in my life, though it was painful being without a paycheck for twelve weeks.

I am an artist and a labor activist. And I think there's a connection. An important social realist art tradition most of us are familiar with is the WPA[5] work that came out in the 1930s and how strong that was. It was the artists' responsibility then and now to speak out. As an art therapist/activist, I believe I have a responsibility to take what my clients are telling me and discern what is theirs and what is the chaos and injustice of the world they live in. If I say the responsibility is mainly the client's, then I am doing something that is not unlike what a bad boss does to her or his employee. I am causing the client to be weakened. A therapist may even wrongly think she or he is empowering the client by giving them an unrealistic idea of what the world is—the sense that it's all the client's doing. It is not. And simply by working harder, they can achieve the American Dream and riches. Usually, they can't. Children in Central America saw bombs dropping. They didn't imagine that. The devastation that occurred in their lives wasn't their choice. It was die or leave—it was that simple. So they left. In their new life, they are in pain. They *should* be in pain and they should be angry as hell. And we should be angry as hell, too.

I see the roles of the art therapist and the activist intertwined. I can't just think of that person in front of me as my client for one hour. I must consider what that person goes home to, what the person's life is about. If I am not doing something to rectify the injustice that's creating the problem in that person, then I'm just hand-holding and frankly

---

5. WPA or "Works Project Administration" was started by President Franklin Roosevelt during the Depression of the 1930s to give work to artists and writers.

I don't want to a part of it. If you do not act, you become accepting of all that happens to you.

THE CHALLENGE: TOWARD COMMUNITY

Maxine Borowsky Junge

The art therapist has a proud tradition as a pioneering individualist. But we believe the time is *now* to move away from individualism toward community, to break through and look at the world we and our clients live in, and to work to change it. A colleague, a Korean-American who grew up in this country, went back to Korea recently. The Koreans he met said to him, "Do not come to help us. Come in solidarity. We do not need your help. We need community with you." The writers here believe we must look to each other, to other creative arts therapists, to other people to form a community—a global community in which human growth is prized. Together we must find the courage to take the necessary actions to ensure this vision.

As art therapists/activists in the human community, with our eyes wide open, we must cherish the transcendent dream of a just and creative society and, using our imaginative hopes, nurture it into being by our action. As art therapists we have unique talents to offer.

REFERENCES

O'Conner, T. (1995). Therapy for a dying planet. In Roszak, T., Gomes, M. E., and Kanner, A.D. (Eds.) *Ecopsychology; Restoring the earth hearing the mind.* San Fransisco: Siera Club Books.

Webster, M. (1986). *Webster's Ninth New Collegiate Dictionary.* Springfield, MA: Merriam-Webster Inc.

Chapter 8

REFLECTIONS ON MY LIFE AS A SOCIAL ACTIVIST[1]

The word "narrative" has become almost as ubiquitous as "creativity." It generally implies a story, perhaps an imaginative one, and usually signifies that there can be more than one story describing or explaining something such as an event. Life stories to make meaning and to understand human behavior and development have a long history in psychology and psychotherapy. Freud's (1910/1961) study of Leonardo DaVinci is an example, along with Erik Erikson's many studies of human lives such as Mahatma Gandhi and Martin Luther (1958, 1969, 1975). More recently, Howard Gardner, (1993) in his book *Creating Minds*, investigates creativity and establishes a theory of multiple intelligences through the life stories of Freud, Einstein, Picasso, Stravinsky, T.S. Eliot, Martha Graham and Gandhi. In my own book, *Creative Realities: The Search for Meanings* (1998), I eschewed the life history approach and instead studied creativity through the artist's work itself as the "map" of the internal landscape.

Nonetheless, life story in the form of life history historically has been an important element of most psychotherapy, counseling, and art therapy. That a person's history is an important forming process of a person's development is obvious. That many people attempt to overcome and survive the traumas of their life is no secret either. But it is only relatively recently, with the embracing of constructivist research

---

1. This essay originally appeared with changes as Junge, M.B. (2007). The art therapist as social activist: reflections on a life. In *Art therapy and social action*. Kaplan, F. (Ed.) London and Philadelphia: Jessica Kingsley Publications. Used with permission.

paradigms that narrative forms of life stories in therapy and as a technique in therapy have achieved legitimacy and importance.

At a time when American mental health seems to be moving toward cognitive perspectives, the life story, paradoxically, is still viewed as an important tool that allows the therapist/listener to capture and understand the context the teller perceives and exists in. Using life story allows the therapist to enter into the essence of the client's world in a deep and important way. This essay is my life story as a social activist. I have twin goals in writing such a personal piece: First, it is my hope that some of these experiences from a long life committed to human service, social justice and activism may strike a chord in others, even illuminate their own life paths and call them to the barricades. Second, it is my hope that I will rediscover myself at age 70 on the path of this sometimes lonely journey. I believe in the courage to speak what I hold dear, even if I am misunderstood. I begin my story by talking about my family, early experiences and what I believe.

MY FAMILY AND CHILDHOOD–ROOTS OF SOCIAL ACTIVISM

I am a 70-year-old, heterosexual, secular Jewish woman. I worked in the art therapy fields before I had words for them or knew their names. But my "official" art therapy work began in 1974 when Helen Landgarten invited me to teach in the Immaculate Heart College's art therapy Masters program. (Before that, I had apprenticed as an art therapist to Helen at Thalians Community Mental Health Center, Cedars-Sinai Hospital in Los Angeles.) Since the 1930s, the focus in art psychotherapy and psychology has largely been on the individual and on individual development. But there was neither the "global village" then, nor today's emphasis on diversity and multiculturalism. The current world has become too complicated for individual thinking and conceptualizing. The obvious paradigm shift needed in art therapy, not exactly new, is toward *a systems approach.* Since I always used my work to address social ills, I have found systems thinking as a different way of considering change to be most helpful and, I think, it should be taught more in our art therapy educational systems. Systems thinking is natural to any painter. A painting is a system in which all parts must work together to make a whole and the whole is more than the mere sum of its parts. To change one thing is to change the whole. For example, to change a bit of color in one section of the painting is to change the whole painting and the rest must be adjusted to fit the change.

I am an art therapist. I am also a painter and a photographer, writer, teacher, systems person, organizational development consultant, family therapist and a social change agent. These "multiple personalities" as some might call them, are integrated and it is actually quite simple: I combine the art of creativity and change in people, families, groups, systems—in myself and in the work I do. Feeling an outsider from an early age, I have always been interested in marginalized people and the "invisible." I trained in social justice and social action at the Highlander Institute in Tennessee and the National Training Labs in Bethel, Maine. (Highlander has been a seat of social action in this country since it was established in the 1920s. Rosa Parks was there the week before she refused to move on the bus and "We Shall Overcome" was written there. NTL originated the first "T" groups or training groups for organizations and businesses.)

I was lucky to be born into a family of artists. I was born and grew up in Los Angeles during the Second World War and Blacklist period in Hollywood, just after The Great Depression which my parents had lived through. In Cheviot Hills, where I spent my childhood, there were few houses and lots of lima bean fields. Motor Avenue snaked through the neighborhood with 20th Century Fox Film Studios at one end and Metro Goldwyn Mayer studios at the other. During World War II, my father rode his bike to work as a contract writer first at one movie studio, then the other. With the neighborhood boys—there were no girls—I enjoyed a vast freedom to play that unfortunately has ceased to exist in urban areas today. Southern California then was a place on the edge of the Pacific Ocean without the constraints and limits of behavior, manners and of feeling that existed in most Eastern cities. Despite this bucolic idealism, an early memory is of watching from the sidewalk, during World War II—I must have been about four—as a cross was burned on the lawn of the other Jewish family on the block. I remember going home to my parents and saying "We aren't Jewish, are we?" They set me straight in a hurry.

I adored my father, a movie writer and professor of screenwriting and playwriting at UCLA. He was a novelist and a founder of the Writer's Guild, a pretty good watercolor painter and a passable violist. He could also listen to his students. But most important for me, I always knew him as a man who stood up and spoke out for what he thought was right. He hated anything that smacked of unfairness. My mother, who had been a theatrical costume and set designer in New York and who ran the WPA[2] theater costume shop for the city of New York at age 21, went deaf soon after I was born and completely deaf after the birth of my brother in 1941. Her deafness was caused by a severe sinus attack in the days before antibiotics or sulfa drugs. As a "stay at home mother" she did a good deal of informal counseling, ironically listening, and encouraging people who were trying to get used to hearing aids. The one she had at the time was very large and there was a five-pound battery pack to support it worn on her leg. She taught a painting class in her garage studio that went on with mostly the same students until she died at age 76 of lung cancer. I consider myself today in my own branch of the "family business."

My parents never issued admonitions about what was right, nor instructed me in any way. They simply modeled a socially active life with social justice as their cornerstone. I took in the lessons even as they were not spoken directly to me. For example, they had many parties and gatherings at the house that were always attended by different races, ethnicities and gender orientations: The Hollywood writers were the "intelligencia." They were invited–told not to talk "shop"– along with artists, historians, writers, psychoanalysts, young and old. What made a good party for my parents were lots of different ideas and a warm inclusiveness.

In those days, there were many places in Los Angeles where Jews were not allowed. As an aware child, I knew that certain private schools and country clubs did not allow Jews. I also knew of one country club that was Jewish and of the Wasp movie director, a good friend of the family, who had integrated it–he would not want to be a member of one that excluded Jews, he said. And he wouldn't tolerate a Jewish one that excluded others. When I moved to south La Jolla with my husband and young children in 1967, for his post-doctoral years at the Scripps Institute, I knew that it had been only in recent years that Jews were allowed to buy houses in that town. It occurs to me that it would be difficult for a Jew to be anything but a social activist.

From my father, I learned to have opinions and ideas and to stand up for them. From my father, I learned to attempt to make things better. From my mother, I learned about listening. From both, against the

---

2. WPA or "Works Project Administration" was started during the Great Depression by Franklin D. Roosevelt to give work to artists and writers.

dark days and unfairness of the Blacklist period, I learned about tolerance.

THE POWER OF ART

When I began Junior High School, I was put in the "dumb" class and stopped going to school regularly. My mother took on the school first—in those days they didn't listen to parents. And when that didn't work—they said I would be more comfortable in that [dumb] class, less pressure, they said—although she might have sent me to a therapist, she sent me to an art teacher Eula Long:

> When I was twelve years old, I attended a children's Saturday art class at the Kann Institute of Art in Los Angeles. The teacher, an energetic gray-haired woman named Eula Long, was interested in the psychological aspects of the creative process and, in particular, was a student of Gestalt psychology. She believed that a supportive emotional environment was essential to the creation of art—that no child's art should be criticized but only praised, and that the teaching of technique was not only unimportant but hindered or even stopped the child's creativity entirely. Those three years of classes were not called art therapy and Eula Long did not refer to herself as an art therapist but I am convinced that that was what she was. I watched my drawings and paintings, at first stilted and self-conscious, take on a richness and excitement that began to be recognized by parents, teachers and friends. With Eula, I had the privilege of experiencing the therapeutic power and possibility intrinsic in art. (Junge, 1994.)

Thus I began my life as a painter and as an art therapist although I didn't know the words "art therapist" yet. My paintings then were filled with people. Much later, when I began to do art therapy formally and saw many clients, my paintings changed almost entirely to landscape. One of my first integrations of art and social change was a paper I wrote in high school: "Daumier, Goya and Ben Shahn: Painters of Social Protest."

Much social change in this country has been tied to music. It is an easier medium to carry along on marches and can meld a group together quickly. Nonetheless, that an image has power and power to make change has long been recognized. The chapters and projects in the book *Art Therapy and Social Action* (Kaplan, 2007) are examples. Artists have portrayed and predicted change. Andy Warhol's soup cans illustrate our culture of consumerism and objects stripped to basics. They reflect a sense of what is presently culturally important, that is hard to bear. Gully Jimson, Joyce Cary's fictional hero of *The Horse's Mouth*, saw a Manet in a store window in London and said "It skinned my eyes for me and when I came out I was a different man"(1965.) No one who has seen Picasso's "Guernica" is likely to escape that image nor think about the Spanish Civil War in the same way again. Goya's "Disasters of War" make peace lovers of us all.

The image in art therapy is an extrinsic reflection of a person's interior landscape. It illuminates what was, what is and what might be. In its concreteness, it illustrates a reality *that can be changed*. In therapy, a person can change the image and may thereby change personal behavior, which in turn can change a family, a group or the world. Images can be used with groups to form a group identity and with marginalized or invisible populations to give visibility, stature and presence in the world. Imagery takes on iconistic importance, symbolic of change. While one may not agree with the Iraq war, the image of Sadamn's statue pulled down is unforgettable.

The issue of *language* is an important one to all art therapists. Unfortunately, spoken language is still the *sine qua non* of the educated person and all too often the language of psychotherapy and of change (despite the fact that soon Latinos will be the dominant majority in the United States, along with Spanish as a spoken language). Language is what is valued and desired. I used to have clients referred to me in a mental health clinic because they would not talk and their therapists became bored. As art therapists we do not need reminding that expressive communication often does not come in language, that many of our clients need imagery and that "creative voices" come in many colors and often do not speak in words at all?

SOCIAL ACTION PROJECTS

In this section, I describe a few social action patterns and that have been ongoing in my life: I have attempted to make things better in the areas of racism and ethnicity and anti-Semitism, women's equality, gender equality and in art therapy as a profession. There will be a description of some projects. But it should be understood that always the "use of self" is central.

Operation Adventure

I wanted to march for civil rights in the South and participate in the Freedom Rides. I knew of Highlander[3] and wanted to go there to train. But I had a young family and no extra money. In 1967, living in San Diego, I used to take my children to John Cole's bookstore–they would play in the "mouse drawer" and with the toys while I rummaged in the books. One day on John Coles' bulletin board, I saw an ad for an art teacher for an enrichment program. I signed on and there met Sandy Turner, a Quaker community organizer. Together, we attempted to turn the group of parents toward an enrichment program in the ghetto areas of south San Diego. When we were unsuccessful, we started our own program.

Operation Adventure was an alternative education program using the arts as our vehicle. We theorized that kids would want to learn anything (including Greek history and myths) if we used art and made the learning relevant and fun. With volunteers, who were not trained teachers, but were interesting people, the program grew in size and success. When I moved back to Los Angeles–my husband had been hired as an Assistant Professor at the University of California at Los Angeles (UCLA)–I peddled Operation Adventure around town. (Sandy moved back to Berkeley where she became involved with the Black Panthers, the Farm Workers and draft counseling against the Vietnam War.) I knew I wanted to do Operation Adventure and hoped that someone would pick it up. It was just after the first Los Angeles riots and Black Power was on the rise. I figured it might be more acceptable for a white woman to be in a Chicano neighborhood than a black one at that time. I ended up in Boyle Heights, East Los Angeles, at the International Institute.

Operation Adventure taught me to speak out for what I believed. In Boyle Heights, Operation Adventure grew big and successful. We received poverty fund grants from the city of Los Angeles. One summer we hired 38 minority college kids to teach the classes and I, the non-verbal one, went downtown to publicly beg the Los Angeles city council for more money to pay them. How could we "enhance self-

---

3. Highlander, originally Highlander Folk School based partly on Danish ideas of adult education, was begun by Myles Horton and Don West in Appalachia in the 1930s to develop labor union leadership. More process oriented than subject it soon became known as a place where blacks and whites could meet together to learn and where civil rights strategies were hatched; it is a school for social activists.

confidence" (a program goal) if we paid our staff so little, I said. That summer though it wasn't much, we were the highest-paid program in L.A.

Additionally, I learned about groups—it was the era of Encounter Groups. With such a diverse teaching staff and a white lady boss, often we had so much conflict that teaching could not go on. Because we didn't know what else to do, my Chicano Assistant Director and I sat everybody down and had our faculty honestly talk to each other. Much to our surprise, relationships improved. (Later, I did some reading about the power of groups and in our second summer, we hired a consultant who regularly ran groups with staff.)

Through Operation Adventure, I met and partied (dancing and parties are very important social action tools for blending groups) with a group of young Chicano men who started the first Chicano literary magazine in the country—*Con Safos: Reflections of Life in the Barrio.* They were lovely people and good friends, but to let a woman, and a white woman at that, onto their staff was not something they did. Operation Adventure went on for about four years, finally morphing into a project with gang kids from Mexico who were alienated from American culture and even the local Latino-American gangs.

Thirty-five years later, I still have contact with some of Operation Adventure's staff and the kids we served. One young woman, a child of Operation Adventure and the low-income housing projects, received her Ph.D. in Botany. Many are lost, in jail, or dead. (I recently heard that a project for gang young men in that area—the cleaning up of graffiti, started by Father Greg Boyle—had shut down, because of drive-by shootings and the fatal killings of two.)

Equality for Women

There are some places on earth where blacks are equal. There is no place on earth where women are equal.
—Jody Fisher, personal communication

I have long noticed the landscape of internalized sexism inhabited by both men and women and realized that even talented women have a hard time. I have long been aware that women are not equal in our culture (or in any culture). I was brought up in a middle-class male-dominated family that was usual for the historical time. Like many of my generation and class, growing up in the fifties, marrying in the sixties and with two small children by the time I was 30, I was supposed to be bright, talented, ambitious and to give it all up for my husband's career. My family story was humorist James Thurber's "a woman's place is in the wrong!" Before the Women's Movement came along and gave permission for my secret strivings, (and those of many women) I tried to stay at home with my young children, but almost went crazy and starting "sneaking out" to take life drawing classes in Arnold Mesches' studio. Art saved my life again.

While "feminism" is a bad name for many in the younger generations, for me it has always meant equality and equal opportunity. In addition, I recognize that our current culture is still rife with internalized sexism, pervading the thinking of many men and also of many women. It is interesting to me that in the early days of the Feminist Movement of this century, there were consciousness-raising groups and assertive trainings–rather challenging notions. These have changed to women as abuse victims and, at best, survivors–decidedly more passive roles apparently more acceptable in today's culture.

Nonetheless, I was surprised when I went in 1970 to talk with the white male Admissions Director of the University of California at Los Angeles (UCLA) School of Social Work. He told me: "We don't take any white, middle-class, middle-aged, Jewish women." Even before that, I had noticed that the Painting Department at UCLA which I had attended as a graduate student had all male instructors except two and was very hard on female students. One woman faculty painted flowers and was ridiculed by male faculty and students alike. The other was ignored; She later became a faculty member at the new campus of the University of California at Santa Cruz, more radical and open and more innovative than UCLA where she finally was appreciated and flourished. (It was the era at UCLA which artist Judy Chicago, a fellow student, has written about.) There are always the little things: In Whidbey Island, north of Seattle where I now live, I am part of a group that puts out a roster. When I first saw it, it contained the male name of the married couple, with the wife's name in parenthesis. (This despite the fact, that it was mostly women, as usual, who came to meetings.) I protested and it was changed. After a health crisis a few years ago, I met with health care workers on Whidbey Island to try to improve the system. I noticed that they had a hard time calling me "Doctor" although they called themselves that. One male doctor stated that he met me at my house because he thought I might be intimidated if we met at an office! At the Dog Park, a retired male doctor, confessed to me (unsolicited) that he was sorry about how he had treated women in his practice. From the days in the '70s when autism was said to be caused by "Refrigerator Mothers" the mental health system has changed. But there is still plenty of mother bashing today as the cause of a child's problems–just listen for it. (And speak out against it!)

Loyola Marymount University, where I taught and ran the art therapy program for many years was first a men's school established by Jesuits. Previous to my coming there, it had combined with Marymount College, a women's institution. Nevertheless, when I started at LMU in 1980 I was told by a male administrator: "The women will be gone soon." Why had our program been "taken in" when Immaculate Heart College, where it started, had closed? I was told that the accrediting organization had strongly recommended that Loyola Marymount have more women and more creative programs. But new ideas or not, old ideas and paradigms do not die: I was on many a search committee in which I was the lone voice questioning what "fit" meant for a faculty member. (Usually, it meant hiring a white male if at all possible.) And every graduation, I watched the emblematic seal on the podium being solely that of Loyola and not Marymount and thereby men, alone. It was only in about 1995 when the LMU basketball player Hank Gathers died on the court, that the TV newscasters began using the terms "LMU" and "Loyola *Marymount*," and so did the University. (And thus, 15 years after the University became coed, women were finally officially included.) As Chair of the Committee on the Status of Women, I initiated and steered the Student Sexual Harassment Policy though the politics of the University, but I do not suffer from the illusion that because it was right, it was adopted: It was a legal necessity. I believe it is my greatest gift to Loyola Marymount.

As an art therapy program, we were outsiders in the male academy. Graduate education was neither welcomed nor thought appropriate. I did an historical analysis of the Jesuits and determined that we were their "shadow" side in that we used art and were, mostly women. When the program came from Immaculate Heart to LMU, we were offered to the art department and to the psychology department. Both declined heatedly. Both departments were in colleges. To be in a college meant that the department and faculty had a Dean, and theoretically a certain amount of protection and advocacy. Probably, because of the accreditation team's urgings, the University decided to keep us, so they made our own department for us in the Graduate Division—which offered no protection but a good deal of autonomy. We were largely invisible which was often to our advantage.

Eventually during California's Marriage and Family licensing problems, there came a time when the University tried to get rid of the art therapy program. With the help of three students, some organizational consultants I knew, and a great deal of understanding of systems and politics, I was able to keep the program anchored in the school, even though another department refused to teach if they changed our degree title, (necessary if we wanted our graduates to remain eligible for employment.) This came about largely through personal politics and a conscious use of self within the university system. While we had not changed the curriculum at all, members of the American Art Therapy Association at the yearly conference, accused us of "losing the art."

In 2004, I wrote a statement for a chair I painted for an art therapy fund raiser:

> Art therapy is predominantly a women's profession and yet, as far as I can tell, the meaning of this is not a conscious fact for most art therapists. In my almost 30 years of training art therapists, most have been women, and many of our clients are women. To understand that the culture in America deprecates women and to help our clients understand politics and that there is still a power differential-- how to approach and change it--are central tenets of feminist therapy and should be central tenets for us all. . . . Although humorous in style and content, the [Superwoman] chair has a serious intent: Perhaps sitting in it will raise the consciousness of women (and men) and enhance their appreciation for all that they do and all they have to do. –Junge, "The Superwoman Chair" (2004)

Anti-Racism, Anti-Semitism: The Inequality of Woman and Man

From my childhood and my days in the ghettos of San Diego and the barrios of East Los Angeles, I have spoken out against these devious inequities. But during my doctoral program at the Fielding Institute in about 1990, I, a student, with three others (one a student and two faculty members) successfully integrated a program faculty by finding well-qualified people of color, shepherding them through a fairly laborious and unusual hiring process and working the system well enough so that when the to-be-expected resistances, of such things as "qualifications" and "fit" emerged, they were dispelled. It was almost a full-time effort and the President of the institution told me that he worried I would never get my degree. (While it may have added to my time at Fielding, it was certainly one of the most important things I have ever done.) This change in faculty composition was a downright threat to the domination of white men. When one group gains power, it is usually true that another loses. For example, African-Americans and women gaining more power, realistically indicates a lessening of white male control. A white male faculty member attempted to head off this shift. "If more women come, as students and as faculty," he said, "then the men will stop coming." While it is my assumption that most white people are well intentioned and do not see themselves as racists, American culture today is rife with internalized racism and unconscious stereotypes. Derald Wing Sue (2001) states:

> This is precisely why it is difficult getting white folks to realize that their attitudes, beliefs, and behaviors may oppress and hurt others. Because they experience themselves as moral, decent, and fair-minded individuals, they find it intolerable to view themselves as oppressors.

On the other side of gender, it is my opinion that one reason we have so many boys today with the diagnosis of ADHD is because we have, as we have always had, *women* teachers. Previously because of male privilege, women teachers were accepting of boys and gave them the upper hand in their classes. As times have changed, girls may be more appreciated and boys less. Certainly, they are medicated for this behavior more and earlier. I also believe there is a good deal of anti-male sentiment in the land and less patience that plays out negatively for boys in the classroom. It is my hope that soon men will begin to question the diagnosis and the current situation before it is too late for many boys.

In my last five years in Los Angeles, I worked in the AIDS/HIV medical practice of Dr. Michael Scolaro. Supporting my gay son's community, I did art therapy with male patients of the practice. During this time, I wrote my article "Mourning, Memory and Life Itself: The Vietnam Veterans' Wall and the AIDS quilt" (Chapter 1 of this book).

A white woman who tries to act as an ally to oppressed groups is often called names and oppressed herself. Recently, I was accused by an art therapist of promoting another "form of exclusion" against people of color. (The art therapist in question was an immigrant from another country who disagreed with my definition of "American born or raised" for a journal series of people of color in art therapy.) As a white female member of an anti-racism team"of multicultural people, I was excoriated. The team told me it was "safer"to lay abuse that was meant for all on a white woman than on others of the team such as African-Americans. In my opinion, white women still have less power than many others do. I was offered my first job out of social work school on a psych ward at University of Southern California/County General Hospital in Los Angeles. Almost as quickly as it had been offered, the job was rescinded because I wasn't a "minority." To do social action work takes a particularly thick skin and the drive to go on in spite of everything. Research has convincingly shown that the more involved in the fray an activist is, the further back they go when they become burned out. We have all suffered and we all display our wounds in our interpersonal and intrapersonal relationships. But some have suffered more.

The Art Therapist With the Art Therapy Client of Different Ethnicity or Race

It has always seemed to me that to be a good therapist, the clinician has to deeply understand the existential world of the client. I also believe that the good clinician not only understands the client's culture but works in the "real world" to make it a more enhancing and nurturing environment. For example, a good therapist needs to be in contact with a child client's teacher–to listen to her, to support her, and, if necessary to help her make changes so the school environment can become a better place for the child. The good therapist always makes the client his/her priority.

With a systems approach, the good therapist as social activist recognizes the family as a culture, and the other people and things that impinge on the client's world and attempts to work to change them as well as the individual client. External events, such as earthquakes, tornadoes, hurricanes, 9/11 and movies may influence progress. Surely, the ubiquity of television as the jointly agreed upon culture of the land, is central. I have been interested in the celebrity as icon and superhero image in which female celebrities opt for breast augmentation against anorexic-like bodies. Juxtapose these images with those of champion female athletes at the Olympics who seem to have no breasts at all. What is the meaning for our clients?

Most art therapists are women (and white women at that). Often clients are not. This dyad poses an interesting and difficult power inequity to begin with. Working with women, the art therapist must help them understand the power inequalities inherent in sexism in the culture and she must, of course, understand them herself and how she might be viewed as part of the power imbalance. This approach is not to squelch strivings, but to offer a reality that can ease guilt and shame. In the era of rugged individualism, it is all too often, the individual who feels shamed, blamed and guilty when it is the culture that constrains.

The same can be said of racism. For a therapist to think she or is he is similar to a client because they may be the same race or background is a mistake. Coming from a position of difference is better. While a therapist may hope for cultural integration, the reality that most people live in today, is extremely racist. I heard race described once as a "mosh pit" of feelings. This can make doing therapy at all a tricky business. In the past, if an African-American single mother and her kids couldn't make it to a therapy appointment because she did not have bus money, it was labeled as "resistance." Hopefully, we are past that. But at a psychology graduate program I taught in, after Loyola Marymount, there are two African-American women on the program faculty. Students chronically got their names mixed up and called one by the other's name. I heard one African-American faculty member state: "We all look alike to them." Feelings are extraordinarily tender and wounds are often at the surface of the personality.

Too much clinical work, I believe, is individually conceived as the art therapists' limits within the confines of the office or studio walls. Often, confidentiality is used as an "excuse." And yet, to be an art therapist is more a "calling" rather than a career choice. (Certainly, it is not much of a money-making proposition.) The therapist can keep confidentiality sacrosanct, still reach out into the client's world, and through the use of self, perhaps even change it. Thomas Szasz and R.D. Laing in the seventies and eighties argued that the proper response to a crazy world was to be crazy. Whether we believe that or not, certainly we could all agree that there is much wrong with the world and much to be done.

MENTORS, ROLE MODELS, INFLUENCES AND MY OWN WRITING

Along with parents and Eula Long, I have been lucky to have had a number of people in my life who taught me, supported me in my social activism activities and who showed me the way. In 1970, a fellow student and friend May Hartman and I, did a questionnaire at our internship agency. As an intervention, we invited the heads of the Los Angeles County Mental Health System to our USC social work class to hear our results. Our professor, Barbara Solomon was the person who taught me "A good change agent doesn't get fired." Sandy Turner, the Quaker community organizer with whom I innovated "Operation Adventure" was a fine role model. She taught me not to practice on my own family or friends. I admired Helen Landgarten, my art therapy colleague and mentor, who consistently pursued clinical treatment for poor people. In my doctoral program at the Fielding Institute, Anna diStefano, Charlie Seashore and Will McWhinney mentored me and taught me much about racism and gender equality. At Loyola Marymount, Virginia Merriam taught me how to stand up for women while Joe Jabbra tutored me in patience, in sticking in, and in kindness. Other influences were my training in social activism at the Highlander Center in New Market, Tennessee, the writings of Myles Horton who established Highlander, where I was taught what I already knew—to work in my own back yard and to be a facilitator of change—not unlike the role that is played by a good art therapist. Also, influencing me were the writings of Paolo Friere (1995, 2000) and Peggy MacIntosh's (1988) article "White Privilege and Male Privilege: A Personal Account of Coming to See Correspondences Through Work in Women's Studies."(I had the privilege of sitting in the room with Friere in his last years, hearing him speak, and doing a drawing of him.)

My history of art therapy (1994) was written because of many years of what I refer to as the "burr in the saddle" syndrome. It was written to right a wrong: I felt that the histories of art therapy then—usually a few pages at the beginning of a clinical book—focused primarily on the Northeastern art therapists. As a Californian, I knew this was not the whole picture by any means. My second book, *Creative Realities: The Search for Meanings* (1998) was written because of a lifelong embarrassment about how the subject of creativity had been approached. I felt that many authors had simply missed the boat. I even had a hard time saying that vastly overused word "creativity" and referred to it as "the 'C' word. (I said this once to a colleague at Loyola Marymount, and he said "Oh. You mean "commitment!") Although much of my published writing had a social action bent, this became more direct in 1989 (with Ault, Barlow and Moon,) when I was on a panel at the Art Therapy Conference called "Social applications of the arts." I focused on the family and stated:

> Many of us in this field, particularly those of my generation, have our roots in the relationship of the arts and social activism. . . . I would like to suggest to you that the time is *now* to renew and intensify our commitment to social responsibility as individual art therapists and as a profession . . . my dream is that in empowering ourselves we can empower others . . . and my dream is that sometime in the future we will truly be free to dream of the transformative nature of the creative process and of the sweeping power of expression and social change that lie within the arts themselves. . . . (Ault et al., 1988.)

In 1993, with Janise Finn Alvarez, Anne Kellogg and Christine Volker, I wrote "The Art Therapist as Social Activist: Reflections and Visions" (Junge et al., 1993). This essay, with changes is Chapter 7 of this book. I wrote:

> From a systems perspective, the role of the art therapist as social activist at a time of deep and crucial change for our clients, mental health systems, our country and the world, are discussed. Despite the fact that art therapists, through our artists' identities, are natural agents of change, our education and strivings for professional acceptance mediate against our natural proclivities in this direction. . . . (Junge et al., 1993.)

In 1999, I published "Mourning, Memory and Life Itself: The AIDS Quilt and the Vietnam Veterans' Memorial Wall":

> Along with the Women's Movement, the Vietnam War and the AIDS epidemic are, I believe, the distinguishing events of the latter half of the twentieth century. They represent two markers of what America means at this unique historical moment . . . the art therapist provides art materials, a listening heart and mind—and a surround in which suffering can exist but be contained . . . [the art product] speaks of continuity in the face of loss and death; it represents and stands for a life. (Junge, 1999.)

This essay with changes, is Chapter 1 of this book and provides its title.

SELF KNOWLEDGE, TRUTH TALKING, HOPE AND COURAGE WITH A BIT OF ANGER THROWN IN, NOT TO MENTION LAUGHTER

A few years ago, with a Social Psychologist, Dr. Charlie Seashore, I presented to my art therapy students at Loyola Marymount what we called "The Good Girl Workshop." Obviously, not just intended for women, we hoped to address what we perceived as a virtually universal stumbling block for all novice art therapists (and plenty of advanced ones, as well.) The stumbling block was *the desire to be liked.* This well-intentioned inclination, if not mediated against is a real problem in doing good clinical work and social action. The therapist may covertly change his or her approach in order to avoid confrontation, conflict and anger and to keep the "transference positive." In my view, this is a dire misunderstanding of the therapy process. Anger is a gift and a motivator for change. In our positive–have a good day–get on with it–culture, in which the word "confrontation" has gotten such a bad name, I'm afraid, we are seeing more of this covert behavior. Even the language has gotten more positive. For instance, I have no trouble saying "challenge" instead of "problem" and embrace the change in meaning, however there are still such things as "problems" and some are insurmountable and to pretend that they do not exist is likely to do ill for our clients.

I believe the art therapist who aims to be a social activist must be self-aware and comfortable in her or his own skin. He/she must not shy away from conflict, nor attempt to bury it. "Consensus" is a catch word today that means that all agree on something. This happens seldom if ever. Sometimes it is the lone voice or action that makes a difference. (Usually, there are others who may agree, but keep silent. A student of mine presented me with a mug with the following quote on it by Laurel Thatcher Ulrich: "Well-behaved women rarely make history.") I often get exasperated about what I consider the endless amount of talking and studying that goes on. Talking and studying are easy; action is what is difficult and takes courage.

The art therapist as social activist must assume that internalized racism and sexism are everywhere and in everyone and she/he must still be a cockeyed optimist. In spite of everything, I still believe change is possible and the world can be changed for the better. I believe that it is the duty of the therapist to try to make things better. We hope that the proclivity and belief in hope and change is in all art therapists. But this is not as obvious as it seems: I once was in a group with a psychiatrist in training who, deep down, did not believe in change—he needed to find another way to make a living. Paolo Friere (1995) wrote:

> I certainly cannot ignore hopelessness as a concrete entity, nor turn a blind eye to the historical, economic and social reasons that explain that hopelessness–[but] I do not understand human existence, and the struggle needed to improve it, apart from hope and dream.

The art therapist as social activist must be brave and courageous. It takes a lot to stand up for unpopular things. Sometimes there are wounds and surely it can be a lonely place. I remember speaking in a group and hearing my voice shake–I went on. Certainly, a touch of humor helps if the art therapist recognizes and expresses the absurdity of it all and can even laugh at themselves. The art therapist who is not afraid of change can become a role model and an influence for others.

A sage said, to do this work there are three rules:

1. Don't push rocks uphill
2. Find a friend
3. Stay alive.

While I have amended the first rule to "don't push *too many* rocks up hill," I believe these are useful edicts for the art therapist. Social activism work can be exhausting and energy draining. And therefore to keep at it–I recommend a cuddle group, in family therapist Carl Whitaker's words–or at the very least, a friend you can speak honestly with. But social activism is the best work there is because like the artist, it is the art therapist's attempt to change the world so that opportunities are more fair and more equitable for all.

> Without a minimum of hope, we cannot so much as start the struggle . . . Hence the need for a kind of education of hope . . . One of the tasks of the progressive educator . . . is to unveil opportunities for hope no matter what the obstacles may be. –Freire (1995.)

REFERENCES

Ault, R., Barlow, G. Junge, M. & Moon, B. (1989). Social applications of the arts. *Art Therapy, Journal of the American Art Therapy Association, 5,* 10–22.

Erikson, E. (1958). *Young man Luther: A study in psychoanalysis and history.* New York: W.W. Norton.

Erikson, E. (1969). *Gandhi's truth: On the origin of militant nonviolence.* New York: W.W. Norton.

Erikson, E. (1975). *Life history and the historical moment.* New York: W.W. Norton.

Friere, P. (2000). *Pedagogy of the oppressed* (Ramos, R.B. Trans.) (20th anniversary Ed.) New York: Continuum.

Friere, P. (1995). *Pedagogy of hope.* New York: Seabury Press.

Freud, S. (1910/1961). The standard edition of the complete psychological works of Sigmund Freud. J. Stratchey (Ed. and Trans.). London: The Hogarth Press.

Gardner, H. (1993). *Creating minds.* New York: Basic Books.

Junge, M. (1994). *A history of art therapy in the United States,* (with P.P. Asawa). Mundelein, IL: The American Art Therapy Association.

Junge, M. (1998). *Creative realities: The search for meanings.* Lanham, MD and New York: University Press of America.

Junge, M. (1999). Mourning memory and life itself: The AIDS Quilt and the Vietnam Veterans' Memorial Wall. *The arts in psychotherapy, 26,* 195–203.

Junge, M.B. (2004). The Superwoman chair. Unpublished statement.

Junge, M.B., Alvarez, J.F., Kellogg, A. & Volker, C. (1993). The art therapist as social activist: Reflections and visions. *Art Therapy, Journal of the American Art Therapy Association, 10,* 148–155.

Kaplan, F. (Ed.) (2007). *Art therapy and social action.* London and Philadelphia: Jessica Kingslcy Pubs.

McIntosh, P. (1988).White privilege and male privilege: A personal account of coming to see correspondences through work in women's studies, Wellesley College, Wellesley, MA.: Center for research on women. Working paper series No.189.

Sue, D. (2001). Surviving monoculturalism and racism. In Ponterro, J., Casas, J. Suzuki L., & Alexander, C. (Eds.), *Handbook of multicultural counseling.* Thousand Oaks, CA: Sage.

Chapter 9

PEOPLE OF COLOR IN ART THERAPY[1]
WITH JANICE HOSHINO

In 2005-2006, I was Guest Editor for four editions of the journal *Art Therapy, Journal of the American Art Therapy Association*, presenting life stories of people of color in art therapy. Janice Hoshino was Associate Guest Editor. There were nine authors and eleven life stories in all. My intention for the series was to honor the many people of color who had contributed to and, in some cases, helped form the American Art Therapy Association (AATA). A few had grown disheartened and left the profession. Although I sent a personal letter to their home address, many people of color never responded to my request, (Perhaps my "whiteness," or that some may have seen me as part of the art therapy "establishment" didn't help.) I was told a few had attempted publication in the *Art Therapy* journal but were rejected. Many have supported an oral history as a way to pass their stories down to future generations.

For the most part, people of color still in AATA banded together in a multicultural committee where, I felt they were all too often, ignored. One committee member wrote me about her surprise that the committee now included anyone with cultural "issues" such as gender,

---

1. Chapter 9 contains excerpts from my guest editorial Stories of art therapists of color. The complete editorial was printed in *Art Therapy, Journal of the American Art Therapy Association* in 2005, *22*, 4. In addition, I have included my response to some letters to the editor about the series. The themes article of this essay concluded the series and appeared with changes as Hoshino, J. & Junge, M. (2006). Themes and reflections on the stories of art therapists of color. *Art therapy, Journal of the American Art Therapy Assoication, 23*, 139–143. Janice Hoshino was Associate Editor for the series. Used with permission.

physical disabilities and religion, which she felt dissipated the original and major focus on the committee's educative function on racism and ethnicity. She said the committee hadn't been asked if it wanted changes. I felt it was important and long past due that the series provide a forum to bring art therapy people of color out of the shadows so others could benefit from their stories, voices, and experiences. After the series in the journal, I hoped the stories would be gathered together to provide an important multicultural monograph to be used by students and others. So far, this has not happened.

In our history as a profession, art therapists have spent remarkable energy establishing ourselves as an innovative, valuable, recognized and legitimate segment of mental health. When I first entered the art therapy business in the early 1970s, one of my primary goals as an art therapy educator was *the development of the profession.* In 1994 I published (through AATA with Paige Asawa) *A History of Art Therapy in the United States.* This was the first history of the profession and remains the *only* history in book form. Although I had been around long enough to know then that some of art therapy's pioneers were people of color who had remained largely invisible, my sources and searches for history, including AATA's archives unfortunately did not afford much of that kind of information. Only one person of color, Georgette Powell, was mentioned in the *History.* This seemed to me inaccurate at best and possibly a terrible wrong. I knew that a number of people had been omitted from art therapy's history and that a great deal more historical investigation was left to do. We know that history is not a matter of merely stating "facts." One is bound by the choices made and by the sources available. As I sat on the floor rifling through the papers at the Menninger Foundation where the American Art Therapy's archives were kept, I was aware that they provided me with a very limited array of historical "facts." This was the reason I titled the book *A History of Art Therapy in the United States.* It was my hope that there would be more and fuller histories to come.

I asked myself: In our struggle to establish art therapy as a profession, had we, like America itself, accepted the tragedy of race by clinging to our racist proclivities? It is no news that the color of one's skin makes a difference and that the darker one is the more likely one is to experience discrimination. Things had changed enough in art therapy graduate programs so that by the 1990s multicultural education was mandated by AATA educational standards and diversity was virtually a catchword. But what this meant functionally was unclear to me. I felt that art therapists–like other mental health disciplines–often remained a naïve lot, well-intentioned certainly, but sometimes unaware and unintentionally insensitive, closeted, distanced, protected even, by the prevailing cultural winds in this country. I well knew that words, no matter how wonderful, do not usually make change; change needs action. The lack of will for confrontation among colleagues, I speculated, caused much but the "niceties" to go underground–felt, but seldom expressed. I thought art therapists and the professional organization (AATA) had little acknowledged and honored our own people of color. It seemed to me then and now, to hear their stories, their difficulties and their triumphs, would benefit us all.

Recently, I saw the musical *Caroline or Change* by Tony Kushner, directed by George Wolfe with a score by Jeanne Tesori. The setting is 1963 in Lake Charles, Louisiana, against the background of young men sent off to the growing war in Vietnam, the Civil Rights Movement gaining momentum, and the assassination of the young President John F. Kennedy, foreshadowing chaos to come. It seemed to me that in the play, Carolyn, an African-American maid for a white Jewish southern family, and her washing machine captured a moment which expressed the decade's essence. One reviewer felt the musical embodied America's soul. Sitting in the audience, watching the play's relentlessness that broke my heart, I was reminded how difficult it is for even well- intentioned people to reach across the twin chasms of race and ethnicity. That white people *are* so well intentioned makes it especially difficult for them to recognize themselves as racists. But the tragedy of Hurricane Katrina has put a suffering public face on poverty and race. Statistics show that poverty in this country has increased in the last years and that most of the poor are African-American.

As I negotiated with the journal and issued a "Call for Papers," an ongoing sticking point for the series was my definition of people of color. From the beginning, I was interested in presenting the life stories of art therapy people of color who were *American born or raised.* I chose this boundary not because I believed others were not discriminated against, but because I assumed that a generation of American-born art therapists of color would likely have had different experiences and had met different instances of racism than those who came from other countries. I also thought that recent immigrants, those with physical disabilities or different gender orientation, to name a few, might have other stories to tell than American born or raised people of color. I felt strongly that the stories of American born or raised art therapy people of color should be told *first.* (My Associate Guest Editor did not always agree with me.)

As a Los Angeles born and raised Jewish-American who moved to the Pacific Northwest in 2001, I had noticed obvious geographical ethnic and racist differences. For better or worse, Los Angeles, for generations has been home to many ethnicities whose parents immigrated here, or, like the descendents of African slaves, came many years ago, but who were born in the United States. Nevertheless, the "multicultural" requirement for university faculty positions, for example, was often met by bringing in a "foreign" professor who may never have lived in the United States at all.

I remembered Maya Lin, the Chinese-American creator of the Vietnam War Memorial in Washington, DC. Lin was brought up in Ohio, but as soon as her design for the memorial wall was accepted, the arguing began: In one aspect of the controversy, she was noted to be "Asian" and "other" not American. That she was a woman was a problem as her design was called as pacifist and feminine (decidedly bad, thought many male veterans). When the people of color in art therapy series was announced, letters came from art therapists decrying my definition and calling it "oppression" and a "new model of exclusion." Some were offended terming it "another piece of tokenism . . . offered by people that are privileged . . . [and] imperialistic."

I wrote:

> Your letters . . . raise important questions about the rubric of "People of Color" and the highly complicated issues about identities of oppression in this country. They express the intense personal and professional stakes that we all have in these matters as scholars. It is not clear to me why, by privileging the recent immigrant of color identity that you haven't fallen into the same essentialist reification that you have seen in my work. Of all the axes of oppression making up contemporary American society, how does one decide what to include and what to exclude? . . . If we include all, we must include gays, lesbians, women, people with AIDS, people with physical disabilities, recent immigrants, the poor, to name a few. But if we go that route do we not erase the specificity and struggles of the American African-American experience, for example?[2]

---

2. First printed in *Art Therapy, Journal of the American Art Therapy Association,* 2006. *23* (1.) Used with permission.

Perhaps I was blinded by my own naiveté; surely, I was not prepared for this form of controversy. I should have remembered the speaker on racism and diversity I heard a few years ago who said that taking on this issue is not like sitting down at King Arthur's Round Table and having a civil conversation. These are complex and extraordinary sensitivities and close to the surface, he said. He likened it to entering the mosh pit at contemporary rock concerts.

A partial list of pioneer art therapists of color includes Charles Anderson, Scuddie and Sarah McGhee, Cliff Joseph, Lem Joyner, Georgette Powell, Gong Shu, Chris Wang and Lucille Venture. A partial list of a later generation of art therapists of color, born or raised in America is Charlotte Boston, Cheryl Doby-Copeland, Robert Grant, Chantal Laran Lumpkin, Sangeeta Levy, Dan Hocoy, Anna Riley-Hiscox, Leonette Joseph, Leonard Lambert, Janet Lew Carr, Janice Hoshino, Gwendolyn Short and Evelyn Yee. (I have unquestionably omitted some; for that I am sorry.)

I am an American white woman of secular Jewish ethnicity. Associate Editor of the series, Janice Hoshino is a bicultural Japanese-American woman. I believe that even the best intentioned of us suffer from internalized and institutional racism—it is in the air we breathe at the beginning of the twenty-first century. I also believe the more conscious we become of our own racism, the more we can struggle against historical inclinations and our cultural milieu. Janice and I hoped that the thoughtful stories from the trenches by art therapists of color would sensitize art therapists and drive us to work to make our profession more inclusive and expansive. Art therapists usually have no difficulty espousing the need for our clients' inclusion in a better society. If the power of the image can change the world, it was hoped that images from the experiences of art therapists of color would inspire us to change our personal connections, our institutions, our society, and the world to become less prejudiced and more inclusive.

The following essay, written by Janice Hoshino and myself, was the last article for the "People of Color in Art Therapy" series in the *Art Therapy* journals of 2005 and 2006. In it, major themes of the various nine stories are collected and described. Here the reader can find similarities in the experiences of the various writers. Among others, their common experience of feeling "different" from the mainstream pervades along with some descriptions of perhaps unintended, but insensitive racism in art therapy educational settings and the profession.

THEMES AND REFLECTIONS FROM THE PEOPLE OF COLOR IN ART THERAPY SERIES[3]

Janice Hoshino and Maxine Borowsky Junge

When Maxine Borowsky Junge conceptualized the idea for a series of stories from art therapy people of color, she wanted to give voice to art therapists who had been part of the profession for a long time, but who might not have been heard by the art therapy community at large. The concept of *legacy* comes to mind. *Webster's Dictionary* (2003)[4] defines *legacy* as "something received from an ancestor or predecessor or from the past." Expanding one's understanding of people, their experiences, journeys, triumphs and challenges may be partially developed through academic pursuit, readings, and other endeavors. This form of exploration, while notable, has its limitations, especially if trying to expand one's understanding primarily through theoretical channels. It is comparable to how Hoshino's psychiatrist father once described his interaction with a famous family therapist: "He worked you hard cognitively, but you could never get a sense of his feelings, his heart." In short, you gain knowledge, but not the personal experience.

The concept of legacy, in our opinion, always factors in an element of time, and poses several essential questions regarding this series: Why have the voices of many art therapists of color remained silent or been silenced for so long? What has prevented them from telling their stories? Was their humiliation and loss too great? Do their experiences of being discriminated against contribute to their shame and silence? What does our profession lose when it remains unaware of or indifferent to contributions made by art therapists of color? These questions may never be adequately answered.

Legacies die when stories become imprisoned in shame, secrecy and silence. Secrecy plays a tremendous role in the loss of stories, which are perhaps abandoned to protect survivors from the pain of their experiences. (Elie Weisel could not speak or write of the Nazi Holocaust for ten years. After he finally began, he wrote a flood of

---

3. Reprinted with changes from Hoshino, J. & Junge, M. (2006). Themes and reflections from the people of color in art therapy series. *Art Therapy, Journal of the American Art Therapy Association, 23*, 139–144. Used with permission.
4. *Merriam Webster's Collegiate Dictionary* (11th Ed.) (2003). Springfield, MA: Encyclopedia Britannica.

books.) Conceivably, those brave enough to tell their stories often find an atmosphere of disbelief or indifference. However, to not do, can contribute to people of color's loss of history, identity, and their specific experience, and leaves us impoverished without an understanding of their journey and their stories. Dangerously, it opens up the possibility of history repeating itself. We recognize this possibility too well from our own family of origin experiences. Hoshino cites the example that the internment of the Japanese-Americans was not talked about spontaneously at home. Secrecy on this particular topic was the norm. Her father only shared this chapter in his life when he wanted to protect her from discrimination or to help her with a required academic assignment, which was highly valued, such as family of origin analysis. Junge is Jewish and counts Hitler's Holocaust as part of her heritage.

What is presented below, while not exhaustive is an outline of the major themes culled from the life stories of the "People of Color in Art Therapy" series which appeared in 2005 and 2006 in the four editions of the journal *Art Therapy: Journal of the American Art Therapy Association*.

Societal Polarization and Family Influences

Early on in their life, many authors recognized societal polarization. Common themes were:

- Memories of violence/social protest
- Memories of racism
- Difference equals "less than"
- Marginality
- Polarization

Several authors sensed that in childhood their existence was different and not explained in the same manner as others. There was the feeling that when living outside the mainstream, existence has shifting boundaries. Doby-Copeland (2006) recalled witnessing the public mourning of John F. Kennedy stating: it was a "time of great polarization." Levy's (2006) early memory was children taunting her, "your daddy is the boogie man; your daddy is the boogie man." Hocoy (2006) noted: "One early realization in childhood was that certain things did not translate, and the nature of my existence was one of living in the margins, a place of continual metaphor." And: "From 'Sesame Street' I heard a voice asking "Which one is different? Which doesn't belong?' I, like many people, was programmed very early in life to think of difference as something lesser and to be removed."

Polarization and early discrimination were often recalled in the context of family memories. Common themes emerged as some authors revealed how the family system integrated into society, and the messages, overt and covert, visible and invisible that they learned. Themes of family childhood experiences included:

- Shame of ethnicity
- Attempt to assimilate into white culture
- Attempt to fit in
- Keeping secrets, sometimes around ethnicity
- Family shame
- Family alliance
- Survival as a family
- Child as cultural liaison for the family

Theorists describe the family as a many-layered mini-culture with values and assumptions about the world and a shared history and purpose. Many life-story authors described such a family system, but in more heightened and specific descriptions and often with more definitive roles. For example, as a child, some were assigned certain roles, like the family translator or the liaison with the outside world for the family system. Joseph (2006) noted: "I came to understand my family's struggle as a kind of war, in which we stood together as allies in the battle for material and spiritual survival." Levy (2006) recalled family shame, and remembered the eagerness "to check the skin color" of each baby born on her father's side of the family. She remembered how her mother hated her sister's kinky hair: "My unhappy mother had awful names for my sister's hair and made daily attacks on her braids. My straight hair was wrapped in cloth strips to make Shirley Temple curls." These messages convey to a child that "life would be easier and more opportunities available if one were light-skinned." Levy's family attempted to pass as white. The obvious meta-message was that they were "less than" and could not be a part of the mainstream.

Some life-story authors are bicultural and described unique challenges with what Levy (2006) termed a "diffused sense of identity." Hocoy (2006) portrayed biculturalism as a "place, where things were 'like' or 'as' other things, but not exactly so." What also becomes apparent is the concept that bicultural people of color may not be accepted by either side, which then further fuels identity conflict. This unfortunate pattern promotes a sense of shame and indignation; the dramatic core of biculturalism then was the inability to have available a built-in support system for those who *could not feel grounded in either culture.*

Dominant Culture

Self-image and self-perception are first developed through influences, messages, and experiences of the family. Whatever, the specific "minority" culture, the dominant culture can play a significant role in perpetuating awarenesses formed early in life. Common messages and themes that emerged for these life-story authors included:

- Falling short of the dominant culture.
- Pressure to assimilate into the dominant culture.
- Pressure to lay aside one's identity.
- Pressure to sacrifice parts of self in order to assimilate.
- Lack of positive images of minorities in media.
- Sense of mental inferiority.
- Choice to remain invisibly visible or visibly invisible.

The dominant culture played a role in many of our author's feelings of shame about their features which were not parallel to American standards of beauty. Joseph (2006) recognized that "the system of capitalism itself was the enemy." Hocoy (2006) found racial discord globally, recalling that in Ghana, religious images of divinity are all white, while government posters encouraged "be proud of your color." Lumpkin (2006) wrote, "One could say the dichotomy is one of being invisibly visible: being accepted but, on the other hand, being constantly reminded of my blackness and separate identity."

Institutional Racism

Many authors wrote about institutional racism. They experienced institutional racism in the following settings:

- Educational settings
- Clinical settings
- Medical profession which does not recognize its own cultural

perspective and tendencies to pathologize
• American Art Therapy Association (AATA)

Boston (2005) wrote: "As an art therapist of color, I am often haunted by the memories of my experiences of discrimination in educational institutions and worksites." Joseph (2006) noted: "institutional, organizational, and individual racism, within [and] . . . outside our profession, affects people of color in need of our therapeutic help. . . . For example, I believe it is inappropriate to persist in applying glib diagnostic assumptions which ignore cultural differences."

Education in Art Therapy

It is always fascinating to find out how individuals learned about and decided to enter the profession of art therapy. All were enthused about art therapy, but had differing experiences in their educational and art therapy programs. Some themes that were notable include:

• Professors of color made a difference
• Experiences of institutional racism in art therapy education
• Universities unaware of their own racism, played this out in program choices
• Many life-story authors pursued doctoral degrees

Farris (2006) recalled that the list of program-recommended therapists provided to art therapy students for psychotherapy included white people, mostly men. Farris's request for a person of color as her psychotherapist was met with the threat of expulsion from her graduate program. Doby-Copeland (2006) examined racial bias with patients and staff in an effort to understand their experiences.

Despite discrimination, hardships and challenges, four of the nine authors, plus Lucille Venture, (Potash, 2005) achieved doctoral degrees—indeed a high percentage and a major accomplishment. The terminal degree in art therapy is the Masters. That people of color in art therapy chose to continue their education implies that they felt they needed more education post Masters and, perhaps, were interested in pursuing university teaching, which typically takes a doctoral degree.

Mentors for Art Therapy People of Color

• Were largely people of color
• Many were introduced to art therapy through mentors

- The decision to become art therapists was because of influence of these mentors
- Cliff Joseph was mentioned more than once as a mentor to many

Mentors, primarily people of color, were very influential in the authors' choice to become an art therapist. They were supportive and helpful as professors and provided guidance through difficult situations. Cliff Joseph was cited as a mentor more than once, while Boston and Short (2006) describe how Georgette Powell befriended Edith Kramer, a major art therapy theoretician. Some authors did not find mentors of color, and often noted feeling misunderstood.

Relationship with the American Art Therapy Association (AATA)

One of the more dominant themes to emerge from the life stories was ideas about the person of color's relationship with the American Art Therapy Association (AATA.) Some of these themes include:

- AATA does not embrace the need for organizational cultural competency.
- Pioneer people of color are often overlooked.
- AATA continues to underutilize resources of minorities (e.g., Multicultural Committee).
- Minorities continue to remain invisible within the professional organization.
- Minorities are often asked to do the work about minorities. Remembered is the book *The Bridge Called My Back* (1983).
- Contributions of people of color are usually overlooked.
- There is a shortage of "minority" art therapists while there is an abundance of minority clients.
- Little, if any, advocacy for teaching white art therapists how to do clinical work with people of color.
- American Art Therapy Association (AATA) journal does not recognize contributions of people of color.
- AATA consists mostly of privileged, white women.
- Research project of art therapy education [in the 1990s] found only 18 black art therapy students nationwide.
- Question of the future of AATA?

Unfortunately, these feelings existed in the early days of the organization (note Boston and Short (2006) writing about Georgette Powell, who helped form the American Art Therapy Association (AATA)). Authors also noted that a shortage of art therapy people of color continues to currently exist. Doby-Copeland (2006) wrote: "Twenty-eight years later, [after the founding] it is frustrating how long it has taken AATA to embrace the need for organizational cultural competence." Notably, the first person of color (Doby-Copeland) was awarded the 2003 AATA Clinician's Award, in recognition for over 25 years of art therapy service.

Art Therapists' Pursuit of Cultural Competence

All life-story authors urgently felt that the priority of cultural competency is crucial in education, work and, as a general principle, in life. They wrote of the need for cultural competency education of art therapists as educators, supervisors and as clinicians. They stressed the need for functional *competence*, not merely written standards of practice. Cited was the difference between words and actions. Doby-Copeland observed: "Discourse is fine but . . . more action is needed."

Slow efforts of employers, the lackluster attitude of the professional organization, and the lack of recognition from white clinicians hurts and disappoints; they have been contrary to people of color's commitment and understanding of the importance of this initiative. The collective voice contends that multicultural competency is indeed a life-long endeavor.

People of Color's Employment and Therapeutic Practice

Many art therapists who wrote life stories worked with disadvantaged populations. (In graduate internships, it is notable that most art therapists are white, while most low-income clients are people of color.) They began work without an art therapist job title, or indeed a personal recognition of what an art therapist is. The previous two were major themes of the autobiographies as well as the following:

- Experiences of client prejudice.
- Supportive colleagues.
- Many art therapists don't know about the effects of racial intolerance in clients and colleagues. It hinders their clinical work.

• Art therapists of color feel a connection with patients due to parallel marginalized experiences.
• Patients acted as social activists.

Compilation of authors' stories revealed an expansive and impressive spectrum of clinical experience with diverse populations. Although life-story authors felt client prejudice existed, they recognized that clients were experiencing marginalization and prejudice analogous to the authors' experiences. Some asserted this created a stronger sense of compassion and connection between art therapist and patient. Many cited that they learned invaluable information from their clients.

Institutional and clinical settings were noted to be culture-bound and culture-biased by several of the authors. Hocoy (2006) contended: "Clearly the enterprise was culture-bound in its Euro-American constructions, values, and assumptions, and culture-biased in its systematic neglect of minority cultures in theory, research, and practice." Joseph (2006) concurred that, "a larger societal context was breeding pathology and needed definition for good therapy to have a chance."

Creativity and New Initiatives as a Way to Cope With Discrimination

Those who have been marginalized and/or experienced blatant racism may feel victimized and made helpless by the experience. Some remain hopelessly stuck in that role. A lucky few channel their frustration through creative processes. Not surprisingly, many of our authors found solace from often constant prejudice, identity confusion and the staggering sense of difference and difficulty fitting in, through the creative process—primarily the visual arts—as a means of coping and expression. Examples include:

• Art as means of expression began early in life, and continues to be an important factor in expression and coping.
• Art was used to create the fantasy of something better—examples include:
  a. Art conveying racial justice against the oppressor.
  b. Art as a fantasy of superhero creations.
• Art as healing.
• Art as social action.

An important method for dealing with adversity, life-story authors wrote, is through utilizing one's own experiences as an instrument to make a difference in the lives of other disadvantaged populations. The collective efforts of these art therapy people of color authors are distinguished and creative. Many prevailed over sometimes desperate feelings of marginalization by creating new avenues in their clinical work, professional organizations, and in the larger society in an effort to make a difference and to advocate for other people of color. The following were all started and supported by life-story authors:

National Alliance of Third World Creative Therapists (NATWCT)
Ad Hoc Committee to encourage minorities to join AATA
Art therapy support group for people of color
Harlem Arts Workshop through the Works Project Administration (WPA[5])
Harlem Hospital Nursing Home
Art in the Park and Tomorrow's World Art Center
International work in Ghana
Creation of new art therapy programs
Consultant to Sudanese refugees in U.S.

The Hope for Diversity in the Future

Although they might be bitter or disenfranchised, our life-story authors of color share an optimistic hope for future diversity. Despite whatever problems they may have personally experienced, they remain committed to this goal. Perhaps it is their attachment to the words of the Constitution, the American dream and their connection to the American way of life. Perhaps it is American history itself, that has encouraged the flames of hope for a better country where all people are truly created equal. We remember the words of a Chicano artist, who had grown up in the United States. From television, movies and the *zeitgeist*, he said, he immersed himself in the notion of the American dream and, in middle age, he still believed it.

A central idea surrounding hope for the future of these art therapy people of color was that multicultural competency is a lifelong process for everyone. The continuous process has similarities that include:

---

5. WPA is the "Works Project Administration" started by President Franklin D. Roosevelt, during The Great Depression to give work to artists and writers.

- Pursuit to understand and embrace culture
- Transformation of going from shame to acceptance
- Encouragement of others to find professional mentors

CONCLUSIONS

The "People of Color in Art Therapy" series provided personal life stories of struggles, triumphs, experiences, and opinions by contributors. While the series was not without controversy, it was approached as an initiative that could provide expansion and consolidation for the art therapy community. It was our hope that readers not only gain an understanding of the individual journeys of these individuals, but also an appreciation of the resilient spirit and inner strength they developed despite considerable, sometimes overbearing, hardships. We hoped this would inspire other future series by art therapy people of color.

We asked the authors the following question: *What can you tell us about your experience of writing your life story for the Art Therapists of Color series?* Difficult feelings emerging were vulnerability, ambivalence and reluctance to contribute to the series. By overcoming these feelings, authors cited a sense of validation and that one's contribution would aid others to become more culturally sensitive. One author responded she was pleased with positive responses from others who had similar experiences. Some *experiences* the life-story authors noted included the following: One author stated when she shared her article with colleagues, they found it to be thought-provoking and sought further information; but some questioned her feelings. Other readers were defensive and distant. One life-story author told us she felt "naked" in what she had written. Hocoy (2006) summarized:

> Writing my life story has been an opportunity to reflect back and examine the cultural threads in my life and realize these threads, which I once perceived as binding and constricting. I now regard [them] as forming the lattice that supports and sustains my very well-being and sense of self (personal communication. (2006)

Through life stories we learned how these art therapists of color coped with discrimination and challenges. They inspire us with their resilience, inspiration, accomplishments, and contributions to the profession of art therapy. Their sense of "gaman" (a Japanese word meaning "quiet endurance") coupled with the breadth of their creative initiatives inspire us to consider this sense of resiliency in overcoming challenges.

We would like to close with a gentle, forceful message: There is much work to be done. We must drive toward continued growth as individuals who embrace, take action and are dedicated to multicultural competency as a lifelong process; this must be a collaborative effort— People of color and their allies of other racial and ethnic backgrounds. We hope the stories of art therapy people of color provide an incentive and a template toward making a difference in our lives, our profession, and more globally, in our world.

REFERENCES

Boston, C. (2005). Life story of an art therapist of color. *Art Therapy, Journal of the American Art Therapy Association, 22,* 189–192.

Boston, C. & Short, G. (2006). Notes, Georgette Seabrook Powell. *Art Therapy, Journal of the American Art Therapy Association, 23,* 89–90.

Doby-Copeland, C. (2006). Things come to me, reflections from an art therapist of color. *Art Therapy, Journal of the American Art Therapy Association, 23,* 81–85.

Farris, P. (2006). Mentors of diversity. *Art Therapy, Journal of the American Art Therapy Association, 23,* 86–88.

Hocoy, D. (2006). Art Therapy: Working in the borderlands. *Art Therapy, Journal of the American Art Therapy Association, 23,* 132–135.

Hoshino, J. & Junge, M. (2006). Themes and reflections from people of color in art therapy series. *Art Therapy, Journal of the American Art Therapy Association, 23,*139–144.

Joseph, C. (2006). Creative alliance: The healing power of art therapy. *Art Therapy, Journal of the American Art Therapy Association, 23,* 30–33.

Junge, M. & Hoshino, J. (Eds.) (2005). Viewpoints: Art therapists of color. [Special "Viewpoints" series]. *Art Therapy, Journal of the American Art Therapy Association, 22,* 1–3.

Levy, S. (2006). Your daddy is the boogie man. *Art Therapy, Journal of the American Art Therapy Association, 23,* 136–138.

Lumpkin, C. (2006). Relating cultural identity and identity as art therapist. *Art Therapy, Journal of the American Art Therapy Association, 23,* 34–38.

Moraga, C. & Anzaldua, G. (Eds.) (2nd Edition 1983). *This bridge called my back: Writings by radical women of color.* New York: Kitchen Talk, Women of Color Series.

Potash, J. (2005). Rekindling the multicultural history of the American Art Therapy Association, [Lucille Venture]. *Art Therapy, Journal of the American Art Therapy Association, 22,* 184–188.

Part IV

THE PROFESSION OF ART THERAPY

Chapter 10

ART THERAPY AS A WOMAN'S PROFESSION

That American art therapy is a woman's profession is no secret. Anyone who has ever attended the professional organization of art therapy, the American Art Therapy Association's (AATA's) annual conference and sat in a hotel ballroom for an opening session notices that women predominantly fill the room. The two major American art therapy theoreticians, Naumburg and Kramer are women. Since AATA's inception in 1969, to 2005 there were 15 women Presidents and three male Presidents. For the highest award in art therapy, the HLM,[1] from 1970 to 2004 there were 24 women recipients and five men. For AATA's Clinician of the Year award, first given in 1990 (through 2004) there have been 19 female winners and one male. Perusing *Art Therapy, Journal of the American Art Therapy Association* for the last ten years, I found that out of 160 total article authors, 130 were female and 30 were men. In book reviews for this period, a larger percentage of men *wrote* the books, but the reviews themselves were written by a preponderance of women. From 1983 when the *Art Therapy* journal began and despite that it was an intense period of feminism in America, there were a very few articles clinical or otherwise in art therapy, addressing women and their issues: I counted nine. When the first art therapy journal, *Bulletin of Art Therapy* began in 1961, the publisher and editor was a woman, Elinor Ulman. The first editor of the *Art Therapy* journal was a man, but the four since have been women. In 1996 under Malchiodi's leadership, a journal issue was dedicated to "Women and Art Therapy." But even in this edition, there was an arti-

---

1. HLM - "Honorary Life Member."

cle called "Men's Roles and their Experience of Depression" by Barbee (1996). While I did not count numbers of males and female faculty in art therapy education programs, I doubt whether I would find anything but overarching numbers of women. Surveying AATA membership in 2003, Elkins, Stovall and Malchiodi found that 91.3 percent were female, 6.2 percent were male and 2.5 percent did not specify. These were predominantly white. I counted membership from the 2004-05 American Art Therapy Association Roster of members, and found that with a total of 4,496 members, 234 were men.[2] This is 94.8 percent female and 5.2 percent male. If my figures are anywhere near correct, female membership is going up and male is going down.

DOES A PROFESSIONAL ORGANIZATION REPRESENT A WHOLE PROFESSION?

Does a professional organization represent a whole profession? Not always, but in this case, it may because most art therapists, most arts healers and most creative arts therapists are members of the American Art Therapy Association.[3] In the 1960s when I was in graduate school at UCLA in the painting department, most of the faculty were men; there were only two women in the department. One woman usually painted flowers and her work was said to be "sentimental." The message was clear to faculty and students, female and male, that neither she, nor her art could be taken seriously or were worth bothering about. The other woman professor, Mary Holmes was an immensely brilliant person who knew more about the arts and culture than any of the men on the faculty and was a remarkable teacher. Although Teaching Assistantships were not often given to women students, I was her Assistant and, formally and informally, she taught me a great deal. Mary was largely ignored in the UCLA Painting Department. She became a founding faculty member at the University of California at Santa Cruz where she lived out her life teaching, lecturing, making art and farming and being revered by her students and colleagues, at what was then, the most radical University of California campus.

2. These numbers in the previous section are, of course, approximate and were counted by apparently male and female names which might not be wholly accurate, but they make the point.
3. "Creative Arts Therapists" are defined as those who use more than one of the arts in therapy.

I had been told in my undergraduate college that I "painted like a man." This was intended to be a compliment and meant to me that I was special and different from other women painters. I didn't want to be a "woman" painter. (To paint like a woman meant sentimentality. Internalized sexism mandates that women also harbor the edicts of the culture which may be anti-woman.) When I arrived at UCLA, I received a large dose of which, some years later, I figured out was sexism, that kept me from painting for almost ten years. When I emerged after those ten years I had morphed into an art psychotherapist. I never regretted that sea change, but I have wondered if the times had been different, or if I attended another of the arts institutions that extended scholarships to me, would I have remained primarily a painter?

In those days, people who wanted to be practicing artists and received Masters of Fine Arts (MFAs) typically took up positions as art instructors in colleges, universities and art schools–if they could get them–so they could continue their careers as exhibiting painters. I speculate that some of those discouraged women art students went into teaching in the public schools or even perhaps into art therapy. At UCLA, women students were not often mentored by male faculty members, not usually represented in exhibits and not usually awarded the few teaching positions in universities and community colleges.[4]

DO WOMEN TEND TO PURSUE ART THERAPY RATHER THAN CAREERS AS PAINTERS AND ART TEACHERS IN UNIVERSITIES AND COLLEGES?

During the time I was a professor of graduate art therapy first at Immaculate Heart College in Hollywood, CA and faculty and Director at Loyola Marymount University in Los Angeles, I interviewed hundreds of applicants eager to attend graduate school. Potential students were mostly women, as are most art therapy students nationwide. Although there are arts prerequisites for admittance to art therapy programs, few applicants are professional-level artists or had been at it a long enough time to develop deep and extensive technical skills.

---

4. Judy Chicago, who was a student at UCLA in those days has written her own view of the sexism there in her first book, originally published in 1975, *Through the Flower: My Struggle as a Woman Artist.*

Applicants often told me they had discovered the powerful use of art as self-expression for themselves during problem times and, with an altruistic bent, wanted to help others. It is my guess that most art therapy students, historically and today, carry these twin passions. Most never wanted to be professional artists. Realistically perhaps, they found the male world of fine art difficult, even impossible. Perhaps they did not even attempt it. Maybe being the relational creatures that women are thought to be, the pleasures of using art in relationship to other people appealed and thus they pursued art therapy.

Sometimes, artists with a strong professional bent, accepted into an art therapy program, eschewed the psychology aspect of art therapy altogether and withdrew to pursue their art. Professional artists have tended to veer away from psychology because many fear it will hinder or stop artistic abilities. In my opinion, this is an incorrect assumption from a long outdated paradigm. It is like the story of the painter who would not pursue psychotherapy because, screwed up though he was, he believed that if he understood too much and became "normal" he would no longer have the need to make art. A prevalent myth is that the artistic personality is close to madness. But this much-believed evil alliance is only a story.

A friend of mine said: "There are some countries where blacks are equal, but there is no country where women are equal" Although we have our first viable female candidate for president, it was less than one hundred years ago, in 1920 that American women finally achieved the vote. (Women gained the right to vote in Ireland and the U.K. in 1928, in Switzerland in 1971, and in Kuwait in 2005.) (Women's Suffrage, Internet, 2007.)

I believe that in the United States the Women's Movement of the twentieth century has been the most important cultural change we have seen in that hundred years. The percentage of women students is now about 57 percent in most universities and colleges today. Trying to achieve gender balance in their student body, it is often more difficult for women than men to gain acceptance to many institutions of higher learning. One institution which does not take gender into consideration for admittance has 67 percent women students giving an indication of what it might be like when gender is not a hindering factor. Nevertheless, men still seem to control much in our culture. We remain a country divided by race, ethnicity and gender. The "Look Test" will do. One does not have to more than look at the people around President George W. Bush and in the U.S. Senate and House to understand what is going on. And look at most of the people writing and producing that cultural panacea, television.

THE HISTORY OF ART THERAPY IN THE UNITED STATES

In 1994 when I published *A History of Art Therapy in the United States*, I had a section in the book called "The Women's Movement as an Influence on Art Therapy." I wrote that although there had been no acknowledgment of this influence on art therapy, art therapy was "created and developed largely by women" and "suffered from many of the same oppressive external and internalized constraints inherent in sexist conditions." (Social work was another "female profession.") A male friend recently said to me that he thought it so obvious that art therapy is a woman's profession that it didn't need to be talked about. While he may be right, I doubt it. However, to my knowledge, art therapy has not been considered in this obvious framework except by a very few and it needs to be.

DEFINITION OF INTERNALIZED SEXISM

Once I gave a research presentation on myths about women at a social work conference. The room was naturally filled with women eager to grow more aware in their understanding. Also in attendance that day were three men. One of my co-panelists thanked the men, but not the women for coming. That women need to be grateful to have their presentation attended by men, and thus validated is internalized sexism in action. Internalized sexism is the "internalization of gender role socialization and sexism" (Major, 2007). Through their own hard work, women have come a long way in this country toward achieving equity and freedom of choice, but that the United States still retains patriarchal tendencies is hardly worth arguing about; the culture even today mandates strong oppression, discrimination and restrictions against women. Women are raised within the American cultural milieu as are men, and as they drink in the surrounding edicts, it becomes part of them and even the most conscious women hardly notice it. Women who come from a culture where they are oppressed tend to take gender discrimination as "reality" and "truth" unless they are consciously able to become aware that this "truth" is something outside themselves that *is* oppressive. Women's stridency is usually what it takes to make social change; it has been difficult for women and men alike. Often, men think they are being "threatened" by women's strivings, and the fact is, they are! Young women today do not like to call themselves "Feminists" because to them it implies an uncomfortable and difficult aggressiveness and stridency. But it has been exactly those qualities that have created change and the possibility for younger women to find a world that is more open to them.

Like others, women and art therapists understandably long for inclusion. They want to fit in. Nonetheless, it is the woman and the art therapist who are able to stand apart and see the milieu for what it is— an inherent inequality of cultural constraints—and who can maintain the potentiality for change in herself and others. Unless a woman is acutely conscious and aware of this boundary, it is obviously impossible for a woman art therapist to help her female client sort out what is culturally induced and what may be intrapsychic.

ART THERAPY PIONEERS AS EFFECTIVE WOMEN

Until relatively recently, the American Art Therapy Association was an all-volunteer organization. For many years it did not have even an Executive Director nor a paid office staff. The first founders of art therapy, many of whom came together to form an association in 1969 at Myra Levick's invitation, were vastly unusual at that time in that most were women seeking professionalism. That was an era when middle-class women, which many of these were, were mandated by the American culture to stay at home and raise families—the tyranny of the post-World War II homemaker and her accepted role as wife and mother. In 2006, Harriet Wadeson and I as editors published *Architects of Art Therapy, Memoirs and Life Stories.* We considered the group of art therapy pioneers wanting to capture their stories as part of the history of the field. Of the 28 art therapists who wrote memoirs for the book, 25 are women. Wadeson and I noted that at the time when art therapy first established itself as a profession, during the 1950s and 1960s, the culture decreed that middle-class women stay home and relinquish desires for anything professional. (Often, the few professional women there were remained unmarried and/or childless, being said to be married to their jobs.) Many of the original art therapy pioneers came of age during these years. How did it happen that these particular art therapy women went against the powerful pull of the tides and ventured out to start a profession? They were people of courage; they were often artists with a drive to create in spite of everything. They were people whose persistence in the face of adversity sustained them. As they pioneered art therapy, Harriet and I proposed that they found a group of professional colleagues and friends who were like them, in that they had "left home and hearth to found a profession of importance and creativity."

Using the Meyers-Briggs Type Indicator Personality Inventory Instrument, I did seven years of research about beginning art therapy students and their identity at Loyola Marymount University. While I never published this study, I found that virtually all of my seven-year sample was strongly "intuitive."[5] No surprise there, but it meant that these students had successfully gotten through a predominantly "sensing" school system and, as many told me, for the first time really felt at home in an educational setting. Most of my graduate students were women. Perhaps art therapy pioneers were too busy creating a profession, establishing education, ethics and professional standards to have noticed who was predominantly doing art therapy. Maybe, as my friend says, it was so obvious that art therapy was a woman's profession that it didn't merit mentioning. Or perhaps the shame of culturally-based internalized sexism pervaded their thinking. (If it is a woman's profession, the culture doesn't need to pay attention.) I believe art therapy as a woman's profession needs to be acknowledged and understood in the profession because this meaning had ramifications, constraints and opportunities for art therapists in the past and will have ramifications, constraints and opportunities for those of future generations. As Faulkner wrote, what is past is never dead or left behind; it is not even past.

Historically, members of art therapy's professional organization are well-known for their vitriolic fights and intense politics–particularly in the early days of the organization. It is my notion that the women who started art therapy were largely unable to "come out of the closet" and openly state their opinions "outside" so they strongly fought–"inside"

---

5. Author's note: "Intuitive" is a type on the Meyers-Briggs Instrument. So is "Sensing."

with each other–some people thought almost to the death. Not able to express rage openly nor freely debate the issues outside, the "ladies" of the American Art Therapy Association acted like anything but ladies. In some way, they must have known that the AATA and the profession of art therapy were *safe places to battle*. Outside, in order to get their educational programs established they knew they needed to "not bite the hand that feeds them." And they did a great job, establishing a plethora of art therapy graduate programs across the country by the twenty-first century, often in male-dominated universities, colleges and institutions. Perhaps, they felt what I call, "The Nice Girl Syndrome,"[6] which kept them from speaking out. Perhaps they felt (realistic) fear. After all, even today women in some places of the world are stoned for some behaviors, decided as aberrant by men. Many of the first art therapists' mentors were men in other mental health professions, such as psychiatry. Although they bravely championed art therapy as a unique innovation, psychiatrists could still be assured that their mentees were unlikely to achieve financial parity or status with psychiatry.

GEOGRAPHY

Geography may have played a significant role in art therapy's development. The United States are a large and often disparate conglomerate with many differences among the states. The Western part of America tends to be thought of as more loose, less wasp and "old money" and less hierarchical in its mental health system. The old joke is that by tipping the United States, all the nuts ended up in California. Born in Los Angeles, I didn't much recognize the vast array of nationwide differences until I went to teach in a more than 100-year-old college in Vermont. The profession of art therapy predominantly began in the eastern part of the United States with the two major theoreticians of the field, Margaret Naumburg and Edith Kramer, practicing and evolving their theories in New York in the late 1930s, 1940s and 1950s. Elinor Ulman, living in Washington D.C., established the first

---

6. "The Nice Girl Syndrome" of course, is not limited to women. In my opinion, it is a culturally induced decree predominantly for girls and women to be pleasing and "nice" that is hard to break out of. There may be very real penalties for doing so. Most novice art therapists experience it and it is imperative that they break out in order to become excellent therapists.

art therapy journal, *Bulletin of Art Therapy,* in 1961. (In 1963, Ulman did a survey of art therapists in the U.S. and Canada and found only 35.) Although Mary Huntoon, Don Jones and somewhat later, Robert Ault were working with Karl Menninger at the Menninger Foundation in Topeka, Kansas–one of the first psychiatric hospitals, this was little noticed in the scant written histories of the day and art therapy remained thought of as a primarily Eastern endeavor.

The first art therapy Master's program in the country was iniated in 1967 by Myra Levick at Hahnemann Hospital and Medical College in Philadelphia. It was not until 1974 that Helen Landgarten innovated the first art therapy program west of the Mississippi River on the West Coast at Immaculate Heart College in Hollywood, CA. I was a founding faculty member of that program. The American Art Therapy Association was voted into existence in 1969. Out of the founding board of ten, seven were women (Junge, 1994). Currently, almost all of AATA's Board and the Editorial Board of the journal *Art Therapy* are Easterners or, at best, Midwesterners (Milwaukee, Chicago) with a few Floridians thrown in. Despite the 2004-2005 AATA membership roster listing 11 and one-fourth pages of California art therapists, of the 26 people listed on the journal masthead, only two are Californians and one of those taught for many years in Kentucky and finally retired to California. Of the 26, 23 or 88 percent are women.

THE MONEY PROBLEM

The meaning and significance of "equity" for women in this country has meant, among other things, pay equal to that of men. Pay for women is not usually equitable even now although things have decidedly progressed in this area. In that inequitable time and in the days of one-salary families, when the profession of art therapy started, many of its pioneers were married women and the cultural edicts proclaimed that married women didn't need to make much money because their husbands supported them. (There was some truth in that.) Pioneering art therapists tended to be offered less money than men and often less than other mental health professionals; they took what they could get to get started and who can dispute that they should have? Despite the fact that art therapy is often more complicated to learn and to practice than other mental health disciplines, because the fledgling art therapist must both learn about therapy and how to do it and about art imagery and it's meaning, the profession still suffers today from this dearth of a living wage. (And I believe this problem in some art therapists leads to a profound lack of self-esteem, a reluctance to be the outsider, and the deepest desire to become more like other, more "accepted" mental health professions.) In this country today, many psychotherapists of different mental health disciplines pretty much perform the same work, but hierarchical pay is considerably different. While consumers of psychotherapy seldom know the difference, from highest to lowest, it goes from psychiatrists, psychologists, social workers, master's level-psychologists and marriage and family counselors and art therapists. (The place it evens out a bit is in private practice.) I have wondered before if one reason there are so few men in the field is because art therapy is relatively low-paying and low-prestige. Also postulated is that the dominance of women in art therapy keeps men from entering as they perceive a "woman's profession" be less important and powerful. And it probably is (Junge, 1994). This was also said about the social work profession when the few men in the field were leaders and administrators, and I have heard it stated anew by male faculty members fearful that the numbers of women students higher than males in colleges and universities will drive men away.

THE FUTURE OF ART THERAPY AS SEEN BY THE PIONEERS

The final question for each memoirist in the *Architects of Art Therapy* book asked the writer to reflect on the future of art therapy as they saw it (Junge & Wadeson, 2006). Many memoirists wrote about the multiple difficulties of balancing work and family while pursuing the career of art therapy. Whatever the difficulties, many spoke of their "passionate involvement" and pleasures that their more than 35-year career had provided for them. They worked for love, certainly not for money, and because they received tremendous enjoyment from their role in the development of a professional art therapy organization and of the art therapy profession itself. Educators felt they lived through the succeeding generations of art therapists they trained, while clinicians viewed, with pride, the progress of their patients and clients. As they looked back, these pioneers felt they had lived lives in art therapy that *mattered*. Edith Kramer, a major theoretician and educator is largely retired at age 90. She has been a life-long proponent of the value of art-making for art therapists; she stated her intention for the future as "to paint and sculpt the world around me with humility, vigor and truthfulness."

Often, art therapy pioneers saw the future in rather general terms. One author said she had no predictions but wrote she wished the arts would be a "major mode of expression . . . [with] art therapists as primary facilitators for reflection, expression and action." Some pioneers noticed and saluted the tremendous growth of art therapy in the past and the expansion of art therapy and expressed their hope that art therapy would continue to grow while keeping open and flexible.

At a practical level, a number of pioneers echoed an ongoing call today for the art therapy profession: the need for systematic and quantitative outcome research studies to "prove" the value and contributions of art therapy to the "outside" world, the mental health and managed care systems. One leader in the field sounded a cautionary note eschewing outcome studies in favor of shining case examples of artist-clients. She felt sure that the "public relations" benefits of these kinds of cases could convince others of the contribution of art therapy far better than research studies. Underlying her proposal is the use of imagery, rather than numbers and words, to reveal and convince of the benefits of art therapy. Many cautioned the field to be especially cognizant and take advantage of opportunities for art therapy's inclusion, such as in public school situations and with returnees from Iraq who may have Post-Traumatic Stress Disorder. One woman rankled about artists attempting to practice art therapy who do not know anything about psychology or psychotherapy and psychotherapists with no studio arts background using art in therapy. Too many practitioners in mental health, they said, do not know to take art and imagery seriously and that the confrontational nature of imagery may at times be dangerous to clients. Mental health practitioners may consider art a light and unnecessary, though often interesting accoutrement or skill or even a technique. This cautionary understanding of potential dangers of emergent imagery is part of the training of art therapists, but not of others. A few writers spoke of the problem of licensure for art therapists connected to employment, but past AATA President Gladys Agell sounded the problem loud and clear. She said, without licensure "employment is in jeopardy" (Junge & Wadeson, 2006).

CONCLUSIONS

Art therapy in the United States was established and began to flourish at a time when money in mental health was plentiful and creative ideas sought out and implemented. (Although I doubt that even in those halcyon days many art therapy pioneers received plush salaries.) Unfortunately, plenty is no longer the case. Bureaucracy, behaviorism and paperwork abound and mental health budgets have been cut to the quick. Most art therapy training programs are in private universities and colleges and most are at the Master's level. This means that tuitions are going up precluding many middle and low-income people from attending at all and those that can afford to attend a training program may graduate with huge debts from student loans. All art therapy educators should consider the risks and difficulties of graduate education and take whatever steps they can to ameliorate the problem. This increase in tuition for art therapy education is occurring at a time when salaries are often on the downswing and unemployment generally is increasing. Elkins, Stovall and Malchiodi's 2001–02 AATA membership survey found that salary information was "roughly identical to those obtained during the 1998–1999 Membership Survey Report." They report (astoundingly) that the largest amount of gross salary reported was $10,000. Not surprisingly, in 2001–2002 they also found salaries "significantly related to gender . . . with males reporting a higher gross salary than females" (2003). Today, employment and decently-paid employment are major issues for the field. I believe, practicalities such as a living wage should be in the forefront today for the professional organization, or art therapy as a profession may not survive.

There is an old joke in art therapy still prevalent today: You tell someone you are an art therapist and they say "what's that?" Students are schooled in what to say back. But the fact remains that it is significantly difficult to tell someone in words what an art therapist does. (Have them create an image, and the value is instantly clear.) Most art therapists do some suffering about this inability to describe their profession in words. I know one pioneer art therapist, and I suspect she is not the only one, who when asked would say she was a housewife, because she was tired of explaining. As evidenced by this joke, in my opinion, if a profession can be said to have self-esteem problems, art therapy is one. At the yearly conference, the main speakers traditionally have been male psychiatrists. To give central presence to psychiatrists and to think that they have something to teach art therapists is patriarchal and out of date. My image is of young women sitting at the feet of the fabled wise man poised to pick up whatever crumbs of wisdom he might drop. There are many wise and experienced art therapists who could teach conference-goers a few things, but they are seldom given such central prestigious forums.

Some years back, a student of mine at Loyola Marymount did her Master's research thesis on resistance to the art by art therapists. Her sample was nationwide and her study found that resistance to the art was typically a result of *a significant lack of confidence on the part of the art therapist.* To my knowledge, there is little if any licensing in America called "art therapy" so we cannot be licensed as art therapists. In many states, to be licensed is the only way to *legally* practice art therapy. To be licensed, committed art therapists must call themselves by another name. Meanwhile, the art therapy profession maintains and acts out its fear that art therapists who become licensed in other fields will surely give up art therapy and attach themselves to their more prestigious and "legitimate" mental health discipline. Unquestionably, it does sometimes happen: An example of this I have seen is the art therapist who earned a psychology degree. Periodically, she appears on one of the morning television shows to talk about children's art. Although she is a past President of AATA, and was an art therapist long before she took up education in psychology, the writing under her name as she speaks says "Psychologist," not "art therapist." I may be wrong, but I believe that if she took this TV designation on and asked to have it changed, it would. Often, what it takes is *speaking out.* I may be wrong again, but I believe that it is particularly difficult for women to speak out because of internalized sexism.

And yet, I know (as do most art therapists) that in every mental health clinic I have worked in, in the workshops I have done nationally and internationally, in the mental health facility I do consultation and supervision for at present, it is the *art therapist* description that fascinates staff members and it is the revealing image that creates the magic that persuades. My own doctoral degree is called "Human and Organizational Systems." I am licensed as a clinical social worker in the state of California. But there is no way I would want to be anything other than an art psychotherapist. I was an art therapist before I had the words for it and will probably remain so until I die. And most art therapists feel the same.

Another student did her Master's thesis on the attitudes of mental health professionals in California to art therapy and art therapists. While conventional wisdom tells us that those who are closer to art therapy and learn to understand how it really works, will appreciate it more, this graduate student, using a large sample, proved the notion. Thus the role of the art therapist, historically and today, is partly educational. Through the use of Self, because of what they do and are, and through the power of the image to intrigue and lodge itself in memory, art therapists help to develop and further the profession and to show its contributions to clients.

It has been my wish for a long time that art therapists would submit proposals to conferences of other mental health disciplines because of the immense public relations factor. (I have noticed that art therapists seldom do this and wonder if it is part of the self-esteem/internalized sexism problem.) We don't need to convert the converted by presenting our work to other art therapists. In my presentations at a variety of conferences, my work has been deeply appreciated by other mental health people and the presentation has often led to further professional invitations. Through presentations to mental health professionals other than art therapists, we display our essential educative function. There are many art therapists who do impressive work and who present well. I believe that this consistently impressive public relations trumps quantitative outcome studies, when the value of most mental health endeavors, except perhaps behaviorism, has not and cannot be "proven" to help.

In my opinion, art therapy as a women's profession should be frankly acknowledged and praised, not hidden in the closet. I consider it something to be proud of and am pleased to be part of it. That art therapy was established and pioneered by women at a time, after World War II, when many middle-class women were bound by strong American cultural edicts to stay home as wife and mother is nothing short of miraculous. Driven by a passion for art and for their innovative profession, these women worked tirelessly against many odds to create a new mental health discipline. It is important that all art therapists recognize and give voice to the considerable achievements of pioneering art therapists who persevered often in the face of crushing adversity. It is past time to step outside the internalized sexism that still exists, controls and restrains us as "nice girls" and slaps assertive women hard in the face when they attempt to cross the line. It is time to praise the founding generation of art therapists who hung in with courage when achievement for women was particularly difficult. Remember: It is less than 100 years ago that women earned the right to vote in America.

Like all women, art therapy women have been discriminated against. But against the odds, they inexorably moved forward. It is time to understand what women in art therapy have achieved. It is time to understand the meaning of art therapy as a woman's profession; and it is time to move forward with that recognition to the future. Art therapists have proven that women can play the necessary politics with the boys. We must recognize and acknowledge the tacit boundaries, but not allow ourselves to be constrained by them. And we must move forward with realism, practicality and with hope.

REFERENCES

Barbee, M. (1996). Men's roles and their experience of depression. *Art Therapy, Journal of the American Art Therapy Association, 13,* 28–34.

Elkins, D., Stovall, K. & Malchiodi, C. (2003). American Art Therapy Association, Inc.: 2001-2002 Membership survey report. *Art Therapy, Journal of the American Art Therapy Association, 20,* 28–34.

Junge, M. (1994). *A history of art therapy in the United States.* Mundelein, IL: American Art Therapy Association.

Junge, M. & Wadeson, H. (2006). *Architects of Art Therapy, Memoirs and Life Stories.* Springfield, IL: Charles C Thomas, Publisher, Ltd.

Major, B. Internalized sexism definition (retrieved from Internet October 14, 2007.) From *People's Institute for Survival and Beyond.*

Chapter 11

RECONSIDERING THE WARS BETWEEN ART AND THERAPY

In this essay, I describe and critique a dominant paradigm in the art therapy profession: Art as therapy versus art psychotherapy. Historically, this dichotomy has served as a method to organize thinking and therefore it has organized antagonists as well who align themselves at the poles and consider themselves to represent one position or the other. This split in thinking was inherent in the early days of the profession and survives today for unexplainable reasons. Art in therapy and art psychotherapy are still positioned as opposing and indeed warring forces in an enduring struggle for dominance. They unfortunately represent a "scarcity" model.

These positions were originally tied to the main theorists of art therapy, Margaret Naumburg and Edith Kramer. Kramer recently termed this "The Historical Rift" and speculated that the difference was more tied to the client ages she and Naumburg worked with, than to any difference in philosophy. She stated that her own work was with children and adolescents who often couldn't or wouldn't talk whereas Naumburg usually saw adults in art therapy (Junge & Wadeson, 2006). Art therapy Masters-level education and training programs, however, often represent one extreme pole or the other in their philosophy and training. Although this difference has been eschewed by many with an admonition that art methods and media be determined by treatment goals and plan, many in the art therapy profession today still hold to these as eternally-lasting oppositional forces.

Art in Therapy Versus Art Psychotherapy is a model. A model organizes our thinking about a certain matter and creates comfort in that we can believe we understand the "truth" but it limits our thinking. Some models are powerful; they exist consciously and tacitly in our minds for eons helping us form ideas and see through a particular lens. (Freud's personality theory is an example.) Some models are merely a mish-mosh of illogical proposals, quickly lost—as they should be—in the clouds of time. A model cannot represent nor define reality. It defines a *piece of reality as interpreted by a theorist*, and after it takes hold, it *limits* our conceptualizations because we use the model's abstraction as a lens through which to focus on a bit of reality. As all art therapists know, the visual image we give to an idea, in turn, defines what we look at and what we see. In my opinion, the art therapy profession desperately needs a new model beyond the Art as Therapy Versus Art Psychotherapy one. It needs a new model with imagery powerful enough to eclipse this old one as an artifact of the past. The new model must capture the imagination of the profession and move it forward.

Art therapists tend to think of the positions of art as therapy and art psychotherapy as mutually exclusive and in our measurement-oriented society with our awareness of limited resources; this is a scarcity model because there is only so much to go around. By definition then, when there is more of one, there must be less of the other.

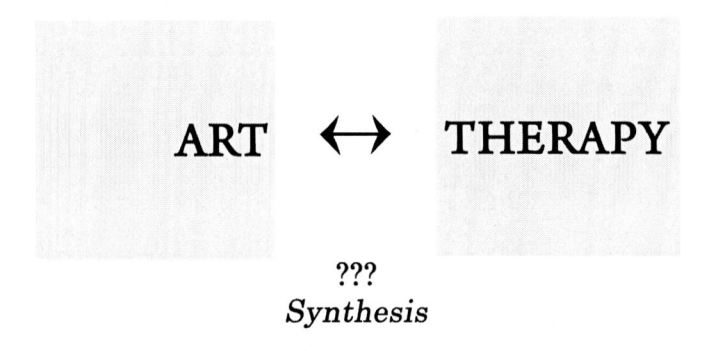

Figure 11-1. "Art as Therapy Versus Art Psychotherapy Model."

In this essay, I trace the roots of the Art as Therapy Versus Art Psychotherapy Model within the art therapy profession and the larger society and take a look at the tacit but powerful assumptions and dynamics implicit in and underlying it. When we live solidly embedded within a powerful world view or reality, like Art in Therapy Versus Art Psychotherapy, we cannot see the forest for the clouds. It is only when change has already occurred at the edges that we may look back and see the shape of where we have been and what has gone before. It is only when we can stand outside and see the whole that we may have departed from, that we are able to envision other possibilities. It is my contention that many of us have already moved beyond the model, but we have not much noticed it because we have not yet seen the emergence of a powerful new model to hold our imagination and explode our thinking. I argue that the old model is no longer a useful tool through which to conceptualize who we are and what we do. But note: a change of world view, and that is what this must be, is remarkably complex and the images through which we organize ourselves and our collective thinking reside deep within us and are hard to shake. They serve the comfortable purpose of providing familiarity and conventions of habit which may have been essential in the past and were important to our understanding.

As a first step, it is my intention to name, to define, to give boundary to the model of Art as Therapy Versus Art Psychotherapy. I will also speculate on some of the reasons why this model continues to provide so much oppositional energy for us and what purpose it serves for art therapists to keep it going. This part of the conversation concerns questions about the identity of the art therapist and the model as an expression of a sexist oppressive society which art therapists, as part of the *zeitgeist* have internalized. Then, I present a second model which we are currently using which I call the Multiple Personality Model, which I believe is also no longer useful. Finally, I will present a new model–frankly a first-cut, which I hope will yield fresh insights and new ways of approaching the art therapy profession as we look to the challenges ahead. I believe that we have placed ourselves in a dark forest which we no longer need, but which we must become consciously aware of so that we may move to the edge of the forest to look toward a vision of new possibilities.

The Art as Therapy Versus Art Psychotherapy argument has often dominated the annual American Art Therapy Association conferences and thinking. Even when it wasn't in the forefront, it was a strong undercurrent and remains so today. The current drive of the American Art Therapy Association is to advocate "cross training"–meaning, the training of art therapists in other mental health disciplines such as counseling. This integration, if it were to happen, is definitely a crossroads which would mean a vastly different future for art therapists and would occur against the loud voices of many experienced art therapists who view it as a relinquishing of the hard-won art therapist identity akin to death. Therefore it seems especially important *now* to carefully address the concepts underlying the Art as Therapy Versus Art Psychotherapy Model. Let me give you an example.

Some years ago, the art therapy Masters program I directed at Loyola Marymount University in Los Angeles changed the name of its degree title from "Clinical Art Therapy" to "Marital and Family Therapy."[1] ("Clinical Art Therapy" was retained in parentheses after "Marital and Family Therapy.") This change was made to keep our graduates eligible to sit for the Marriage and Family Therapy License in California. To change the name was a severe loss for us, but we saw it as a necessary adaptation to the prevailing winds of change in the state and that it was imperative to keep our wonderfully-trained graduates viable in the shrinking mental health job market. We did not believe that the name change would result in students abandoning their art therapy heritage or identity, nor indeed their art.

Soon I began to hear strong, loud voices at conferences and in the art therapy literature bemoaning the loss of art in the California programs and warning of dire dangers of this nationally. Despite the fact that the doomsayers imagined such a future, their cries had no basis in reality or fact. (This fear of "loss of the art" seems a persistent, ongoing, if somewhat paranoid, fear in the life of the art therapy profession.) I believe this notion still exists and is prevalent today. As the Director of the Loyola Marymount art therapy Masters program, I often spoke out asserting that this was not the reality–the "facts" didn't seem to make a difference. The "facts" were that art in the curriculum was not changed in any way from the program originally approved by the American Art Therapy Association's Education and Training Board in 1979. In fact, the name change allowed us to include *more* opportunities for engagement with the art process within the classroom and academic program. The concern that art or art therapy was totally or almost totally removed from the curriculum was simply

---

1. The other art therapy programs in California made this change as well.

ridiculous. Indeed, at the strictly quantifiable level there was *more art* than there had been in previous years.

Nevertheless, the idea that art was fast disappearing from art therapy seemed embalmed in stone and in the profession's collective consciousness—it strikes me as an ongoing fear which drives too much of what organized art therapy does. (I believe there to be some kind of *guilt about art* evidenced by many art therapists. The amount of discussion that continues about how much or how little is, in my opinion a form of denial combined with resistance to embracing the future.) At one annual conference of the American Art Therapy Association, the major opening panel of the general session was titled "Death of Art therapy." The panel followed this line of thinking: Most panelists felt we were headed down the road to Armageddon because of our profound longing to become other kinds of mental health people and our having ceased to hold art dear. (I'm sure the irony is not lost on you of art therapists being so defined by and attached to words.)

Soon after, Patricia Allen's article appeared in the American Art Therapy Association journal titled "Artist in Residence: An Alternative to Clinification for Art Therapists." With this paper—very important for the profession—Allen virtually single-handedly started a studio art movement, wherein clients would come into art therapists painting studio and work along side of them. In this way, Allen maintained, the art remained central while words were irrelevant. Allen placed herself and her colleagues square on the art side of the Art as Therapy Versus Art Psychotherapy model and therefore against art psychotherapy (Allen, 1992). Allen, who had been one of the "Death" panelists defined "clinification" as the art therapist acquiring the skills and coloring of other mental health disciplines while steadily abandoning art. Allen asserts that the clinification approach depends on verbal discussion and intervention and not on the art image. She stated that art psychotherapy doesn't use the art therapist's art background, and that any well-trained clinician can do it. Allen cited Ault's 1977 conference presentation, the title of which was "Are You an Artist or a Therapist?" This was a useful question in 1977, but I propose that it is no longer a useful question because the implication is that if you are one you cannot be the other.

Allen's clear and elegant formulation takes a side in the war and defines many of the explicit and tacit assumptions underlying the Art as Therapy Versus Art Psychotherapy Model. While it is not my intention here to argue against Allen's position, I cannot go forward letting stand her contention that any reasonably trained clinician can do art therapy. With a stroke of her pen, Allen eliminated 60 years of theory, almost 40 years of Masters-level art therapy training and millions of hours of carefully thoughtful and compassionate integrated art therapy practice.

Frankly, I find it insulting to be accused of "losing the art" because I am an art psychotherapist–always have been and always will be. I have been a committed artist since I was 12 years old and I continue to be. This includes my ongoing work as a painter, but it also involves my creative process through everything I am and do. Helen Landgarten who invented the term "clinical art therapy" has been a painter throughout her life. Other examples are Robert Wolfe who is a psychoanalytically-trained art therapist and a fine sculptor and Robert Ault who, after he left teaching at Emporia State University and being an art therapist at the Menninger Foundation in Topeka, Kansas, opened his own art school where among other things, he painted every day and exhibited regularly. The counter examples are many.

From an historical perspective, the Model of Art as Therapy Versus Art Psychotherapy evolved in two ways. First, it came from the art therapy profession's history still alive in the generations of art therapists trained by the two great pioneers and theoreticians Kramer and Naumburg. While their ideas were undoubtedly around before in the *zeitgeist*, most art therapy educational programs historically and today mainly attach themselves and their philosophy to one or the other ideas of these women. The second way is the art therapy profession's natural embeddedness in the prevailing ideas of western cultural dualism since Galileo and Newton, the Renaissance and the Age of Reason.

THE STRUCTURE OF DIALECTICS

The structure of the Model of Art as Therapy Versus Art Psychotherapy is a dialectical one, and I'd like to make a brief foray into epistemological and philosophical roots of dialectics for further understanding of where art therapists are getting our history. There are two distinct bodies of theory relating to dialectics. First, there is the Aristotelian dialectic which assumes a given set of premises and offers tools of logic with which to decide the issue at hand. This method is about proofs and aims to establish a *truth.* The second body of dialectical theory, based in the Hegelian perspective, assumes an *historical evolution* in which two opposing forces contend with each other. The first force is the already accepted thesis or ideology (I assume this is the *art as therapy* position. The second force, in this case *art psychotherapy*, is positioned against it and, according to Hegelian dialectics, both are eventually replaced with a new synthesis.) This is a theory about power. Why have we needed a power theory in art therapy and why has it had such staying power?

The history of organized art therapy through its professional organization of the American Art Therapy Association (AATA) has been a history of intense, strong personalities, mostly female, and of many internal wars. One of the ways in Western thought, we most powerfully define ourselves is through our contact with the *other—often* thought of as "the enemy." We need a psychological awareness of where we end and they begin in order to exist; we need to know certainly that we are *different* from them. (An example is that when the Soviet Union after such a long time, ceased being our cold war enemy, Americans often flailed about, in search of ourselves. Another, more recent example is the current President, George W. Bush's definition of "the axis of evil" implying that the United States is "the good one.")

Origins of the Model of Art as Therapy Versus Art Psychotherapy

You can't have a war without an enemy and war can serve an important unifying function. Note America's designation of the Iraq war and terrorism as our enemies. War keeps both parties engaged on the field of battle and with enough energy going to try to stay alive. In addition, it keeps armies of soldiers solidly aligned behind the generals—Kramer and Naumburg, in this case.

In the long war of Art as Therapy Versus Art Psychotherapy we have had some pacificists and conscientious objectors. We have also had defectors who left the field and went to the edges—went AWOL in disgust and even despair weary from battle. But strangely, the center has held and marvelously the art therapy profession has *stayed alive.* Although AATA may be an organization of individualists, most of us do not drift off to join other camps. We do not become full-time artists or full-time psychotherapists *sans* art.

Art Therapy

(Art) Education Kramer	(Art) Psychotherapy Naumburg
Emphasis on creative process	Artwork as symbolizing communication, projection of inner world to outer
Little or no verbalization	Verbalization leading to understanding and interpretation

Figure 11-2. "Two Pioneer Art Therapy Theorists: Origins of the Model of Art as Therapy Versus Art Psychotherapy."

The dialectical Model of Art as Therapy Versus Art Psychotherapy can be understood as an ideological battle for control and power within the profession, which had a tremendously important purpose and which holds within its design our resistance to letting it go. Because, as we battle, we face each other and *stay connected*. Embracing, we stay locked irrevocably in mortal contact. With the *other as different* we can know and define ourself and our own boundary. And most essentially, we can know ourself as *not alone* in the world in the most profound of existential terms.

I wonder if the "Death of Art Therapy" panel and Allen's sounding of the "clinification" alarm may have been as much a defensive maneuver against a perception of an evolving sense of loneliness as it was about a system of ideological truth. Allen warns that the survival of the field depends on the art therapist's deep connection to art. And she implies that the psychotherapy side of the model is without art.

ART VERSUS THERAPY IS A MALE MODEL

A dialectical model is a decidedly male model. The descriptive terms are individualistic, competitive, non-relational and are often about war. The two sides of the dialectic coin are not about dialogue or conversation. They are about two lawyers with loud voices trying to shout each other down. Synthesis is supposed to happen only after eons of historical time. In my opinion, in art therapy this synthesis occurred long ago, but because of the stranglehold exerted by the model, few have noticed.

The Women's Movement was probably the most important of the twentieth century and there has been much change. Nonetheless, we still primarily live in a patriarchic society and often wear patriarchic garb without even noticing it. Most art therapists are women; many would define themselves as feminists. Unfortunately, this does not preclude our exhibiting internalized sexism from the culture and unconscious attachment to habitual male ways of thinking and being, on which much of our formal and informal education has been based. Attachment has been long recognized as an important survival mechanism. Sometimes it is called "identification with the aggressor" or, in this case, the oppressor.

To visualize another model, we might take the component parts of our art therapy systems including ourselves, and reformulate an image within the quite different context of evolving notions of feminist conceptualizations. The image might emerge from our own stories of who we are and what we have experienced and we would tell it to each other. It could be collaborative, relational, community and contextually embedded. It could be less individualistically and competitively based, less reductionistic, less analytical in motive and less separated. It could be an open systems model with permeable boundaries able to open and close, to be frankly nurturing and frankly instrumental as needed. It could be both container and contained. Empathy would be the tool for knowing and for the relating of the parts.

THE ART THERAPIST'S IDENTITY: ARTIST AND THERAPIST

Art therapists tend to define themselves using a parts model: for example, they are therapist, artist, teacher, clinician, healer. This reductionistic and partialized model of discrete, bounded wholes assumes art therapists are a collection of parts bounded off from each other. Models like this which divide us into parts without attempting to help us understand how the parts relate to each other, dance with each other, meld into each other toward integration, or even disappear altogether, in my opinion are not useful images for the evolution of art therapy identity or practice. I believe most art therapists would describe themselves as some sort of integrated whole, but the visualization of the parts model keeps us from seeing ourselves this way.

Art and our identity as artists contain essential meanings to us and to our profession as a whole, and most of us came to art therapy through our own experience of art's profound ability to heal. Nonetheless, I am interested that many students and art therapists of long standing, experience tremendous conflict and even guilt about their involvement in art therapy as if it were an immense betrayal of art and of their core identity—as if being an art therapist was some dirty little secret. Some years ago, a student of mine wrote of her tremendous struggle in finding "peace" as an art therapist. She stated that she identified herself as an artist, not a weekend painter, or a creative person. For her, undertaking education to be an art therapist involved losing her art. She called it "the abandonment" of one's art.

My doctoral work involved a study of creativity in visual artists and writers (Junge, 1994). It will come as no surprise that for all the artists I interviewed, art provided the core meaning for their lives and always had. The calling to be an artist often comes early and is the envelope of identity through which all else is sifted. One artist in my study, a well-known movie writer, playwright and novelist, told me of his sense memory as an infant, of being held in his mother's arms at the movies. His writing throughout his life was a return to the containing protection and pleasures of his mother's arms. A family doctor and friend for years always began our conversations with "Are you painting?" It was very clear to me that anything I might do was not as valuable as my life as a painter. When Harriet Wadeson and I recently researched retired art therapists, we found that many felt guilty about not doing "enough" art, now that they ostensibly had time (Junge & Wadeson, 2005).

Tinkering with depths and vicissitudes of identity found in the dynamics of these stories is no easy matter and should not be taken lightly. I believe not nearly enough attention is paid to the ramifications of identity shifts and struggles in art therapy training programs. There is the additional issue for women artists and thus for many art therapists—the problem of sexism historically and as it continues today. Given the restraining edicts of the culture, its lack of support and ambiguous messages, it is something of a miracle that women artists have survived at all. I believe we can understand many women art therapists' conflicts and guilt over abandoning their art as a *culturally overdetermined* blaming of themselves as victims because there has not been adequate recognition of the remarkable weight and pain of the chains in which women artists work. Cohen (1983) in her article "The Woman Artist: Struggle for Self-Realization postulates that it is actualizing her strong creative urge which hurls the woman toward conflicts which usually are oppositional to other women's roles and that her creative gifts can become additional burden and even a threat to the evolution of personality. Chicago (1975) a well-known pioneer of feminist art wrote of her own struggles as a woman artist.

So where does all this leave us?

- With a model pitting art as therapy against art psychotherapy which through its structure and implications encourages and supports this burden and this split.
- In a mental health profession which is predominantly women.
- In a culture where women are oppressed.
- In a culture where women artists are doubly oppressed.
- In the art therapy profession where most are women who are culturally oppressed and where many continue to grapple with stunningly deep and painful conflicts about their art.
- In a struggling profession where the work is difficult and underpaid.

And in a profession in which we work within a dominating, oppressive paradigm or model which offers us little solace or support and which, in fact, often tears us down. It is an outdated paradigm which does not deepen nor enrich our work lives, but instead quantifies them into measurable but never enough parts (e.g., the current Supermom image.) It is a paradigm which does not support *our need for each other as collaborative beings or our longings for community*. Although the paradigm may be outdated, most art therapists exist within it and within the constraints and mandates of the cultural *zeitgeist.*

In my opinion, art therapists understandably have a serious self-esteem problem. The Art as Therapy Versus Art Psychotherapy paradigm holds us within a model of individualism, competition and armed battle against the *other* as enemy. If one "wins" the other loses; but truly both lose. It is a model in which an enemy is ultimately necessary to the existence and maintenance of the identity of both sides, but it is a war which no one can ever win.

TOWARD AN ALTERNATIVE MODEL

As I have argued in this essay, models organize our thinking and simultaneously limit our thinking and knowing. They arrange our conceptualizations in a comfortable habitual way to help us defend against the chaos at hand. They can also provide blinders in that they only let us see a certain designated landscape within their boundaries, helping us with our fears and creating a kind of "comfort zone" wherein sameness and consistency give pleasure at their predictability. McWhinney (1992) in his book *Of Paradigms and System Theories* writes of the advantages:

> Human societies of today need—as much as they ever did—relevant and contemporary symbolizations of their universe, their values, their assumptions and their archetypal exemplars. They need these symbols to provide coherent systems of belief and to resolve current issues. These accumulations of belief coalesce into a world view . . . through which, order, meaning and a sense of control and ownership are maintained.

The dialectical model of Art as Therapy Versus Art Psychotherapy is inadequate, outdated, and psychologically damaging. It is a hindrance, not a help, in resolving the complex issues which art therapists face today. We need powerful visions and images to lead us to imaginative ways of thinking and seeing. A new model should not be divisive, but must include person, practice and community. It should be relational, interactive and enhancing in attitude and values. I propose that the art therapist should be a *creator of meanings*. The model should contain open systems which evolve over time and which envision and support a systems perspective of the art therapist and art therapy practice immersed within the world. And it should include the quality for system *change* and thus for *model change*.

Profound world changes have stirred us all as we move into a new century which will present new challenges. It is a moment for imagination, innovation and boldness. But then, art therapists have always been good at that.

REFERENCES

Allen, P. (1992). Artist in residence: An alternative to "clinification" for art therapists. *Art Therapy, Journal of the American Art Therapy Association, 9*, 22–29.

Ault, R. (1977). Are you an artist or a therapist?-A professional dilemma for art therapists. *Proceedings of the 1976 annual American Art Therapy Conference: Creativity and the art therapist's identity.* Baltimore, MD.

Chicago, J. (1975). *Through the flower: My struggle as a woman artist.* Lincoln, NE: IUniverse, Inc.

Cohen, T. (1983). The woman artist: Struggle for self-realization. *Women & Therapy, 2.* New York: The Haworth Press.

Junge, M. (1998). *Creative realities, the search for meanings.* Lanham, MD, New York, Oxford: University Press of America.

Junge, M. & Wadeson, H. (2005). The wit and wisdom of the retired art therapist. Research study presented at the conference of the American Art Therapy Association, Atlanta, GA.

Junge, M. & Wadeson, H. (2006). *Architects of Art Therapy, Memoirs and Life Stories.* Springfield, IL: Charles C Thomas Publishers, Ltd.

Malchiodi, C., Allen, P. & Cattaneo, M. (1991). Art therapy: Post-Mortem. *Proceedings of the 1991 annual Art Therapy Conference, Image and metaphor: The practice and profession of art therapy.* Denver, CO.

McWhinney, W. (1992). *Paths of Change.* Newbury Park, CA. Sage Publications.

Chapter 12

THE ART THERAPIST AND AGING

Age doesn't matter much unless you are a cheese.
—Billie Burke

*Happiness is not in the mere possession of money; it lies in
the joy of achievement, in the thrill of creative effort.*
—Franklin D. Roosevelt

*Every loss diminishes one's life—and somehow redoubles
one's responsibility.*
—Fritz Stern

Aging goes against the American grain of eternal youth and vigor. While in other countries aged people are often revered and respected as having lived long enough to achieve considerable wisdom, in America, one is expected to remain eternally young and especially women are congratulated for appearing so. It is said that a man looks mature, but a woman has "let herself go." For most Americans, wearing the visible signs of aging is a fearful prospect. Do wrinkles present the viewer with a future of inevitable death? In a death-denying society, is this why aging is so fearful? The multitude of creams promising youth and an absence of wrinkles and the growing prevalence of cosmetic surgery eschew aging and are intended to turn back the clock for a people perhaps fearful of death.

In the MTV culture, whatever wisdom elders may offer is usually not sought, wanted or valued. The saying "Old age is not for sissies" has been multiply attributed, not the least of which is to the actress

Bette Davis. Gloria Steinem, upon being complemented for not look-ing her age is said to have stated: "That's what 50 looks like these days." Preparing for a 70th birthday last summer, my daughter told me she had read that "70 is the new 40." (She figured that made her 11 and I certainly didn't feel 40!) I consulted with a doctor last week who was surprised at my (advanced?) age. "I thought you were in your 50s," he said. I know of one art therapist who endured many cosmet-ic surgeries and who shaved ten years off her real age, in favor of retaining the perception of youth and the ability to have employment. She may have been absolutely correct about the employment part.

While many of these comments about looking younger than one's chronological age were intended as complements, they not-so-lightly conceal a subtext which proclaims that aging is nothing to be desired and should be warded off as long as possible. Have a look at the myr-iad ads for anti-aging creams and potions in the women's magazines. Ageism reigns and flourishes in America. This is despite the "senior" population growing ever larger, longevity hugely increasing and the first of the baby boomer generation born in 1946, which has applied for social security. An example I know of is a university which attempted to gain a form of accreditation. Despite glowing reports from site teams, they were consistently rejected. With a smart lawyer who based his potential case on the fact that the university was pri-marily for mid-career people, and who threatened to sue for the dis-crimination of ageism, it won and they were given the accreditation they sought.

In my estimation, seniors today are social pioneers. They are the first and largest generation of elders who, thus far, have remained largely invisible to developmentalists. Much of what is supposedly "known" and thought about this age group is shrouded in myth and legend.[1] In this sense "myth" and "legend" equals stories but not truth. Gratefully, there is now the remarkable opportunity to push aside the fogs of legend and learn some truths about this cohort. Attention must be paid.

What is even designated "senior" is often in question. The American Association for Retired People (AARP) can be joined at 55 because they are defined as "seniors." Previously, terms such as "The Aged,"

---

1. Author's note: For a compelling read concerning the myths of old age, I suggest *Beyond Nostalgia: Aging and Life Story Writing* by Ruth E. Ray.

and "The Elderly," were used. We all were expected to retire from our useful years of work at 65 (implying that any use we had to anyone or anything was over) to finally achieve our "Golden years"–which meant we could live out whatever time we had left as we chose. Whether there was any truth in the previous description, it is certainly not the case today. For example, many seniors work full-time or part-time far past any accepted retirement age. Financially, they cannot afford to do anything else. The last life stage, however it is described or positively framed, whether one believes in an afterlife or not, is about understanding the meaning of one's life as lived, achieving a useful present and exploring a realistic future which no longer stretches unknown for many years and–to put it frankly, if uncomfortably–which inevitably ends with death.

As the English language has gotten steadily more positive, the term "Senior" is used because, theoretically, it does not designate negativity. Seniors, whatever they are called, in other countries are revered for their wisdom and suffering gained over a long life. In the United States, at best, seniors are supposed to be sitting around enjoying having nothing to do, playing golf or cards or cruising on a ship to far ports if they have money, bothering nobody preferably and reviewing all the past history of their life. Or at worse: Seniors are a "burden on our family" as part of the sandwich of the "sandwich generation" or living in an assisted living center because they can't live on their own anymore and they can't live with children and this is a way for them to retain some sense of independence. Assisted living is often paid for by children of seniors. They do not matter very much to anyone, except perhaps the old person's family. Whatever contributions the person might have made are thought to be long over. Accomplishments are finished. My Aunt Sis is 100 years old. She is the last of her family of origin to be alive. She lives alone in the apartment she has always lived in. She has a caretaker to help her. She was married–her husband died a number of years ago. She worked in a rental car business, had no children and played golf every day until quite recently. She still walks, with a walker, but she walks.

Historically, very little of the influential developmental literature went further than a person's forties. For example, even Erik Erikson in his important work *Childhood and Society* (1950, 1963, 1968) ostensibly about growth throughout the life cycle, predominantly stopped writing specifics and virtually ended describing his notion of developmental crises in a person after they achieved a synthesis of the intimacy versus isolation crisis[2] in young adulthood. It is my theory that it was only upon reaching the end of his 40s and entering into his own middle and later life that Erikson (and some other developmentalists) finally realized that human growth and development occurs as an ongoing phenomenon even into late life, even until death. Erikson revised his early work to include more developmental phases only when Erikson himself, got old enough to know that development doesn't end with young adulthood. Later, Erikson added another stage of "grand generativity" in his own older years. Then there were the developmentalists who postulated a "mid-life crisis."(We might speculate, that they were having their own.) Even feminist thought virtually ignored the generation of elders as having meaning and still developing. It is only more recently that adult development (as opposed to *child* development) has become a subject worthy of investigation at all (Smelser & Erikson, 1980; Stevens-Long, 1988; Berger, 2001). Gender bias is ongoing. It is true that some mental health literature has focused on aging but it has been the pathology of the elderly that was written about. "Normal" senior development has been mostly invisible. At the first part of the twenty-first century:

- People are living longer than in any previous generation.
- The link between age and retirement is eroding.
- As has been known for a long time, women tend to live longer than men.
- There are more "seniors" than ever before.
- Supposedly, there are or will be more jobs with seniors inhabiting them because they can't afford to "retire" among other reasons.

Assumptions about aging and old age are based on the idea of retirement about age 65. After that, it is said, elderly lives may be pleasant, even stress free. Despite the fact that the notion of a predicted retirement age is growing less and less likely for most people, the myths about aging still prevail. For many years, I gave a slide presentation of art therapy across the developmental life span called "An Introduction to Art Therapy." Preparing to give this presentation to a

---

2. Originally, Erikson proposed a 7th stage of "Middle Adulthood," ages 40-65 and an 8th stage of "Maturity," age 65-death and outlined the two crises that went with each stage, but very little was written about them as contrasted to the stages of the earlier years.

group last year, I went over my slides and was shocked to see that the only artwork I had about the aged was about the past and the idea of life review. But research has raised questions about the universality, even the use for many at all of life review. Research reveals that older adults were no more likely to engage in life review than those in younger generations. Having aged myself, I have, hopefully, acquired more open eyes, and I know that most American seniors do not live in the past, but hold tight to the present and even look forward to the future. The generations of art therapists in their seventies and eighties lived through tumultuous times in the United States–the assassinations of John Kennedy, Martin Luther King, and Robert Kennedy, the up-heavals of the sixties, and 9/11 to name a few. And they have learned from them. This cohort of seniors has a great deal to teach us all about how to live, how to work and how to love; what they have to give is wisdom.

In 2005, at the annual conference of the American Art Therapy Association (AATA,) Harriet Wadeson and I presented our research about the retired art therapist.[3] Our research inquiry was driven by the fact that these days the profession of art therapy has its ever-expanding share of "seniors" in their "golden years." Harriet's and my research was our attempt to highlight this cohort as an important, thoughtful and contributing segment of the art therapy profession–experts who have much to teach us–we speculated–if we only ask. Finding our respondents through an announcement in the American Art Therapy Association *Newsletter*, the American Art Therapy Roster (2004–05) and the list of AATA's Honorary Life Members, we used qualitative methods. Our sample was composed of 31 respondents who were mostly female, self-selected, and primarily in their sixties and seventies. We wanted to explore the current lives of these art therapists, to find what they had learned along the way and what they had to say to future generations. Retired ourselves, we hoped to avoid the stereotype of the forgotten senior in art therapy.

We intended to start our conference presentation with a well-known art therapist who had taken up tap dancing for sheer pleasure in her retirement. We invited her to dance and she accepted. Shortly, before the presentation she told us that she had injured her foot and would be unable to tap dance. This seems to me the perfect metaphor for

---

3. The presentation of research was called "The Wit and Wisdom of the Retired Art Therapist."

aging: The mind is vital and wants to experiment with new skills and ideas, to explore brand-new territories but the body doesn't always support the mind. I make a joke about a "body transplant." But the reality is that there are many wise art therapists thankfully still with us to learn from. They retain agile minds and creative opinions forged from thoughtful years of experiences. There are still many from the pioneering generation who began the professional organization, the American Art Therapy Association.

In our study, we asked about reasons for retiring from professional life. Many people wrote about the changes in university departments and clinic attitude and philosophy, negative administrative politics and funding cuts. One person wrote of "seeing too much sexual abuse in young people"; "forty-three years was enough!" she said. After retirement, the financial hardship for many is considerable—particularly for single people (few have pensions) and many reported that the lack of professional contacts and challenges are tremendous losses to them. About their current contact with art therapy and the American Art Therapy Association (AATA) one wrote "[Art therapy] really doesn't exist for me. I'm still plugged in but feeling a growing distance," and: "AATA doesn't know me nor seem interested except for collecting my dues," "I do not go to the annual AATA conference because it is too expensive."

We are past the era when agencies or universities footed the bill for conference attendance. Long ago, discounts for students were discussed endlessly by AATA and never done, to my knowledge. Now AATA desperately needs discounts for aging art therapists, if they want them to attend the annual art therapy conference; many cannot afford it. The message so far is that the organization doesn't care about their attendance. Another respondent, answering the question about connection to art therapy said: "I read the journal—that's it. I still identify strongly with the field, but I'm happy to be out of the political wrangling."

For positive changes about retirement, respondents wrote: "[I] am my own boss with more choice and less stress," "More freedom, less responsibility, more artwork," "Birthing new friendships," "Wiser and being the master of my days," "More creative—time to create and play," "Still learning." Under negative changes, respondents wrote that they missed students, professional associations and camaraderie with others through the creative process and they missed socially relevant work. Most felt there was a tremendous prejudice against retired people, and that older people tended to be "invisible" even to the art therapy profession. They worried about children and grandchildren and about their own health and "keeping energy up." Guilt about not doing their own art "enough," pursued art therapists even into their retirement. This guilt about artwork is a consistent and ongoing cry for the professional art therapist throughout the working life and it looms large for those who have retired. I have noticed that by becoming art therapists, art therapists seem to feel that at some profound and primitive level they have abandoned their art. "I should do more of my personal art" they say. Perhaps this guilt is inherent in the profession and even acts as a motivating drive for the art therapist to help clients find the pleasures of imagery and creativity. Many in our research about retirees wrote about the need to stay involved with their own art and "not let chores get in the way."

As to the wisdom they wanted to share with succeeding generations of art therapists, one respondent wrote: "Art therapy is a wonderful field, but a difficult profession." Others said, "Stick with it. It is an honorable profession," "Assert yourself." "Stay the course," "Congratulations on choosing a very rich and enriching profession" and "My greatest memories include patients." Of the two major theoreticians in art therapy, Margaret Naumburg died in 1983 and Edith Kramer now in her 90s spends much of her time creating her own artwork.

But of the wise art therapy pioneers who wrote their memoirs in *Architects of Art Therapy* (Junge & Wadeson, 2006) most are still with us. Many are vital, energetic people with important ideas to share. Many still practice art therapy. I know of one who in her eighty-fifth year has established a dynamic group for unwed teenage mothers. This group is offered in the first art therapy clinic in America in a university setting and will have as an important side effect, bringing into the university a whole segment of the population not usually invited nor comfortable there. Many seniors are the art therapy writers, movie-makers and thinkers of the profession. They have been the movers and shakers and have not "retired" from that.

Aging art therapists include many past presidents of the American Art Therapy Association who first established and expanded the profession. Among them are those who initiated and promoted education and training programs for art therapists, and educational and professional standards and ethics. (There are now more than forty art therapy masters-level programs and two Ph.D. programs in the United States.) They ably fought adversity and battles, internal and external, and have prevailed and they have learned from their vast experiences. That art therapy continues to exist as a profession and AATA continues to expand in membership is largely due to their efforts. Their acquired wisdom is a precious gift and, I propose that it should not be lost to the newer generations of art therapists, but must be actively sought, honored and preserved. It is our very important and stimulating history.

A Korean friend and I talked about the respect for the aged in her country and the apparent lack of it here. Senior art therapists as social pioneers are treading underbrush and paths where the road is not yet established. In my estimation, they are also creating and contributing an important developmental life stage with contributions still to make to the art therapy profession and to the world. It is my sincere hope that American art therapy can buck the prevailing tide against making the elderly in our midst invisible and be as innovative as the art therapy pioneers were, to take full advantage of our own cohort of art therapy seniors. They offer us knowledge, wisdom and downright good ideas honed from the hot fires of the creation of a profession. I have found these pioneers to be generous, supportive, dedicated and consistently passionate about art therapy. Against many odds, they continue to care. To ignore them would not only be a shame; the art therapy profession's loss would be a tragedy.

REFERENCES

Berger, K. (2001). *The developing person through the life span.* New York: Worth.

Erikson, E. (1950, 1963). *Childhood and society.* New York: W.W. Norton & Co.

Erikson, E. (1968). *Identity, youth and crisis.* New York: W.W. Norton & Co.

Smelser, N. & Erikson, E.(Eds.) (1980). *Themes of work and love in adulthood.* Cambridge, MA: Harvard University Press.

Stevens-Long, J. (1988). *Adult life: Developmental processes.* Palo Alto, CA: Mayfield.

Part V

CLINICAL APPLICATIONS OF ART THERAPY

Chapter 13

THE BOOK ABOUT DADDY DYING:
A PREVENTIVE ART THERAPY TECHNIQUE TO HELP FAMILIES DEAL WITH THE DEATH OF A FAMILY MEMBER[1]

Grief rituals such as traditional funerals and memorials allow the expression of emotional reactions within a unique context and thereby can help stimulate both the mourning process and the restoration to normal life. Creating a book about the deceased is described in this essay. By making a book which is permanent, stable and continuing, family members are given permission to express and communicate their many feelings of grief within the explorative safety of the therapeutic milieu.

Rituals consist of symbolic acts and often objects with symbolic value may be used. Being able to work with the symbolic act or object involves both an intense focus and a certain amount of distance and can free up the investment of psychic energy for real life activities. A book is a container of memories, feelings and of a specific history. Like a life, it has a beginning and an end and can provide a symbolic way of working on the sense of loss caused by death in the family. This may be particularly important in helping young children gain some level of understanding and comfort.

This essay was first printed in 1985 in the days when Kubler-Ross and her colleagues were beginning to restate the tremendous impor-

---

1. This essay is reprinted with changes from Junge, M. (1985). The book about daddy dying: A preventive art therapy technique to help families with the death of a family member. *Art therapy, Journal of the American Art Therapy Association*, March 4–10.

tance of an appropriate grieving as a necessary and significant act of a life. From about 1975 on, we experienced a cultural revolution in our attitudes toward death and its vicissitudes with a resulting proliferation of thought and literature about death and dying. From the pioneering work of Kubler-Ross (1969) and others we gained important new insights including that of the impact of death on those left behind.

When this article was first published, it described the book technique with families trying to survive a death. In the years since publication, I and many art therapists have used the book technique, not only with families, but also with other people undergoing separation or death–such as families and individuals undergoing divorce, or a potential death from AIDS or cancer. The fact of the book's reality and concreteness in the world seems to give considerable comfort as a "gift" left behind, while the process of book-making enables the system to remain open to the inclusion of the difficult subject of death and therefore creates a timely intervention to evoke the experience of grieving.

Before Kubler-Ross' clarity of vision, death was tucked away in the closet and children were often shielded from its desperate difficulties. Then for a time in the last days of the twentieth century, death and dying became "popular" and was a focus in mental health practice. In the years since, in my opinion, mental health focus has transformed again and in our current culture of "get on with it," "have a good day," and the sense of forced optimism resulting in the "happiness movement," death and grieving are once again in the closet. Although now we are more likely to allow children at funerals and memorials and to have hospice care and facilities for elders and dying people, we still know little about aging and the end of life, despite the dramatic aging of America. For example, "Life Review," which was accepted in the developmental literature as what elders wanted to do, turns out to be a myth for many. Many seniors want to look not backward, but forward.

Ongoing intense grieving is difficult for Americans to see or cope with. For the most part, current language avoids the matter. We seldom hear the word "death." It may be too direct, painful and final a word. Animals are "put down" or "put to sleep. "Passing on" or "passing" or "passing away" are terms more likely to be used than "death" or "dying." These terms often imply a comforting afterlife which many believe in and many don't. Children may be told little more than that the one who died is in heaven. Yet violence, especially gun violence, proliferates in this country and children arrive in our therapy offices having witnessed or experienced the death of a parent.

This essay describes an art therapy technique which is sensitive, honest and encourages a family to focus on their grief, not look away from it. Through the book, it offers enough distance to make important grief possible. I present a clinical art therapy technique to help a family cope with the death of one of its members. The making of a book in which all the family participates is highlighted. A theoretical rationale about bereavement is proposed and two case examples are described. The approach of the "The Book About Daddy Dying" is presented as a model for dealing with the attendant feelings of death in a family. But perhaps its most important benefit to the family is its preventive mental health function, in that appropriate grieving can ward off later problems. In addition, the book's potential as a vehicle for family ritual to aid in the transition from one life stage to another will be discussed.

INTRODUCTION AND THEORETICAL RATIONALE

The importance of the expressive mourning process and its role in successful adaptation in later life to separations and losses, has been emphasized in the psychological literature starting with Freud's seminal work *Mourning and Melancholia* (1917). It has long been well-known in mental health circles that failure to mourn or inadequate mourning by a parent may later result in possible pathological problems in parent-child relationships. Obviously problems may not arise in all cases of death in a family, nor may there result pathology or symptomotology, as a reaction to any crisis is strongly influenced by past and present life experiences, ego strengths and coping mechanisms. However, over the years, the consistent and increasing presence in my clinical practice of families who need help dealing with and communicating about the death of a family member leads me to the notion that we need a reconsideration of the issues involved, as well as the development of new and effective interventions and strategies to deal with loss.

Studies on stress levels' effect on the development of illness have found that the death of a spouse or partner is the greatest stressor there is. The remaining parent whose spouse has suddenly died needs to cope with changed financial, emotional and domestic roles and responsibilities and an uncertain future at a time when she or he is most unable to do so. It is a time when questions from children may not be welcomed nor answered as to the facts of the death, cremation or burial, and so forth. Children may find themselves distanced, isolated and lonely at a time when it is most important that they are able to connect with the remaining parent.

Sometimes the circumstances of death, such as a violent one or a suicide, may be cause for shame and may make the subject of the death itself taboo. Or a surviving parent may mistakenly, and with the best of intentions, want to spare children the pain of loss and therefore not share their own feelings with them. A family covering-over process can be all too likely: the remaining parent overwhelmed with his or her own feelings of sadness, abandonment and confusion, finds it difficult at best to help the children effectively grieve. The surviving parent's silence can convey to the children that death is secret and frightening and cannot be openly discussed. After the intense emotional reaction of the first few days or weeks, the loss may be covered over to become a taboo subject, a hidden and uncommunicated reservoir of pain and secrecy which can lead to the development of family dysfunction and psychopathology.

The reaction of the child, or children, to a death in the family depends on many factors including age, emotional and cognitive development and the emotional closeness to the dead family member. The death may result in loss of residence or change in schools and friends. The child may not only have to cope with the primary loss, but also with her or his feelings of distance from, even abandonment by the surviving parent who, because of the situations noted above or others, is significantly unable to be emotionally available and withdraws from the child. Thus the child experiences a second, perhaps even more devastating loss and has no avenue of communication with which to question or understand. Family therapists have found that the most influential factor in the child's reaction to the loss of the parent and the development of family dysfunction, appears to be the ability of the remaining parent, despite difficult feelings to stay emotionally open and not create distance from the child.

Herz in Carter and McGoldrick (1980) cites four factors which affect a family's reactions and adjustments to a death. These are: (1) the timing of the death in the life cycle of the family; (2) the nature of the death (is it expected or unexpected? Was there a long term of caring for the dying family member or was it a sudden death?); (3) the family position of the dying or dead family member and the emotional significance to the family; and (4) the openness of the family system. Difficulties can arise from a lack of openness in the family system; crucial is the ability of family members, particularly the surviving parent, to be able to be nonreactive to the system's emotional intensity. Despite this intensity, communication of thoughts and feelings must go on. The book described in this paper is a technique to permit family expression and communication and to prevent the premature closing down of the family system.

CASE EXAMPLES

The following case examples show the process of making a book with two families. The first example describes the development of the book idea because of the clinical needs of a particular family. It describes a "nuclear" family with two young children experiencing the death of the father by suicide. The second case example concerns a divorced family, in which the young divorced father died suddenly of cancer; it is intended to underscore the flexibility of the book technique in its adaptability to use with various family constellations.

Case 1: The F. Family

Ms F. came to the mental health clinic with her two young sons, Jimmy, age four and Mark, age seven, two months after the suicide of her husband, Mr. F. who had a lengthy history of depression. The month before his death he had been a patient in a psychiatric hospital where his doctors said he was improved and no longer suicidal; they planned to release him. Ms F. disagreed with the psychiatrist's assessment and asked that her husband be kept for a longer time at the hospital. This was refused. Three days after his release, Mr. F. ingested an overdose of medication and died.

As presenting problems, Ms F. cited intense and ongoing depression in herself. She felt overcome with guilt that she had been unable to convince her husband's doctors of the seriousness of the situation, as well as intense anger at the mental health system. Both sons were described by their teachers as being pervasively sad and unable to concentrate on school work.

The F. family was assigned for therapy to a staff psychologist who saw them for four sessions, which she felt were of little help. Mother wept copiously through those sessions and said she also cried at home whenever she thought of her husband. Naturally preoccupied with the loss of her husband she was unable to disconnect from her constant ruminations long enough to focus on her two young sons and their grief. In session, the psychologist observed that the boys made occasional attempts to gain their mother's attention, but seemed to grow increasingly detached and withdrawn at her lack of response. The psychologist contacted me with the hope that a family art therapy task might serve to focus the family together in a more productive way.

As I thought about the F. family system, it seemed to me that something more than the usual art therapy techniques were needed to symbolically contain the overwhelming thoughts and feelings evoked by the father's suicide. Although there was clearly the overriding need for catharsis to allow for acceptance and support, Ms F's inability to control her feelings in any way had caused her to withdraw from her sons and they from her. Using a structural family theoretical framework, it seemed necessary to help Ms F., if possible, reconnect with her sons, so that she could begin to help them with their loss, as well as perhaps gain some sustenance from them. Appropriate defenses would be supported and confrontation of fragile ones would be avoided. As I look back, however, the book idea may have emerged because I knew education was highly valued in this family and Mr. F. had read nightly to his sons.

The psychologist and I met with the family, to suggest that they make a book together about Mr. F. This would include their memories of him, both good and bad, and events together as a family before his death, questions and answers about the death and, of course, all their feelings. I asked the family to bring in photographs of Mr. F. to include.

We met weekly for six weeks and worked together on the book in the sessions. During our work together Ms F. grew increasingly capable of concentrating and helping her sons to do so. Thus her nurturance of them resumed. The distancing device of making the book and the focus on its pages seemed to allow a damming up of the previous spilling-over feelings in mother, giving her more control and more comfort and thus allowing more room for her sons' feelings. Sometimes the family worked individually and sometimes together on one piece of paper around a central theme. The separate pages remained in a folder with the therapists each week and we told the F. family that when we finished the book, we would get it bound for them to take home.

In the sessions, family communication was emphasized and questions were asked and answered and re-asked and answered again. This was my first experience in working with a very young child undergoing the experience of the death of a parent, and although many developmentalists tend to emphasize the young child's lack of conceptual ability and thus the inability to understand, I found that Jimmy was *trying* to understand. His repeated questions, as well as his ongoing involvement in the work of the book, convinced me of this. With Jimmy I came to believe that the young child must find some way to make sense out of his dramatically changed world in order to be able to go on.

At the end of the six weeks, family and therapists agreed that the book seemed finished. (The six weeks time frame, while reminiscent of a crisis model, was not preplanned, and we would have continued with the chapters as long as it seemed useful.) The therapists agreed to "get the book put together" and we arranged a last meeting. We mounted the newsprint pages on sturdier paper and put four notebook rings through the pages to keep them firmly together. At the last meeting, the family talked about its feelings of doing the book and both family and therapists expressed that they had shared a difficult but special experience together. We recommended that the book be kept in a safe place at home where any family member could read it at will, but that the book be read together by all three remaining family members at least once a week.

One year later, Ms F. called at the insistence of Jimmy who had told her "the book is falling apart and needs to go back to the clinic." We asked Ms F. to bring the boys and the book in for a re-evaluation.

Indeed, the book *was* falling apart literally. We wondered was the family also? The family told us that they had read the book together almost every night for the year. Ms F. stated that the book had given the family an avenue for communicating about Mr. F. and a vehicle whereby they could continue the expression of feelings of all kinds.

Each family member had individually read the book as needed in her or his own way and it was the only thing in this now single parent's house consistently returned to its "safe place" on the shelf.

In our re-evaluation sessions, we created new pages for the book about what had happened to the family in the year since Mr. F.'s death. Ms F. was now attending a widows' group. She had started graduate school with a goal of a career as a teacher. She had recently had a few dates and in the month before the call to the clinic had spent a weekend away from the boys for the first time. The boys had remained with a baby-sitter for the weekend. Jimmy and Mark had settled down in school and were doing well except for occasional spells of "moodiness." Mark still tended to be overaggressive at times and Jimmy had occasional nights when he wet his bed. But generally all family members seemed to be progressing appropriately in their mourning process. Jimmy's urging that the F.'s come to the clinic was seen as an anniversary reaction to Mr. F.'s death, probably exacerbated by Ms F.'s trip away. We took the book and reinforced the binding with notebook "reinforcers" and sent the book and family home with the recommendation that they call us as needed.

At the two-year point, we received no phone call, so we decided to follow-up ourselves. Ms F. reported that all was well. She was still having trouble adjusting to her role change as a single mother feeling overwhelmed and harried at times. She had finished her graduate work and acquired a teaching position which was very rewarding to her. She was still attending the widows' group and had recently begun a relationship that she said "might become very important." Both boys were doing well at school and with friends. Mark, the older had begun to successfully stay overnight at the houses of his friends. Jimmy was not ready for this yet, but his incidences of bed-wetting were down to practically nothing. Both boys had big brothers through the Big Brothers' organization.

Ms F. said that in the second year, they had continued to read the book together though not as often, and that she would sometimes find one or the other of the boys, usually Mark, engrossed in it. She said that they sometimes still cried when they read the book, but that the pain had diminished. The book stayed in its safe place on the shelf for whichever family member might need it. Ms F. expressed her gratitude for the book and later wrote the Director of the Clinic a letter expressing her thanks.

Case 2: The H. Family

The family was being seen in treatment for problems of stress and family disruption at the time of the divorced 32-year-old father's sudden death from cancer after a long illness. The family consisted of Ms H., a single mother with two daughters, Ruthie age five, and Sharon age seven. Also, attending therapy meetings periodically was Ms. H.'s live-in boyfriend. Because of the divorce, this book was viewed as *belonging to the two children.* Mother was included with her children in almost every session as a *therapeutic ally*; she worked hard to help her young children with their feelings of loss.

After the divorce, Ms H. had become a self-supporting single mother with two young children, who typically experienced role overload; the family style tended toward chaos. However, the divorced parents managed to remain on good terms and the girls had regular weekly contact with their father. Ms H. had even contributed financially to help her ex-husband with medical bills and Mr. H. had been included in several therapy sessions with his daughters. Mr. H.'s death was unexpected in spite of his long illness and there had been little anticipatory grieving.

We met in the therapy room to begin the book soon after the family's brief memorial service, and the making of it continued for slightly more than three months. Ruthie and Sharon were invited to bring in photographs to include and simple materials such as markers, crayons, and collage pictures were offered. At times the therapist suggested specific directives. At other times free drawing was encouraged, as themes emerged indirectly. Verbal exploration, discussion and writing on the artwork were encouraged to extend communication. At times, Ruthie and Sharon directed me or their mother what to put on the picture and we wrote it for them.

The weekly therapy sessions were usually attended by Ms H. and her daughters. Because of the divorce, occasionally the two girls met alone with the therapist to allow freedom for information and feelings that might be difficult for the children to say in front of their mother. Communication was enhanced when the girls later shared these pages with their mother. The artwork centered around typical issues of grieving, separation and loss. Following are chronological, though not consecutive, examples of artwork from beginning, middle and ending phases of the book.

The book began with a page of Sharon's (age seven) writing:

Daddy died Sunday. He was lying sick in bed when all of a sudden the door sprang open and two little girls came in. The nurse had to wake him up because right before they came, daddy had just had a shot. And right after they left, he died.

Figure 13-1 by Sharon, shows the visit to the funeral home. Pages in the first section of the book, along with feelings of grief were often informational in tone. In the middle phase of the book more ambivalent expression prevailed and often combined loss and anger.

Figure 13-l. "Daddy at the funeral home" (Sharon).

Figure 13-2 shows pleasant memories of past times, together with loss. Also in this section appropriate underlying anger began to surface.

Figure 13-2. "Memories of Daddy" (Ruthie).

In Figure 13-3 "Daddy Lying Sick in Bed," a spontaneous drawing, Ruthie showed her vivid and mixed feelings. She told me about the picture and I wrote the words on another sheet of paper for her:

Daddy's in pain. He feels sad. I wished [sic] he would say "Hi" to me. I felt mad that he didn't say "Hi" to me because I wasn't tall enough for him to see me. I held his hand. I wanted to kiss him but it was time to go because he fell back to sleep. I felt mad that I didn't get to kiss him. But there was another reason I didn't get to kiss him. I was scared cause he looked scary. He had his mouth open and he was breathing hard and he was moaning.

Figure 13-3. "Daddy lying sick in bed" (Ruthie).

Sharon's drawing of the aggressive video game "Me (Packman) [sic] Eating Up Daddy's Dreams" depicted her normal rage metaphorically (Figure 13-4). In the last month of making the book, Ruthie expressed a reunion fantasy and a wish to have a tangible part of her father. She wanted an ash. Figure 13-5, done by Ruthie in a last session, "Daddy is as nice as a butterfly" shows Daddy floating away, smaller than the butterflies and in the distant top corner.

During his illness, Mr. H. had been involved in a cancer support group utilizing techniques of guided imagery and drawing. After his death the girls had asked to have his drawings and were given them. Both children often mentioned his drawings during the course of our therapy time, as if their father's imagery on paper, now in their possession, had provided some tangible evidence of his presence in their lives They often drew "his pictures" in their book.

Figure 13-4. "Me (Packman) [sic] eating up Daddy's dreams" (Sharon).

Figure 13-5. "Daddy is as nice as a butterfly" (Ruthie).

For the last page of "The Book About Daddy Dying" Ruthie and Sharon chose to render together one of their father's drawings. Sharon illustrated three arches (Figure 13-6) with a handwritten "I love you Daddy" covered by a paper flap (perhaps representing their lost father, the shape resembled a tombstone). Over the arches a vibrant red sun, drawn by Ruthie, is setting into dark blue clouds. The sun has a few spiky points reminiscent of the spikes of hair, typical of the girl's portrayals of their father's head, bald from chemotherapy. It is my speculation that the three arches represent the remaining family group with Mr. H. as the setting sun in the distance.

Figure 13-6. "I love you Daddy" (Ruthie and Sharon).

In the last session, we took the calendar and counted up how long it had been since the day of Mr. H.'s death. The girls wrote: "Daddy died March 14th on Sunday, 14 weeks and two days, three months and a week 100 days ago today," and the book was finished.

A year later, I met Sharon and Ruthie in the clinic waiting room where they were waiting for their mother, who was now participating in a women's support group. Sharon's first words to me were "We still have the book!"

CONCLUSIONS

Each life transition in the developmental phases of a family requires more or less drastic changes by all family members and death demands a uniquely difficult adjustment. The art therapy technique described is based on a family systems approach. It has as its goal the openness and flexibility of the system at a time of great family crisis and change. The book is seen as preventive as well as ameliorating in that if grief is incompletely resolved by the premature closure of the system, family dysfunction and the development of psychopathology can result. I believe that a book such as this can be an instrument of important family ritual to aid in a successful transition.

In making the book, family members are given permission to express, communicate and work on the many feelings of grief within the safety of the therapeutic milieu. They enact and create an important symbolic ritual which gives both focus and distance to their intense feelings.

A book such as that described is a permanent, stable container of memories, feelings and of a history. Like a life it has a beginning and an end and can provide a symbolic way of working on a deep sense of loss. We began and ended our sessions. We began to make and finished making the book's pages. We began and ended reading the book and we began and ended the first year and continued on to the next. And throughout, the book remains in a "safe place" on the shelf to remind us of our beginnings and our endings and our constancy in the face of them. It is a book made by those still living and is representative of the acknowledgment and permanence of important feelings and memories and that those we love live on in our memories and feelings. This acknowledgment can be crucial in the process of saying goodbye, for it is the beginning of letting go and of going on.[2]

REFERENCES

Freud, S. (1917 [1915]). "Mourning and Melancholia," in *The standard edition of the complete psychological works of Sigmund Freud*, Vol. XIV (1914–1916). London: The Hogarth Press, 1957.

Herz, F. (1980). The impact of death and serious illness in the family life cycle, in Carter, E. & McGoldrick, M., (Eds.) *The family life cycle.* New York: Gardiner Press.

Kubler-Ross, E. (1969). *On death and dying.* New York: McMillan Publishing Co.

---

2. My father read to me nightly when I was a small child. He died when I was 30. I spent many years working on my grief. This clinical work and article paralleled and enabled my own grief work.

Chapter 14

FAMILY ART EVALUATION AND THERAPY

MY BACKGROUND AS A FAMILY ART THERAPIST

I consider family art therapy my specialty. Having been a family art therapist for more than thirty years (since 1971 to the present,) I have practiced family therapy and family art therapy in clinics and in private practice. For the last few years, I have done consultation and clinical supervision for a mental health clinic on Whidbey Island, in the Pacific Northwest where I now live. Sometimes I demonstrate family art therapy and in late 2005 I did a three-session seminar about family therapy.

I went back to school for my master's in my thirties because I was bitten by the family therapy bug and in my graduate internship I was lucky to fall into the major training center for family therapy in Los Angeles–Cedars-Sinai Hospital, Thalians Community Mental Health Center. In addition, I was lucky to be "found" and trained by a revered staff member there, pioneer art therapist Helen Landgarten. Helen, one of the pioneers of art therapy, coined the term "clinical art therapy," and innovated the first art therapy graduate program west of the Mississippi at Immaculate Heart College in Hollywood, CA. Helen virtually invented the concept of "the directive." Luckily for me, she was well-versed in thinking, conceptualizing and practicing family art therapy.

I joined the art therapy graduate program at Immaculate Heart as a teaching faculty member soon after it began; directed by Helen Landgarten, it was family art therapy focused. The program moved to Loyola Marymount University in 1980 where I continued as professor and Associate Chair and eventually, I was department chair there for many years.

Virtually my first personal therapy experience was family therapy. My son (now in his early forties) was 18 months old. My daughter was in kindergarten. We were referred by the school director to therapist Helen Reid. Full of motherly guilt, I called for an appointment and she said to bring the whole family in. I realized immediately, although I didn't have "therapy words" for it at the time, what an important intervention that was; it immediately shifted the "blame" away from one person—often the mother, or the "identified patient." In Helen Reid's office, the family dynamics played themselves out through the immediacy of in-the-room behavior. And so began my life-long romance with family therapy.

Since the 1930s of the twentieth century the focus in art psychotherapy and psychology has largely been on the individual and individual development. In art therapy educational programs, beginning on the east coast, the emphasis was usually psychodynamic training which if neo-Freudian, and not strictly Freudian, was advanced. There was neither the "global village" then, nor today's emphasis on diversity and multiculturalism. Boundaries were usually the individual's psyche and the United States, Caucasians were seen as "the norm." This artificial model of boundaries was widely taught and felt in the mental health community as a whole was a deeply embedded "truth." It reflected our prevailing and vastly influential philosophy which emerged from the manifest destiny of the opening of the western United States. It proclaimed our perspective of the grand and brave individual, usually male, carving out the wilderness. It was a limited, white perspective.

Now at the beginning of the twenty-first century, hopefully we have learned something and have moved forward; we know our current world has become too complicated for individual thinking and conceptualizing. We are aware of a multitude of differences in world views. We have moved away from psychotherapy as natural science which we now see as an important approach, but not necessarily *truth*, nor the *only* approach. In my opinion, the obvious paradigm shift needed in art therapy, not exactly new, is toward a systems approach. Systems thinking is most helpful and, I think, should be taught more in art therapy educational systems. That much training in art therapy and psychology is still individualistic is drastically outdated. But merely to invite family members into the consulting room does not family therapy make. *It is a matter of a different way of thinking about change.* Systems thinking establishes a different method from individual thinking of considering *change* and is natural to any painter; a painting is a system in which all parts must work together to make a whole. To change one thing is to transform the whole. For example, to change a bit of color in an artwork is to transform the whole painting and the rest must be adjusted to fit the change. To put it simply; a system is a parts/whole concoction in which the whole is greater than the sum of the parts. Consider a horse. Simply putting all the parts together does not create a horse. *Boundaries* are artificial and metaphoric limits which may be drawn around a family, a neighborhood, or in much larger terms–the solar system. But it is evident that boundaries are mental constructs, are created and are not usually innate. All parts within the boundary influence the whole and these parts must be taken into consideration. For example, Hurricane Katrina must be understood not as a single episode, but as an influential happening of a particular and specific time and place which directly impacted certain people of New Orleans, but which the ripples of were felt by many. And most people today would agree that the federal government's lack of timely intervention, through the ripple effect, created both psychological and functional implications which still impact the people of New Orleans and our nation as a whole.

Language is an important issue for all art therapists and all psychotherapists. Art therapy is sometimes thought of as "non-verbal." Typically, this means that one does not talk when one does art therapy and spoken language is not part of the process. I do not use it that way in my practice, nor do I consider art therapy non-verbal. And there are plenty of other art therapy practitioners effectively using language as part of their work. But the created art image is non-verbal, often primitive and from-the-unconscious communication and if the art therapist is able to "read" the non-verbal communication, she or he can gain a description of the person or family's inner life inaccessible to words.

Unfortunately, spoken language (English) is still the *sine qua non* of the educated person and all too often the language of psychotherapy and of change. Language is what is valued and desired. (I had clients referred to me in a mental health clinic, because they would not talk and their therapists became bored.) As art therapists we do not need to be reminded that expressive communication often is not couched in language and that many of our clients need imagery to get to their deeper feelings. We know "creative voices" come in many colors and sometimes do not speak in words at all.

After observing the power of groups in an alternative education program I innovated in the 1960s in the barrios of East Los Angeles, "Operation Adventure," I wanted to find out more about groups. About 1969, I attempted to take the group course at the Group Psychotherapy Institute, but was told it was full, so I took a family therapy course instead. Through the two-way mirror, I watched a talented therapist, Joan Schain, work with a family over a ten-week period and I was fascinated. At the end of the class, I asked Joan if she would train me—it was the era of paraprofessionals. She said: "I would, but you wouldn't have anything when you finished. Why, don't you go back to school?" And so I did.

Probably I was already a systems thinker when I went to school—I have come to feel one either has the "gene" for systems or one doesn't. I got wonderful training in systems thinking at Cedars—in particular from the Director Dr. Saul Brown, and my clinical supervisor, Dr. Ellen Ruderman and, of course, from Helen Landgarten. I often had the opportunity to observe families through the two-way mirror and watched therapists working with them—invaluable education both about families and about how to do therapy with them. I learned family art therapy as Helen Landgarten's apprentice. It is my strong belief that without a supervisor who really knows and supports family therapy, it is very difficult to get through one's, quite natural, resistance and almost ubiquitous individual training.

I wanted to go to Philadelphia to study family therapy with Salvador Minuchin in his Child Study Institute there, but I had young kids, a young husband, and no extra money. So basically, I learned family therapy through doing and reading everything I could get my hands on, and saw video tapes of major figures in the field working. I had a close friend and colleague as interested in family work as I, May Hartman, and we met regularly and "consulted" with each other. I began teaching family art therapy in the early 1970s. Those were the days when famous family therapists often came to Los Angeles to give demonstrations of their work to mental health professionals with a "live" family. I was lucky to see most of the masters in action. Some I wanted to emulate and some I didn't want to be anything like, but it was immensely useful to have those live models to work from.

Family art therapy has been a part of Masters graduate programs in art therapy for many years. Nonetheless, in training programs, it has tended to be one course and a matter of inviting family members into an individual's therapy session, to gain information for the therapist or toward a particular individual goal and it has not usually been systems thinking. Family art therapy in graduate art therapy training has tended to be a sidebar of the more traditional psychodynamically-oriented art therapy. Much art therapy literature on family art therapy has been individual papers in a journal or a chapter in a book demonstrating it as an offshoot, or one-of-many approaches to art therapy. There are very few books on the subject. The art therapy program at Loyola Marymount University in Los Angeles is the only one I know of with a family systems focus throughout.[1] (This occurred because three of the main faculty and the Chair were family thinkers who were experienced and passionate about family work and were well trained in family art therapy.)

HISTORY AND DEVELOPMENT OF FAMILY ART THERAPY

Hana Yaxa Kwiatkowska (1978) invented and established family art therapy at the National Institute of Mental Health, part of the National Institutes of Health in Maryland. She worked in the psychiatric branch of the Institute with families of schizophrenic children and other mental disorders. While much of her actual work was done in the 1960s and 1970s and although she published articles about art with families, she did not publish her book on the subject until 1978 (*Family Therapy and Evaluation Through Art*). Kwiatkowska joined the National Institute of Mental Health in 1958 and began to use family art with schizophrenics and their families, *as evaluation*. She asked each family member to draw a separate family picture. Essentially emphasizing the revelation of intrapsychic processes through the art, Kwiatkowska discovered that the material could be reviewed with the family for the purpose of clarifying dynamics and patterns of interaction. She used this information to create a number of research projects. Kwiatkowska developed a research protocol with schizophrenics and hysterics and a family art evaluation procedure.

---

1. The art therapy graduate program at Loyola Marymount University also prepares students to take the Marriage and Family Therapy Licensing exam.

Helen Landgarten's *Family Art Psychotherapy* was published in 1987. Focusing on her clinical cases and from a psychodynamic and systems approach, Landgarten described her cases from her perspective as a family systems art therapist. In 1993, Debra Greenspoon Linesch edited *Families in Crisis: Overcoming Resistance Through Nonverbal Experience*. This book consists of a number of family-focused chapters with a range of problem populations. Each chapter is by a separate author which originally was a Masters thesis in the Loyola Marymount Art Therapy program. There is a beginning chapter by Linesch titled "Family Systems and the Creative Process" and an ending chapter which takes "The Second Look." In 2001, Doris Arrington published *Home is Where the Art Is*. In 2004, Shirley Riley and Cathy Malchiodi presented *Integrative Approaches to Family Art Therapy*. *Family Art Therapy: Foundations of Theory and Practice* by Christine Kerr and Janice Hoshino was published in 2007. (The reader is referred to Chapter 13 in this book "The Book About Daddy Dying: A Preventive Art Therapy Technique to Help Families Deal with the Death of a Family Member.") Of the nine authors mentioned above, four were professors at Loyola Marymount University and were trained as family art therapists at Cedars-Sinai Hospital in Los Angeles.

ASSESSING THE FAMILY

To create a viable treatment plan, in the first sessions the family art therapist must assess the family's needs as a whole. This does not mean evaluating *individuals* within the family, but understanding the interpersonal style and needs of the family as it enacts its process in the therapy office. The therapist can be pretty certain that the process acted out in the consulting room is the same as that acted out by the family at home. To aid this process, I always use a family art task in the first session.[2] Following are general theories I use in assessing and planning treatment goals and procedures, the modified first family art therapy task, and a case example.

My works rests on the central assumption that *everything has meaning*. Therefore, I consider how I introduce myself and when I introduce

---

2. My version was modified from Landgarten's (1987) art task. To make the task somewhat shorter than Landgarten's, I felt, was less confusing and confrontive for the family and took better advantage of therapeutic timing. (For a slightly different assessment, the reader is referred to Landgarten's *Family Art Psychotherapy*.)

the sometimes extensive paperwork to the family. Even what is conveyed and to whom in the first phone call is essential. Exactly who is seen in the first therapy session and when are important and have meaning to the family. For example, I try to not reinforce the notion of the "identified patient" as the carrier of all problems in the family. Despite the fact that individual children are often presented to the therapist as the problem I only see this person within the *context of the whole family.* Often, I intentionally do not speak first to the "identified patient (i.p.)" because one of my first goals is to "sink" the identified patient back into the family system and work with it as a whole. I can usually achieve my goal by the amount and nature of attention paid, or not paid to the identified patient. If a therapist only sees the identified patient, it reinforces the family's idea of the problem as residing in one person and this notion will be tremendously more difficult to change.

MY THEORETICAL FRAME

1. *Systems thinking*
2. *Structural thinking* (Salvatore Minuchin and Jay Haley's structural mapping. I have found this most useful for mapping a family after the first session and planning change.)
3. *Developmental stage thinking* (At what life stage in family life is the family? For example, a family with small children, married a few years, or not married is different from a family with adolescents.)
4. *Humor* (I believe you can do anything if you use humor–this is a playful approach to a family that most likely has forgotten how to play.)
5. *Relationship building with the family as a whole.* (It is very difficult, perhaps impossible, to see one family member regularly and not "side" with that person. And even if you don't, the family will see you that way. The "family therapist" must remain that; if an individual needs to be seen, another therapist should see them or they may be seen occasionally within the family context after that has been well established.)
6. *Art* can be integrated with any theory or used to further whatever goals. (Art is usually useful and pleasurable for the family. In my therapy sessions, it is not a "choice" for them; it is "how I work" and is used in every session.)

7. History and the Unconscious. I believe these will be enacted by the family in the present. I have done long history taking sessions with a parent, but they were always within the context of the system, after the first family session and usually really are a therapeutic strategy about making a relationship with a difficult parent. It is not usually the "facts" that are important, but how they have become part of and are manifested in the family's culture.

FAMILY ART THERAPY ASSESSMENT PROCEDURE

First Intervention: The Phone Call

Get the whole family in. "Whole family" means everybody who lives in the family home, or grandparents who are raising the children and may have a lot of interaction with the family. Often mothers are the "front person" for the family and may tell you the father won't or can't come. The therapist should not accept this at face value, but should talk to the father himself. The therapist should tell him how important he is to the family, and that he needs to be part of the session. Usually, this works, if the therapist is confident about it.

Second Intervention: The First Art Therapy Session

Use the family assessment protocol in the first session. If there is paperwork, do it or have the family do it after the session. What if you were having a dire family crisis or problem which had caused you pain and anxiety, probably for weeks and were faced with a stack of paperwork before you could see the therapist. It might appear that the therapist is more interested in paperwork than in the family. The therapist should make every attempt to ameliorate contextual necessities with the family, but obviously needs to fulfill the requirements of the institutional system.

First Question in Session:

The first question is usually addressed to the non-identified patient sibling: "What did your parent/s tell you about why you're here?" This question enables the therapist to assess communication in the family, as well as clear up any confusion. Remember to use language that the child can understand.

Warm Up for Art:

1. Materials: Each family member on an 8 1/2 x 11 paper, markers
2. Time: 10 Minutes total

3. <u>Art Directive</u> (To the family): Take a marking pen and make your initials big on the page. Now finish them, add to them, decorate them in any way you want.

4. <u>Discussion</u>: Each family member is directed to hold his/her drawing up so others can see. Therapist tells the family that the artist can say anything they want about the picture and others can ask questions. Therapist can speak about the importance of names.

Afterwards, therapist collects and retains these works.

Family Mural

1. <u>Materials</u>: Paper, hung on wall (so that family must get up from table – 18 x 24 or more)
   Masking tape
   Markers

2. <u>Time</u>: About 10-15 minutes for drawing and 10-20 minutes for the discussion after.
   Children's ages should be considered when deciding how high to hang the Family Mural paper

3. <u>Art Directive</u> (To the family): You are going to do a drawing together as a family All families do them differently; however you do it will be fine. I'm not going to talk while you work. Afterward you will give the drawing a title, a name, and write it on the picture. Then we will discuss the experience. There are four rules:
   1. Each family member must have a different color marking pen
   2. Choose one color marking pen and keep it throughout the drawing.
   3. Take turns
   4. No talking

When the family has finished with the drawing, therapist will need to prompt about the title (They can talk about that–tell them that.)

The *Family Mural* provides a visible concrete product of the family dynamics. The one-marker rule makes it possible to see where each family member is and if the rules are broken. Therapist and family can talk about what happens when rules are broken in this family and at home. Both content and process of the picture are important.

4. *Discussion*
   The family discusses the mural first.
   Then therapist joins in.

Therapist picks up one major family dynamic and states it (e.g., I observed from the picture and the marker colors that no one helped anyone else.)

Therapist asks for general reactions about the mural and the session and makes next appointment, if there is one.

The first session may end here.

Second Family Mural

Only if time.

Family members can talk, otherwise directive is the same.

The two mural experiences can be compared.

(I don't usually do this, because I find it confusing for the family and because I don't usually have time.)

CASE EXAMPLE: THE H. FAMILY

The H. family came to therapy referred by the school because of their son Billy, age 13. According to his teacher, Billy's problems at school included lack of focus, wandering about the classroom, not doing his work, and directing a good deal of anger at peers. The H. family included Lance, age 19, Lisa, age 18, John, age 15, Jeremy age 14, the identified patient Billy, age 13 and Tony, the youngest age who was six. At first glance, I could see that the H.'s were coping with teenagers ready to leave the family, and with younger children whose needs were quite different. Ms H., age 43, had recently gone back to work as an Administrative Assistant after being a stay-at-home-mom for many years. Mr. H. was a 43-year-old computer software salesman. The family was seen as a whole for 15 sessions once a week. Art was used in every meeting enabling simultaneous communication by all in this large family. Structural family theory was used to assess the family dynamics and plan for change.

Observation of Family Process

Although the rules for the Family Mural do not specify images of individual family members, the H. family decided to draw its family members on the mural paper. Mother urged Tony, the youngest to start first. He drew a Christmas tree in the center of the page and was the only one not drawing a member of the family. Each family member drew separately. No one engaged cooperatively on anyone else's drawing. Each drew the person they felt most aligned with or wished to be aligned with, thus graphically designating family sub-systems: Mom drew her youngest son as a small child with a blanket indicating her close connection to him. The two oldest teenagers as the subgroup closest to separation drew each other near the top left corner of the mural. Dad drew Mom as a faint yellow profile—she was barely visible. In the discussion afterward, he said that he had drawn her away from the family at her new work. Billy, the identified patient, noticing that Dad had been left out of the picture, drew him bottom left, far away from mom and in another avoidant profile. Billy, drawn by his next older sibling, is in red. He is shown in his room listening to CDs. He has earphones on and the music looks loud; but the earphones keep him separated and from hearing or being heard, by the rest of the family. Billy is drawn as the largest on the page, but he is encapsulated by a red line creating a boundary between him and the rest of the family.

Figure 14-1. "H. Family Mural."

Discussion with H. Family After the Mural

Mother noticed how separate all family members seemed, "Almost like they are floating." She connected this separateness with her own sense of despair and her fear that if her family really knew how badly she felt, they would be devastated and would distance themselves further. She said this had happened in her family of origin when her mother was psychiatrically hospitalized for a long period and her family had drifted apart. This mother of six children said she felt like "one of the kids" and not a parent at all. Father was seen as the family "punisher." He acknowledged this role, but said he felt lonely. He said "I'm more used to working with computers than with people, even my own kids." The oldest child, Lance, age 19 was in junior college, but still lived at home. He spoke of his concern that "my family needs me," perhaps giving a clue to his difficulties in leaving an already amorphous family unit. Billy, the identified patient was viewed by the family as "the loud one." I told the family that Billy's loudness at home and problems at school were indeed an important message to his family. The behavior was *positively reframed* by suggesting that it was Billy's way of signaling a wish for more closeness, communicating and attention in his family. "Perhaps," I speculated "Billy wishes to take off his earphones and come out of his capsule, and help others in the family come out of their more invisible capsules as well."

After the Family Mural: The Art Therapist's Thoughts About the Family

The initial family task revealed issues of separation-individuation, closeness-distance and fears around the expression of pain, sadness and anger which were to prove ongoing themes in the family's treatment. Strong feelings were not permitted in the H. family except in the youngest, Tony and in Billy. An unstated rule about control seemed to be that it was safer to act like a machine. When strong feelings *were* allowed, they were seen as "babyish" as with Tony, or pathological as with Billy. The H. family's attractive exterior façade covered family secrets and served as a defense to wall off anger and depression. Billy had assumed the role of anger-carrier for the family. Mother's distance from the family was felt most acutely by the youngest, Tony. With his bids for attention and clinging he showed that he was feeling potentially abandoned and was attempting to keep his mother from leaving altogether. Ms and Mr. H. exhibited very little connection or affection between them as a couple.

Creating a Treatment Plan

After the Family Mural, the therapist formulated the following plan for family art therapy, including goals, objectives and artwork:

1. Enhance family connectedness: By promoting communication and free expression. In order for anyone to effectively separate from this family, it had to first be brought together.
2. Create an alliance and working relationship between the parents—the "architects" of the family: Help them deal more effectively with all their children.
3. Disengage the youngest child, Tony, from the parental unit: Help establish Tony's ties with his siblings, (so that he might be released from the burden of holding Mother together).
4. Transform Billy's role as "anger-carrier" for the family: If family members were allowed more space for all kinds of expression, each could claim his or her place and Billy wouldn't need to continue this role.
5. Artwork: Structured directives tailored to a task-oriented and problem-solving approach in which everyone in this large family could simultaneously express their thoughts and feelings.

CONCLUSIONS

Doing family art therapy, I have had the advantage of good training, good supervision, good therapy and a family which taught me a lot. I also enjoy chaos, carnivals, circuses, and finding my way out of the morass—probably necessary for a family art therapist. I am outlandishly fascinated by the imagery a family creates and consider it, often a projection of their inner reality. I have been a conscious parent and a conscious therapist. It is my belief that family therapy is the treatment of choice for children up to adolescence and sometimes after for the very simple reason that children are strongly influenced by environment. Although children as young as three are sometimes seen individually in clinics these days, often it is the parent/s that needs parenting help. Ignoring this need and working with the child alone is likely to do more harm than good. It is often the family that has a large part in injuring "the identified patient." I consider that it is the family as a whole that is *hurting* and in pain and for effectiveness, must be included in the therapy work. Seldom is individual therapy with children effective, in my opinion, and often the therapist colludes with a parent who may not know any better and who brings in a child with the request "fix him." Family work is more effective and usually quicker. Individual therapy with a child, if it works at all–and we have little "proof" that it does, takes much longer and is likely to be ineffective because the child, theoretically settles back into the same injurious context as before.

REFERENCES

Arrington, D. (2001). *Home is where the art is: An art therapy approach to family therapy.* Springfield, IL: Charles C. Thomas.

Landgarten, H. (1987). *Family art psychotherapy: A clinical guide and casebook.* New York, NY: Brunner/Mazel.

Linesch, D. (1993). *Families in crisis: Overcoming resistance through nonverbal experience.* Philadelphia, PA: Psychology Press.

Kerr, C. & Hoshino, J. (2007). *Family art therapy: Foundations of theory and practice.* New York: Routledge.

Kwiatkowska, H. (1978). *Family therapy and evaluation through art.* Springfield, IL: Charles C Thomas.

Riley, S. & Malchiodi, C. (2004). *Integrative approaches to family art therapy.* Chicago, IL: Magnolia Street Publishers

Chapter 15

BRIEF PSYCHODYNAMIC FAMILY ART THERAPY

Instead of traditional psychodynamic psychotherapy's focus on history and the past as causal links to the present, brief family therapy focuses on the *present* as enacted by the family in the consulting room and on the *future*. Brief therapy proposes that problems are solvable and changeable. It maintains that knowing the root cause of problems is not crucial in making present and future change. Rather than a search for pathology or its development, brief therapy highlights *solutions* and family *strengths*.

With the mental health field driven today by managed care and community mental health facilities, it is often easier to get insurance coverage for acupuncture treatment than for mental health service. Positive outcomes for therapy treatment are of great importance for those that pay for them and community mental health centers possess a mandate to provide effective services to large numbers of people. Brief therapy is often the treatment of choice.

Short-term psychotherapy[1] works better for many families today in the increasingly hectic and sometimes chaotic lives that many people live. There is little time or money for longer-term treatment and longer-term therapy which strives for personality and ongoing behavioral change, unfortunately, historically has not proven its value or effectiveness. Brief therapy, in that a family can identify a specific goal, work toward that goal, achieve it and leave therapy to try the new

---

1. The terms "short-term therapy/psychotherapy" and "brief therapy" are used interchangeably.

solutions in their ongoing life seems a better fit for the contemporary lifestyle. Brief psychotherapy also seems to fit better with current managed care systems and with mental health institutions stressed for time, money and efficacy. After successful work on their most essential problem, perhaps later the family returns to therapy to work on another problem or asks for longer-term work; perhaps not. What may be of most help these days to families is a series of focused, short-term treatments.

Brief therapy is based on the premise that it is not the therapy itself, or the short time spent in the therapist's consulting room that is important, but the *outside world* in which a family lives its ongoing life. Brief therapy is time-limited and has a beginning and a designated ending known to both family and therapist from the beginning of treatment. Sometimes these limits enhance the therapy. The art process and product can be particularly useful in short-term therapy because it quickly cuts through the abundance of material a family may present and, with imagery, quickly brings what may be most urgent into a focus available for both family and therapist to see. Through a timely art intervention and with a sensitive and direct art therapist, imagery helps form a visible, specific definition of the problem to be worked on that can be "seen" With the concrete presence of the art, an art therapist can help the family establish a visual record and image of their specific goal. Because language is already an abstraction, often the family's words are more difficult than art to move from generalization to the specific. Art imagery immediately brings the specific into acute focus.

Historically, short-term therapy was seen as second-best or even substandard by many practitioners, including art therapists. Training was usually long-term, psychoanalytically-based and the psychiatric community was slow to change. Superficiality, symptom substitution and no ongoing change were the usual accusations. But even Freud's techniques were often implemented over a series of months and no longer. Now at the beginning of the twenty-first century with mental health budgets cut to the quick, rampant paperwork and the necessity to treat large numbers of people with successful outcomes, there has come the obligation for clinicians, whatever their belief in long-term treatment, to modify their tactics and be accountable. In crisis theory terms, the constraints on mental health care can be viewed, as an event causing disruption to the old order which has opened the way for creative reorganization and the opportunity for innovative growth in brief therapy approaches.

Many consider that the three main innovators of psychodynamic short-term therapy are Malan, Sifneos and Davanloo (Messer & Warren, 1995; Cooper, J., 1995). Much of what I call "the second wave" of family therapy: solution-focused therapy (de Shazer, 1985) narrative therapy (White & Epston, 1990) therapy for drug and alcohol (Berg & Miller, 1992; Berg & Reuss, 1998) and cognitive-behavioral therapy treatment (Dattilo, 2005) focuses on behaviorally oriented, functionally operationalized brief treatment. The different forms of brief treatment aim at a small problem area and are usually problem specific such as sexual abuse (Dolan, 1991; McGoldrick, 1998) or age specific such as children or adolescents (Bertolino, 1999.)

Time, as a variable in psychotherapy treatment has long been known to be unimportant. Historically, the concept of *time* in psychotherapy tended to mean the longer the therapy, the better. The emphasis on time grew out of Freud and the historical emergence of psychoanalysis as a treatment of choice for those with time, money and the desire to make "real" (personality) change. An analysand could spend four or five times a week in analysis over a period of as much as nine years. There was little, if any, research to prove the claim of "more change comes with more time." Nevertheless, many clinicians today still retain the belief that a long time is an essential element of good therapy treatment.

The literature focusing on brief family art therapy is minimal. Riley (1999) in her book *Contemporary Art Therapy with Adolescents* has a chapter called "Short-Term, Solution Focused, Art Therapy Treatment." (Riley termed herself a "postmodernist art therapist.") In *The Arts in Psychotherapy*, an international journal, no article on brief family art therapy was published from 1996 to the present. While some art therapy journal articles have been published on family art therapy generally, to date no book on brief family art therapy has been published.

Brief treatment is not simply a short version of long-term psychodynamic therapy. Different in approach, methods and goals than longer-term therapy, the potential value of brief therapy depends on the therapist's ability to help the family *partialize* and *operationalize* its goals. While it may have deeper underlying goals, the treatment itself is tied to behavioral operations in the real world. As an example of moving toward partializing in the therapy session, I describe this conversation between the client and the therapist: The art directive was "Pick out pictures out of the collage box about what you want *different* in the family." At the art therapist's direction, clients chose pictures, glued them down and wrote words or sentences under the pictures about why they chose them. Art images allowed family members to concretely envision changes–both conscious and unconscious–but now the art therapist must use words to make the images less general and with more specific meaning to family members. The art therapist asks:

> *Therapist*: I see you wrote "communication" under that picture. What is it you want to communicate? ("Communication is a catchword and a generalization with little specific meaning. The therapist attempts to help the client make the word specific and operationalized. The therapist will work with the client to make the concept of "Communication" small enough and behavioral enough so it can be worked on.)
>
> *Client*: Oh I don't know. Just that we talk and hear each other better.
>
> *T*: Exactly what is it that you want to say?
>
> *C*: I want to say "I am angry."
>
> *T*: What are you angry about?
>
> *C*: I am angry that the front door is always left open.
>
> *T*: Who do you want to tell that you are angry that the front door is always left open?
>
> *C*: I want to tell my son.
>
> *T*: What exactly are the words you would you like to say to your son?
>
> *C*: I am very angry that you always leave the front door open.
>
> *T*: What might he say?
>
> *C*: You never said anything to me. What's the big deal?
>
> *T*: Your answer?
>
> *C*: I am saying it now! I want you to always close the door when you go outside.
>
> *T*: Good! Now I understand why there is a door in your collage picture. Say these words to your son directly and tell me next week, how it went. Or: Turn right now to your son [who is in the family session] and tell him exactly what you want.

If matters had been left at the general term "communication," the family's ability to problem solve and potential to change would have been drastically compromised if not impossible altogether. While many individuals who enter our consulting rooms tend to speak in generalities, I believe that it is the therapist's job to take steps needed to make the generalities specific enough to be worked on in brief family therapy. Often a generality is a defensive and unconscious way to cover a unique, specific and important meaning.

Additionally, brief therapy depends on the therapist's ability to come to speedy conclusions and decisions, to be direct and assertive and to move quickly, skills which often are not enhanced in the usual therapy training. The psychodynamically-trained therapist, all too often secretly (or not so secretly) may believe that short-term therapy is useless. Thus training, experience in and a commitment to short-term work by the therapist, are imperative. In addition, therapists may need to battle their own training and forceful desires to acquire *understanding* before they can then adequately proceed to therapy. In brief therapy, one usually proceeds without "full" understanding. Therapists may struggle with a belief in the worthlessness of short-term work and only do it as a "prologue" to a longer involvement, which may make the short-term work all-but-worthless. To a large extent, positive outcome of brief treatment depends on the ability of the therapist and family to make contact, to rapidly develop an alliance and to provide hope. Empathy, support, education and encouragement are essential. There are many challenges for therapists in doing this kind of work, and a learning period with good clinical case supervision is certainly called for and is necessary.

ART IN BRIEF THERAPY

Art is flexible and adaptable to any needs of brief therapy and greatly enhancing to it. But I have come to feel that it is the factor of the *permanence* of the art product that is crucial to short-term treatment. Long after therapy is finished, the art remains an image in the memory of the client and the therapist. "I don't remember much about the first session," the client says, "but I sure remember that picture my mom drew." The image and the physical experience of image making, remain long afterward in the mind's eye and body and often become part of a family's collective consciousness. A stalled family that has long forgotten how to have fun–if it ever knew–gains pleasure from the art making. Along with the memory of the image, the actual physical presence and on-going existence of art retained and "protected" by the therapist or family can be a remarkable positive factor, representative of hope and the continuing possibility of change.

During the late 1970s and early 1980s, I worked in the Child and Family Psychiatry Division, Thalians Community Mental Health Center at Cedars-Sinai Hospital in Los Angeles. The short-term therapy program there innovated at that time was called Family Evaluation Team, or FET. In the years of the program over 225 families were seen. The Family Evaluation Team was based on a crisis model and on multiple impact family therapy then being done in Texas in which families from outlying districts who could not come to the clinic on any regular basis would come attend therapy for a few intense days. A team of therapists would meet with the family using various approaches and techniques in an attempt to shake up the family system, teach new and alternative behaviors and give the family many things to try in the long months between clinic visits. An art therapist, Virginia Austin, was a member of the Houston group and used art therapy in brief treatment with good results.

The Family Evaluation Team at Thalians met with each family for a total of five hours. The first hour was an *Assessment Session* in which the family's concerns were clarified and focused goals for treatment set. One to two weeks later the family met for a three-hour *Intervention Meeting*–a workshop in which the family would explore new behaviors toward their focused goals. At the end of this meeting, specific tasks and homework were often given and an appointment was made for approximately two weeks later. In the final *Review Session* the family considered its progress toward its goals and therapists reinforced the family's positive gains. Della Selva and Malan (2004) researching brief therapy suggested that the crucial ingredient for change might be the factor of the therapist's enthusiasm for the process and for change.

The families we saw in FET were not screened for motivation, insight or "appropriateness." Many were multiproblemed with years of difficulties behind them. There was an abundance of single-parent (usually the mother) families. A few families had had years of treatment in long-term therapy and thick file folders in our clinic; they openly stated that five hours of therapy was a waste of time. I was trained in longer-term psychodynamic therapy and it took me awhile to begin to enjoy this very different form of psychotherapy. But eventually, enjoy it I did. I liked thinking quickly on my feet and I liked being direct and assertive. Finally, I found it to be a style of treatment that fit my personality. To me brief therapy was sometimes chaotic, sometimes depressing but always alive–as alive as the families themselves–and always exciting. It sometimes "worked" where years of therapy before had failed, because it quickly cut through the many layers of problems which might have enabled the family to "understand" but not to change–what I call: attending therapy to keep from changing; and it got the family working again. In particular the art was remarkably helpful in brief family treatment.

In the years since the Family Evaluation Team, I have worked in art therapy with many families in planned short-term treatment. My theoretical orientation is systemic and dynamic. I strive for symptom alleviation, behavioral change and a better sense by the family, of the dynamics of the family as a whole. Each family brings to the therapy session its own history and dynamics as a family system. It is my conviction that many behaviors played out in the present are rooted in the past, but plumbing the historical past for information is unnecessary and time wasted because the family will enact its own history in the here-and-now of the sessions. The therapy room is always filled with family-of-origin ghosts and ghosts are best dealt with in the present.

CASE EXAMPLES

Following are case examples from first sessions of brief family art therapy. In all cases, these pictures helped the family achieve a concrete focus on its goals for therapy.

The M. Family, Caucasian with five children, ranging in ages from seven to 18 came to the clinic, referred by the school, because of the youngest child's lack of focus, not doing his work and hitting other children. I watched out the window as the M. family arrived. One after another they seemed to spring forth from the small Volkswagen bug, in no way spacious enough for all. They reminded me of the clown cars at the circus in which hundreds of clowns spring from an apparently tiny car. Figure 15-1 is a family drawing which revealed how crowded and undifferentiated this family was. For example, when I introduced myself and asked for each family member's name, father stopped me to say: "It doesn't matter. We are just the M. family." Despite the large house they drew, the family said it was what they *wished for* not what they had. They actually lived in a three-bedroom apartment bursting at the seams with teenage energy. Treating this family as individuals rather than the undifferentiated mass they presented seemed essential and that was my stated goal for them. Parenting teenagers is different from parenting young children and older teenagers are different than younger adolescents. These parents had a lot on their hands! Art therapy and the family drawing gave all family members equal footing to represent themselves and their needs. From the intense intervention workshop, came individualized goals and homework for each family member concretized in "Prescriptions" written on a pad and handed to each at the end of the session as they walked out the door. Art provided simultaneous, yet individual expression as each family member exercised autonomy over his or her own drawings and selection of materials. When the family returned for its final session, they were asked to individually draw "things that were different or better and things that were not."

Figure 15-1. M. Family Drawing Revealing a Lack of Differentiation.

In this family drawing, a Caucasian mother, father, twelve-year-old son and six-year-old daughter graphically revealed their feelings of isolation from one another. In the discussion after the drawing, despite the conglomerate title "Us," family members noticed that all the figures were separate and no one had helped another or drawn on any one else's figure. The rule that each family member take only one marking pen and keep it throughout the drawing, usually implies that family members must help each other and cooperate by adding their own color to another's work. The J. Family agreed that they wanted something different and made cooperation their goal. In the intensive workshop, they went on in other pictures to experiment with methods of interacting enabling them to explore ways of cooperating with each other.

Figure 15-2. J. Family Drawing–Revealing Isolation.

A depressed, single African American mother with two teenaged sons, wanted to talk to them about their father who had attempted suicide and then left the family some years before. The family was directed to "pick out pictures from the collage box about your father/husband leaving the family." Each family member worked on her/his collage. They chose collage images, glued them on the page, and wrote a word or sentence under each picture about what it meant. Then each family member shared his or her picture with the others enabling them to talk together for the first time about this difficult family experience. The art enabled them to communicate together about the leaving and express and explore their feelings. Because she talked "from" the picture, it also allowed this mother to speak to her sons about their father, which she had never been able to do before because of her own very mixed feelings; it had remained an unspoken family secret and a taboo subject. It turned out that the sons had known about the facts of their father's departure, but that it could not be freely talked about by the family made it go underground to become an evil and untouchable secret.

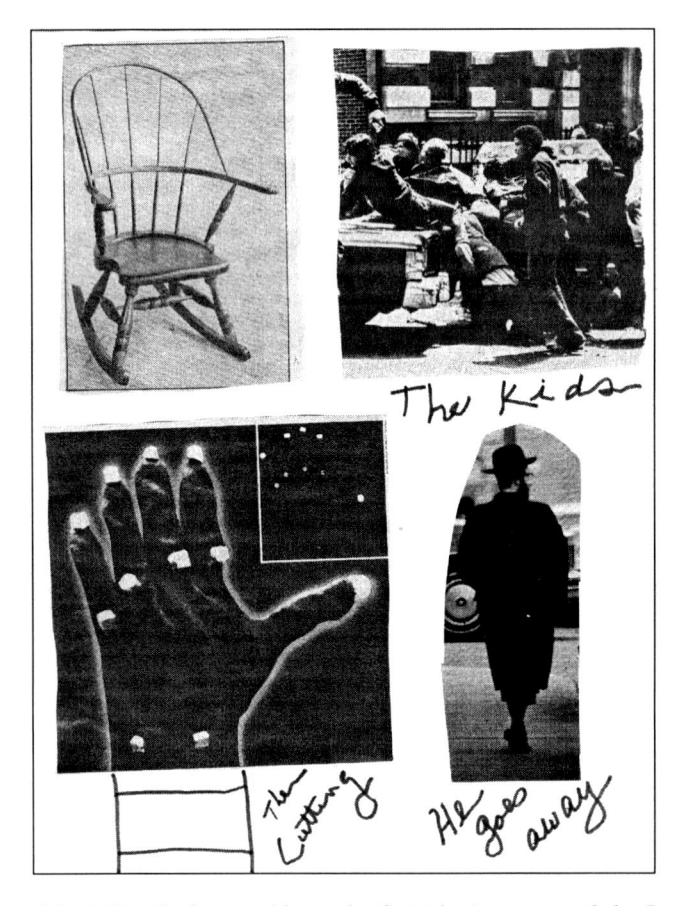

Figure 15-3. A Family Secret: About the Suicide Attempt and the Leaving.

The family drawing revealed the family life space of this Caucasian family: It portrayed a mother entangled with her twelve-year-old son and revealed the isolation and loneliness of the stepfather, who had been married to the mother for many years but had not been able to penetrate the dyad. Mother took up a major amount of the space of the drawing. She drew the large tree dissecting the middle of the page.

The son drew his school on one side of the tree and the stepfather drew on the other. He drew a very small tree stunted by the shade of the huge central tree. Through the family mural, both mother and stepfather expressed their wish to be closer and to not spend so much "energy on F.," the son. In the intervention workshop, the couple drew a series of pictures together in which they experimented with dual interaction. The twelve-year-old son F. was placed outside the therapy room with the therapist, and observed the parents working together on the artwork through the two-way mirror. He was instructed to give them feedback afterward on how they were doing in reaching their goal of turning toward each other.

Figure 15-4 A Mother's Place in the Family Needs Changing.

Ms T., a widowed Caucasian mother, seldom left her apartment. She came to the clinic with her seventeen-year-old son complaining that he was out all the time, didn't come home when he should and that she was lonely. The picture they drew together symbolized the relationship of the two. The son went over the lines of the house to em-phasize that there are two houses, not one, although the mother tried to keep the picture only one house. Ms T. knew her son would leave home eventually as he grew into manhood and, in fact, she con-sciously wanted him to have his own life as an adult, but since her hus-band had died, she said she had focused all her energy on her son and was finding herself very depressed at the thought of his leaving. It turned out that what Ms T. meant by "out all the time" was that her son was on the swim team at his school and had daily practices after school. Behind the house, he drew a pool, giving a clue to his interests and to the conflict with his mother. Artwork provided a visible, unchanging reference point as Ms T. was encouraged to start a life for herself separate from her adolescent son. In a very real sense, nor-malizing the separation interaction and helping the mother learn to nurture herself were goals of the brief therapy.

Figure 15-5. One House or Two?

REFERENCES

Berg, I. & Miller, S. (1992). *Working with a problem drinker: A solution focused approach.* New York: Norton.

Berg, I. & Reuss, N. (1998). *Solutions step by step: A substance abuse treatment manual.* New York: Norton.

Bertolino, B. (1999). *Therapy with troubled teenagers: Rewriting young lives in progress.* New York: Wiley.

Cooper, J. (1995). *A primer of brief psychotherapy.* New York: Norton.

Dattilo, F. (2005). The restructuring of family schemas: A cognitive-behavior perspective, *J. Marital & Family Therapy.* January.

Della Selva, P. & Malan, D. (2004). *Short term dynamic psychotherapy: Theory and technique synopsis.* London, England: Karnac Books; new edition April 2004.

de Shazer, S. (1985). *Keys to solution in brief therapy.* New York: Norton.

Dolan, Y. (1991). *Resolving sexual abuse.* New York: Norton.

McGoldrick, M. (Ed.) (1998). *Re-visioning family therapy: Race, culture and gender in clinical practice.* New York: Guilford Press.

Messer, S. & Warren, C. (1995). *Models of brief psychodynamic theory: A comparative approach.* New York: Guilford Press.

Riley, S., (1999). *Contemporary art therapy with adolescents.* London and Philadelphia: Jessica Kingsley.

White, M. & Epston, D. (1990). *Narrative means to therapeutic ends.* New York: W.W. Norton & Co., Inc.

ABOUT THE AUTHOR

Maxine Borowsky Junge, PhD, LCSW, ATR-BC, HLM, is Professor Emerita at Loyola Marymount University, Los Angeles, where she taught for 21 years and was Chair of the Department of Marital and Family Therapy (Clinical Art Therapy). She began her art therapy involvement in 1973 at Immaculate Heart College in the program innovated by Helen B. Landgarten, which was the first art therapy graduate program west of the Mississippi. She has also been a faculty member in psychology and art therapy at Goddard College in Vermont and Antioch University-Seattle and presented papers and workshops nationally and internationally. Along with working at many clinics including Cedars-Sinai Hospital, Thalians Community Mental Health Center in Los Angeles, Dr. Junge has had a private practice since 1973. More recently, she has included organizational consulting. She has contributed chapters to art therapy and psychology texts, the latest being "The Art Therapist as Social Activist" in *Art Therapy and Social Action*. She has published widely for more than 30 years. Her favorite articles appear, substantially revised, as essays in this book. In 2006, Dr. Junge was Guest Editor for a series of nine life stories of art therapy people of color for *Art Therapy, Journal of the American Art Therapy Association*. Her three books before this one are *Architects of Art Therapy, Memoirs and Life Stories* which she edited with Harriet Wadeson, *Creative Realities, The Search for Meanings,* and *A History of Art Therapy in the United States*. The *History* is the only one of its kind and is used in graduate programs across the country. Dr. Junge is the recipient of awards, including an "Award for Excellence" from the South Bay Contemporary Art Museum and Harbor-UCLA Hospital and the Social Justice Award at Fielding Graduate University. She received three nominations as "Woman of the Year at Loyola Marymount University. Trained as a painter through graduate studies, she is an exhibiting painter, draftswoman and photographer. She lives on Whidbey Island in the Pacific Northwest where she consults to a mental health agency, paints and writes.